THE CHRISTIAN Grandma's idea book

Hundreds of Ideas, Tips, and Activities to Help You Be a Good Grandma

Ellen Banks Elwell

CROSSWAY BOOKS

WHEATON, ILLINOIS

The Christian Grandma's Idea Book: Hundreds of Ideas, Tips, and Activities to Help You Be a Good Grandma

Copyright © 2008 by Ellen Banks Elwell

Published by Crossway Books
      a publishing ministry of Good News Publishers
      1300 Crescent Street
      Wheaton, Illinois 60187

Interior design and typesetting by Lakeside Design Plus
Cover design: Amy Bristow
Cover photo: Getty Images

First printing 2008
Printed in the United States of America

Unless otherwise indicated, Scripture quotations are from *The Holy Bible, English Standard Version*®, copyright © 2001 by Crossway Bibles, a publishing ministry of Good News Publishers. Used by permission. All rights reserved.

Scripture quotations marked NASB are from *The New American Standard Bible.*® Copyright © The Lockman Foundation 1960, 1962, 1963, 1968, 1971, 1972, 1973, 1975, 1977, 1995. Used by permission.

Scripture references marked NIV are from *The Holy Bible: New International Version.*® Copyright © 1973, 1978, 1984 by International Bible Society. Used by permission of Zondervan Publishing House. All rights reserved.

The "NIV" and "New International Version" trademarks are registered in the United States Patent and Trademark Office by International Bible Society. Use of either trademark requires the permission of International Bible Society.

Scripture references marked NLT are from *The Holy Bible, New Living Translation*, copyright © 1996. Used by permission of Tyndale House Publishers, Inc., Wheaton, Ill., 60189. All rights reserved.

Scripture references marked TLB are from *The Living Bible* © 1971. Used by permission of Tyndale House Publishers, Inc., Wheaton, IL 60189. All rights reserved.

Library of Congress Cataloging-in-Publication Data

Elwell, Ellen Banks, 1952–
    The Christian grandma's idea book : hundreds of ideas, tips, and activities to help you be a good grandma / Ellen Banks Elwell.
        p. cm.
    Includes bibliographical references.
    ISBN 978-1-58134-946-7 (tpb)
        1. Grandmothers—Life skills guides. 2. Grandmothers—Religious life. 3. Grandmothers—Family relationships. I. Title.
HQ759.9.E48 2008
248.8'45—dc22

                                              2007040621

VP	16	15	14	13	12	11	10	09	08
	9	8	7	6	5	4	3	2	1

To my mom, Betty Banks,
with loving regards from her eleven grandchildren.

Chad Elwell: Grandma loves us, cares for us, sets an example for us, feeds us, and is leaving a wonderful legacy for us. When we were kids, and she prayed with us, she oftentimes reminded us to thank God for loving us.

Nate Elwell: I love spending time with Grandma because she is such a good role model. She instills in us the importance of having a close relationship with the Lord, and she reminds us how much she prays for us. Grandma has a strong spiritual foundation in her life, based on the Word, prayer, fellowship with others, and generous giving. She has sheet after sheet pinned to her bulletin board of the missionaries that she and Grandpa support. Grandma's strong foundation bleeds over to her physical strength, too. When I was in little league, someone hit a foul ball into the stands, and my grandma was there to catch it . . . bare-handed!

Brit Elwell: When I met my future grandmother-in-love, I was completely taken with her energy and spunk. She has a natural love for life and people, and her energy is infectious! My favorite memory with her is when she put on my four-inch red patent high heels and posed for pictures! She has a twinkle in her eye and brings great joy to all who know her!

Jordan Elwell: One of the things I love most about my grandma is her drive and enthusiasm for life. She and my grandpa took me and three of my cousins to London one summer, and at the end of each day as we cousins collapsed at the hotel to take naps, Grandma was still running strong, ready for more, with more energy than anyone else! Her zeal is more than just tangible energy, however. I know that my grandma's untiring support is with me through the mountains and the valleys, in the best times and the worst times of my life. My grandma would go to the end of the earth and back for me, and words cannot describe what that means to me.

Nick Banks: When I think back to the time Grandma and Grandpa took me on a trip to the United Kingdom, I remember enjoying time spent talking with Grandma in the backseat of the car as we rode all the way from Scotland to London.

Anna Banks:
A heart of gold,
A smile to unfold,
A grace to save,
A love to crave.
One who delights,
In those nights,
We spend together,
That last forever.
Playing board games,
Sometimes card games,
But we want you to know,
That we love you so.

Brent Pflederer: Grandma has a way of making each of her grandkids feel like they are her favorite. However, we all know she is extremely fair with all of us and treats us all with the same love. Grandma bakes the best gingersnap cookies and aims to feed me as much food as possible, whether I'm over there for Thanksgiving dinner or to fix a computer problem. It's *great*.

Sarah Pflederer: Grandma always makes it her mission to fill me up with as much food as possible. I enjoy riding my bike over to her house, and whenever I'm there, no matter how busy she is, she stops so she can hear what is going on in my life. Above all that, Grandma has been passing on her strong faith to all of us ever since I can remember. From the Bible stories she read us when we were little, to the example she's been setting, to the prayers I know she prays for me daily, Grandma has never stopped combining her job of being a wonderful Grandma with her strong faith. I love my grandma!

Brittany Korell: Grandma is always serving others and never thinking of herself.

Aleena Korell: Grandma is the Energizer Bunny to me. She never stops and has fun doing things for others. She is a great role model for me, and I hope that I will be half as kind and caring someday as she is now.

Janine Korell: I like to visit Grandma. She has a big house. It's fun to play pick-up sticks with her. Grandma loves God with all her heart!

Contents

Preface

*W*ith the help of more than two hundred grandmas, moms, and grandchildren from around the world, I have attempted to write the book I'd like to read. Years ago, when I compiled *The Christian Mom's Idea Book*, I wished I'd received those five hundred wonderful ideas *before* I had children. So after one of our sons, Nate, married his lovely wife, Brit, in 2006, I began gathering wisdom and advice for a stage of life yet to come—becoming an effective Christian grandma. For this book, I've collected over eight hundred ideas, thoughts, and stories from (1) grandmas of all ages and stages, (2) moms who described things their mothers or mothers-in-law did with or for their children, and (3) grandchildren from kindergarten on up to adults.

One ten-year-old boy wrote, "I call my grandma 'Nana' as a special name. She is always there to love me. She is not old at all—she is only in her 50s. My grandma likes to drink coffee in the morning. At night, she likes to sing. She watches us all the time when our parents are gone. She likes to laugh and play around. She likes kids around the house. She will always be there for me. She will love Jesus all the time."

Many grandmas around the world spend time with their grandchildren, give gifts to their grandchildren, and share family traditions with their grandchildren. Christian grandmas have unique opportunities to influence grandchildren for good. By following Christ and pointing their grandchildren to a relationship with God through Christ, they bless and serve the present generation as well as generations that follow. Their investments of time, love, and God's Word make a difference both now—and forever. "My Grammy's love for me," wrote young mom Janna Hickel, "gave me a glimpse of Christ's love for me. She loved me despite my shortcomings and, when you're loved like that, you can't help but love back."

Chapter 1 of this book explores some things the Bible has to say about being a grandma. Chapters 2–20 (arranged alphabetically from *Activities* to *Vacations*) explore what two hundred people from three generations have to say about being a grandma. Within these pages, you're invited to enter the worlds of grandmas, moms, and grandchildren from Singapore, England, Australia, Nigeria, Peru, New Zealand, Burkina Faso, The Netherlands, South Korea, Pakistan, Taiwan, Switzerland, Indonesia, Italy, Ethiopia, the Philippines, Austria, Mexico, Japan, Iran, Namibia, Sweden, India, Jordan, South Africa, Canada, Siberia, Finland, Romania, and the United States of America. As I have received their contributions, I've been enriched more than I could have imagined. No grandma could ever incorporate all these ideas into her life, but I hope you'll discover some that work for you. If your heart is stirred as you read—mine was as I compiled—I offer thanks, again, to the people who were willing to put their thoughts and experiences into words.

Special Thanks

The people who contributed to this book are acknowledged on pages 12–14. Without them, this resource would not have been compiled. Some people offered me such an abundance of material (one grandma sent sixteen typed pages!) that their names could almost have appeared on the title page: Nancy

Brown, Nancy Ector, Grace Anderson Elwell, Joyce Fahs, Carol Findling, Marge Gieser, Kita Heslinga, Janna Hickel, Esther Jeychandran, Dee Kijanko, Gloria Leff, Rebecca Lutzer, Brenda McDonell, Kajsa-Lena Nyblom, Carolyn Walter, Janice Whitbread, and Ranie Yesudian.

I'm grateful to authors Nanci Alcorn, Gracia Burnham, Cynthia Heald, Rebecca Lutzer, Francine Rivers, and Margaret Taylor—and even some of the menfolk, Sigmund Brouwer, Gary Chapman, Bruce Howard, and Jerry Jenkins—for contributing grandma vignettes to this book.

I appreciate that educators Chad Elwell, Jill DiCicco, and Julie Reynolds gathered grandma thoughts from students of various ages. Jim Elwell, Chad Elwell, Nate Elwell, Brit Elwell, Jordan Elwell, Gail Pflederer, Barbara Korell, Ruthie Howard, and Shelly Wildman reviewed portions of the manuscript—a huge help. For organizing things on my computer and getting me out of a few quagmires, I owe Jordan Elwell more treats from Taco Bell. And most of all—to my husband, Jim, I'm grateful that you brainstormed with me, encouraged me, prayed for me, and picked up pizza and salad from Lou Malnotti's on evenings when I didn't cook.

Ellen Banks Elwell
Wheaton, Illinois, 2007

Acknowledgments

I want to thank:

The Grandmas: Yoanna Abu-Rahmeh *(Jordan)*, Lynne Ahrenholz *(USA)*, Hope Akpokene *(Nigeria)*, Jean Allen *(USA)*, Jean Amsler *(USA)*, Marybelle Bauer *(USA)*, Nancy Botts *(USA)*, Mary Kay Brooke *(USA)*, Lois Brorson *(USA)*, Cari Brown *(USA)*, Nancy Brown *(USA)*, Cindy Chole *(USA)*, Dawn Clark *(USA)*, Joanna Conley *(USA)*, Marilyn Dinkel *(USA)*, Nancy Ector *(USA)*, Karen Elifson *(USA)*, Grace A. Elwell *(USA)*, Edra Estabrooks *(USA)*, Joyce Fahs *(USA)*, Carol Findling *(USA)*, Sally Florence *(USA)*, Gladys Gavin *(New Zealand)*, Carol Genet *(USA)*, Cornelia Gheorghita *(Romania)*, Marge Gieser *(USA)*, Denise Gill *(USA)*, Cocky van den Ham *(The Netherlands)*, Kita Heslinga *(USA)*, Martha Hoke *(USA)*, Linda Horton *(USA)*, Ruthie Howard *(USA)*, Ruth Howell *(USA)*, Esther Jeyachandran, *(Singapore)*, Ems Johnsen *(South Africa)*, Mary Grace Johnson *(USA)*, Susan Johnson *(USA)*, Diane Jordan *(USA)*, Dee Kijanko *(USA)*, Marilyn Kitchell *(USA)*, Betty Knoedler *(USA)*, Emma Korell *(USA)*, Kristin Kriegbaum *(USA)*, Gloria Leff *(USA)*, Nancy Lewis *(USA)*, Sherri Litfin *(USA)*, Rebecca Lutzer *(USA)*, Shirley Mathews *(USA)*, Ruth McDonald *(USA)*, Brenda McDonell *(USA)*, Kajsa-Lena Nyblom *(Finland)*, Betty Nyman *(USA)*, Betsy Pearson *(USA)*,

Valerie Pearson *(Australia)*, Carole Pflederer *(USA)*, Mary Phillips *(USA)*, Zin Poppe *(USA)*, Flo Schmid *(USA)*, Becky Schulz *(USA)*, Linda Smith *(South America)*, Marilyn Strutz *(USA)*, Beverly Stubbs *(USA)*, Margaret Taylor *(USA)*, Debbie Van Der Molen *(USA)*, Marilyn Vaughn *(USA)*, Joyce Walta *(USA)*, Janice Whitbread *(Canada)*, Lois Widder *(USA)*, Janis Williams *(USA)*, Ruth Wit *(USA)*, and Ranie Yesudian *(India)*.

The Moms: Cindy Augustine *(USA)*, Karen Bagge *(USA)*, Jan Bastian *(USA)*, Sarah Bradley *(USA)*, Alicia Brummeler *(USA)*, Angela Castaldo *(USA)*, Julie Clum *(USA)*, Janna Hickel *(USA)*, Barbara Korell *(USA)*, Melody Kube *(Russia)*, Linda Jensen *(USA)*, Candy O'Donovan *(England)*, Esther Ouoba *(Burkina Faso)*, Gail Pflederer *(USA)*, Claire Shume *(Australia)*, Julie Sohmer *(USA)*, Laura Swoboda *(USA)*, Cathy Thill *(USA)*, Rebecca Thomas *(USA)*, Moronke Thompson *(Nigeria)*, Penny Thrasher *(USA)*, Lilla Ann Toelcke *(USA)*, Karin Tuurie *(USA)*, Carolyn Walter *(USA)*, Jennifer Wheatley *(USA)*, Shelly Wildman *(USA)*.

The Grandchildren: Seyi O. Abodunde *(Nigeria)*, Lisa Anderas *(USA)*, Eleah Augustine *(USA)*, Katie Augustine *(USA)*, Anna Banks *(USA)*, Nick Banks *(USA)*, Myles Barnes *(USA)*, Abby Bennett *(USA)*, Josh Berg *(USA)*, Luke Berg *(USA)*, Ryan Berg *(USA)*, Anna Brummeler *(USA)*, Jacob Brummeler *(USA)*, Bailey Byers *(USA)*, Carissa Cruz *(USA)*, Sara Dax *(Austria)*, Olivia Daylor *(USA)*, Leandre Dentlinger *(Namibia)*, Eli Dossett *(Austria)*, Nadine Dunsing *(USA)*, Marvin Elequin *(Austria)*, Brittany Jensen Elwell *(USA)*, Chad Elwell *(USA)*, Jordan Elwell *(USA)*, Nate Elwell *(USA)*, Charlie Faulkner *(USA)*, Sam Fox *(USA)*, Roanne Paula Garcia *(Philippines)*, Lee Gayoung *(Korea)*, Mariam Gilani *(Pakistan)*, Kristiana Hatcher *(Austria)*, Kristine Hayden *(USA)*, Jackson Hayes *(USA)*, Elise Herbert *(USA)*, Ryan Heslinga *(USA)*, Hannah Hickel *(USA)*, Janna Hickel *(USA)*, Mark Howard *(USA)*, Steve Howard *(USA)*,Weston Howard *(USA)*, Han Byeol Hur *(South*

Korea), Rachirael Augustin Jacob *(India)*, Benjamin George Jeffrey *(United Kingdom)*, Baylor Johnson *(USA)*, Christopher Jones *(USA)*, Mandy Jungels *(USA)*, Miranda Kalinowski *(USA)*, Dong kwan Kim *(South Korea)*, Alexandra Kirchner *(USA)*, Aleena Korell *(USA)*, Brittany Korell *(USA)*, Janine Korell *(USA)*, Michael Kvick *(Sweden)*, Samantha Lapid *(Philippines)*, Alli LaReau *(USA)*, Patricia Lehner *(Austria)*, Philipp Liebentritt *(Austria)*, Victoria Linner *(USA)*, Will Litfin *(USA)*, Paul Manuel *(Philippines)*, Kelly Moon *(South Korea)*, Ethan Mosley *(USA)*, Erik Mueller *(USA)*, Saron Mulugeta *(Ethiopia)*, Alwin Jose Murickananil *(India)*, Reza Nasseri *(Iran)*, Samar Nasseri *(Iran)*, Jericho David Norman *(Austria)*, Jordyn Marie Nunnally *(USA)*, Mia Nyblom *(USA)*, Hannah Pabinguit *(Philippines)*, Benjamin Paul *(United Kingdom)*, Jack Peacock *(USA)*, Gracio (Rio) Permata *(Indonesia)*, Brent Pflederer *(USA)*, Sarah Pflederer *(USA)*, Jordan Pittman *(USA)*, Erin Polderman *(USA)*, Weston Poling *(USA)*, Kenny Ponquinette *(USA)*, Christopher Porter *(USA)*, Paola Ramirez *(Mexico)*, Annika Reynolds *(USA)*, Wilson Reynolds *(USA)*, Austin Richards *(Austria)*, Jonathan Sabella *(Italy)*, Joe Schuette *(USA)*, Melody Scott *(USA)*, Anna-Joy Setran *(USA)*, Laura Shume *(Australia)*, Maddi Shume *(Australia)*, Sophie Shume *(Australia)*, Keeley Slamans *(USA)*, Bryan Smith *(USA)*, Anah Southard *(USA)*, Natalie Stewart *(USA)*, Bavishya Subramanian *(India)*, Yurika Suga *(Japan)*, Josef Suhonen *(Sweden)*, Emily Toelcke *(USA)*, Ben Van Dixhorn *(USA)*, Jack Van Dixhorn *(USA)*, Lily Van Dixhorn *(USA)*, Megan Van Dixhorn *(USA)*, Immanuel Wicaksano *(Indonesia)*, Jannica Yu-Jan Wu *(Taiwan)*, Zach Zabran *(USA)*, and M. J. Zepeda *(USA)*.

One

Legacy

I felt close to my Grandma Banks from as far back as I remember until the day she died. That was a long time, because she lived to be 103. She was a kind, wise, and patient woman. One of the best gifts she gave me was my dad, who shares her wonderful temperament. Grandma Banks stood about five feet short and was pleasantly plump. Maybe that's why she felt so soft. My siblings and I still chuckle about a time in our childhood when Grandma said to our youngest cousin, "Oh, Kim . . . your grandma is fat." "Grandma, you're not fat," Kim replied. "You just have a lot of body." I can still picture my grandma laughing. She tilted her head back when she laughed, listened carefully when people around her spoke, and took her calm presence along wherever she went.

Shortly after her parents moved from Germany to the United States, Grandma Banks was born as Minni Ottallie Biesenthal. Her family continued to speak German at home for some years. When I was a little girl, Grandma taught me how to count in her mother tongue: *eins, zwei, drei, vier, fünf, sechs, sieben, acht, neun, zehn.* . . . At Christmas time, she was fond of singing "O Tannenbaum" and "Stille Nacht." Because Grandma was such a peaceful person, I assumed that she had enjoyed a pleasant childhood. When I was a teenager, though, Grandma shared with me that when she was twelve, she received news one night that her Dad had died. He had been drinking heavily, fell off a neighbor's porch, and died instantly. She told me that as difficult as that time was for her family, they felt some relief when her father was gone. He had treated the family poorly. While sitting there listening to Grandma at her dining room table, I got very still. I felt badly that she hadn't had a kind father like I did. My young mind wondered how a woman who grew up with an unkind dad could be such a loving grandma.

Grandma Banks's formal education took her only as far as the eighth grade, but she was an intelligent woman. She liked to reminisce about the years she worked for the president of the Farley Candy Company. Mr. Farley, Grandma told us, taught her to avoid using the same word twice in any letter or document that she typed—good advice for all writers. Grandma was more than intelligent; she was wise. She often said, "I try to learn one new thing each day."

On my mom's side, Grandma Wright was a strong, conscientious, and resourceful woman. She had a full head of striking auburn hair, which my youngest son, Jordan, inherited. Because Grandma Wright lived in California, and I was born in Chicago, I saw her only a few times before she died at the age of seventy-seven. Although my memories of her are limited, the one tangible thing of hers that I have is a small wooden plaque with white letters raised in relief: *Only one life, twill soon be past, only what's done for Christ will last.* "To me to live is

> *Five Best Things about My Grandma:*
>
> 1. *She is nice.*
> 2. *She cares when I'm sad.*
> 3. *She is fun.*
> 4. *She never says, "Don't cry!"*
> 5. *But the best thing is that she's mine.*
>
> *(Grandchild, Austria, age 10)*

Christ." Phil. 1:21. The plaque is tangible—the truth behind it eternal.

Over the years, my mom told my siblings and me about how Grandma Wright regularly baked bread from scratch and sewed clothing for her family. It's a good thing that Grandma Wright was so industrious, because she and my hard-working Grandpa raised eleven children during the Depression. My mom was number ten. Sadly, in addition to being a hardworking man, Grandpa Wright was a hard-drinking man. Those were difficult years for the whole family. But in the midst of trying times, something good was also happening. "God," my mom often says with a catch in her throat, "was drawing me to Himself." God used His Word (Mom started going to a church one of her sisters had attended) and His people (many of my mom's Christian friends and their parents prayed for her and encouraged her during those years) to help her grow.

To this day, my mom is overwhelmed at how God reached out to her with His grace and mercy. So am I, because her faith in Christ subsequently pointed my dad to faith in Christ. As they have served God together over the years, they've blessed me, my siblings, and our spouses, as well as each of our children and generations yet to come. When my mom was being drawn to Christ as a teenager, I wonder if she had any idea of the rich legacy she and her future husband would leave for generations yet to come.

What were your grandmas like? Did you ever have a chance to meet them? All grandmas leave legacies, whether or not they have an opportunity to meet their grandchildren. Kristiana Hatcher, a young friend from Austria, wrote this about a grandma she never met:

> My mom's mom died before I was born. Still, I feel as if I know her from the stories I have heard. The best gift my grandma gave me was a small bit of advice she gave my mom years ago. When my mom was a teenager, she felt gawky and ugly. Don't all teenage girls? Her hair

17

was too thin, too straight, too limp. She didn't have the full, curvy body craved by those of us who look in the mirror and are depressed by our flat chests and nonexistent hips. All of these traits she passed on to her only daughter—me. But my grandma knew that those things mean nothing. She understood that there is so much more to a girl than thick hair and feminine curves. What makes us who we are, as women, is our character, not our stumpy hair and invisible eyelashes. My grandma gave my mom a piece of advice which my mom, in turn, imparted to me: We can't control the way we look. We can't make a wish and wake up beautiful. But we can decide who we are going to be, and how we're going to use what God has given us. Today, my mom is a missionary, reaching the world for Christ. And I can look in the mirror and smile, thinking of a wiser woman.

Some of your grandma memories might be heart-warming, some might not. Some contribute pleasant memories to a family's lore, others leave behind painful words or unfulfilled dreams. Although we're all affected by the choices of previous generations, none of us is trapped. Each day, we face new opportunities to choose, and the choices we make influence present and future generations.

Joyce Walta, a grandma from the United States, reflects on the legacy her grandma left:

"From my grandma, I learned that my job on this earth was to care for God's creation, and let others know, by my life, words, and actions, of God's love and redemption." From South Africa, Ems Johnsen wrote, "The legacy I would like to leave my grandchildren is that of memories. How will they remember me? I want to be joyful, to revel in the wonder of God, and to know and enjoy my grandchildren as God knows and enjoys me." Shirley Mathews, a United States grandma, expressed, "I am realizing how profoundly a grandchild changes me. This little girl has reminded me of the brevity of life and the need to influence another generation for Christ."

When it comes to advice about leaving a good legacy, the Bible is our richest resource available. Whether we dip into the prophets, the psalms, or the epistles, a couple of principles keep surfacing: *Remember God's Word and God's wonders and tell them to future generations*:

> Only take care, and keep your soul diligently, lest you forget the things that your eyes have seen, and lest they depart from your heart all the days of your life. Make them known to your children and your children's children—how on the day that you stood before the LORD your God at Horeb, the LORD said to me, "Gather the people to me, that I may let them hear my words, so that they may learn to fear me all the days that they live on the earth, and that they may teach their children so." (Deut. 4:9–10).

Remember God's Word and God's Wonders

One morning I was studying Genesis 37–50, a gripping account of Joseph's life. After reading how Joseph had been betrayed by his brothers, sold into slavery, and dumped into Pharoah's dungeon for two years, I realized that Joseph would have had plenty of bad memories to mull over. I mused that he had his moments. I also wondered what good memories were stored in his brain—remembrances that would have been encouraging, not painful. What life stories did he have from the past that might prompt him to believe that God would provide for him in the future? Joseph didn't have the Bible; it hadn't been written yet. But it's safe to assume that his parents had told him the story—probably more than once—of how God had blessed his great-grandparents, Abraham and Sarah, with a son in their old age. Joseph may have experienced sweaty palms and wide eyes when he heard the account of Abraham and Isaac's trip up to Mount Moriah to make a sacrifice. I wonder how he felt when Grandma Rebecca described what it was like to fill umpteen water jugs for Abraham's servant (and camels!) only to find out that God was arranging for her and Isaac to become husband and wife. I imagine that stories of God's faithfulness to Joseph's grandma, grandpa, great-grandma, and great-grandpa helped him to hang on to his faith during some very difficult months and years. In remembering, Joseph would have realized that if God could be trusted to take care of them, then God could take care of him, too.

My grannies are good Christian influences to me and give me someone to look up to. (Grandchild, Australia)

Today, we have much more than the stories passed down to Joseph. We have a feast of accounts to remember—the whole Bible! A little girl who regularly observes her grandma's love of the Bible was sitting and scribbling in a notebook one day, her Bible open next to her. When her mom walked by and asked her what she was doing, Kenedy answered, "Oh, I'm just 'Bible-ing' like my Mimi (Grandma)." This young girl has seen her grandma *remembering* God's Word—dwelling on it, treasuring it, and holding it dear.

In remembering God's Word, we remember His wonders—things He has done that are amazing, astonishing, or stunning; parting the waters of the Red Sea, feeding the five thousand with five loaves and two fish, and the ultimate wonder of Jesus' death and resurrection out of love for us. Some of God's wonders are also seen in our daily lives. "Grandma Knoedler," wrote Steve Howard, "has always reminded me of God's faithfulness. When I was growing up, she would call me (or e-mail me) on the anniversary of some event—for example, my falling out of the triple bunk and cracking my chest—and remind me of how the Lord has protected me over the years."

Another grandma gathers stones of remembrance, based on the Scripture passage in Joshua 4:21–24: "And [Joshua] said to the people of Israel, 'When your children ask their fathers in times to come, "What do these stones mean?" then you shall let your children know, "Israel passed over this Jordan on dry ground." For the LORD your God dried up the waters of the Jordan for you until you passed over, as the LORD your God did to the Red Sea, which he dried up for us until we passed over, so that all the peoples of the earth may know that the hand of the LORD is mighty, that you may fear the LORD your God forever.'"

"I make a point," says Marge Gieser, "of painting a small stone with some sort of identifying symbol or figure commemorating amazing events in our family life that speak of God's mercy and power on our behalf. A few examples are the three-month premature birth of our twin grandchildren, a four-year-old who somehow swallowed a needle that thankfully lodged in his appendix instead of his bowel, and a three-year-old who miraculously saved his one-and-a-half-year-old brother from drowning in our backyard twenty-four-inch deep pond. (At that time, the three-year-old was badly delayed in speech, but that night, he clearly and distinctly said, Jesus helped me.) Another time, when an eleven-year-old grandson was seriously injured on a canoe trip, there was an amazing and sudden assembly of people to help us—a miracle of God's grace evident to us all, most of all the eleven-year-old. I expect that the stones will

> *Grandma Knoedler is the type of person I love so dearly because I see so much of Christ in her. This is why I call her as often as I do—because she is a person I truly love in addition to her being my grandmother. She is a joy to have in my life. (Adult Grandchild, USA)*

21

slowly pile up in years to come as there are more incidents of God's amazing grace and mercy. They will be there so that the children can ask, what is the meaning of these stones? Then, we can all recount the stories."

Tell

We are to tell God's Word to the next generations—to live it, to rehearse it, and to communicate it. The New Testament book of 2 Timothy refers to Timothy's grandma, Lois, as a shining example. "I am reminded of your sincere faith, a faith that dwelt first in your grandmother Lois and your mother Eunice. . . . But as for you, continue in what you have learned and firmly believed, knowing from whom you learned it and how from childhood you have been acquainted with the sacred writings, which are able to make you wise for salvation through faith in Christ Jesus" (2 Tim. 1:5; 3:14–15).

"Lois played a great role in the lives of her daughter and her grandson," wrote Ranie Yesudian, a grandma from India. "Her faith was like an Olympic torch passed on from generation to generation." Timothy's grandmother, Lois, and his mother, Eunice, planted seeds of God's Word in his young heart, preparing him to see his need for a Savior.

One of the reasons that Timothy could firmly believe the truth of God's Word was because of the credibility of the messengers—"knowing from whom you learned it." When children and grandchildren see the truth and grace of Christ worked out (although imperfectly) in us, they often want to believe in Him, too. By God's grace, we can do that for future generations.

One young mom, Carolyn Walter, wrote this about her mother: "From the day that each of my sons were born, their grandmother (my mom) has been whispering Bible verses into their ears. I would hardly have thought to have done this during those early days while learning to manage a newborn under immense sleep deprivation. But as I watched my mother relieve me and take my colicky son in her arms and rock him while reading aloud from the Word of God, I remember thinking . . . I hope I'm a grandmother like that some day!"

> We will not hide these truths from our children;
>> we will tell the next generation
> about the glorious deeds of the LORD,
>> about his power and his mighty wonders.
> For he issued his laws to Jacob;
>> he gave his instructions to Israel.
> He commanded our ancestors
>> to teach them to their children,
> so the next generation might know them—
>> even the children not yet born—
>> and they in turn will teach their own children.
> So each generation should set its hope anew on God,
>> not forgetting his glorious miracles
>> and obeying his commands.
> Then they will not be like their ancestors—
>> stubborn, rebellious, and unfaithful,
>> refusing to give their hearts to God.
>>> (Ps. 78:4–8, NLT).

Psalm 78 suggests several reasons why we're to remember God's Word and wonders, telling them to future generations:

1. So they will set their hope in God.
2. So they will not forget God's glorious works.
3. So they will obey God.
4. So they will learn from the past and not repeat the mistakes and rebellions of their forefathers.

So They Will Set Their Hope in God

Now that I'm in my fifties, I've lived long enough to be convinced that the hope of the world is not found in the goodness of mankind. I only need to look as far as my own heart to know that. I see my selfishness daily. If it weren't for the forgiveness and hope that Jesus' death and resurrection offered me, there's no way my heart could be changed. Through faith in Christ, though, I became His child, and my heart continues to be renewed. That is the hope my husband and I heard from our parents. That is the hope our children have heard from us and their grandparents. We pray even now that generations to come will set their hope in God, too. It doesn't always happen that way, though. Sometimes, the hope of one person in a family may not be immediately evident in the next generation, but is realized again several generations later.

My grandma loves God with all her heart. (Grandchild, USA, age 10)

That was the case for Ravi Zacharias, an international Christian apologist.

In 1858, a young Nambudiri [Indian] woman who had five brothers came into contact with Christian belief and was fascinated by what she heard. Evidently, she had been speaking with the missionaries at the Basel Mission, a German-Swiss Christian mission in her village. When the rest of the family learned of her interest, she was strongly rebuked, threatened, and warned not to visit the mission compound anymore. As I understand it—and as was told to me by my grandaunt who lived to the age of 103—on the day after this reprimand, as soon as her brothers left for work, my ancestor went to the missionaries to tell them she could no longer come. But while she was there, news arrived that a cholera epidemic was spreading rapidly throughout the village, which meant that everyone was ordered to be quarantined—wherever they were at the moment. She could not leave the mission compound, and her brothers were not permitted inside to take her home. So she had to remain there for several weeks, much to her family's displeasure. During that quarantined period, the young Nambudiri asked all her questions about Jesus Christ, and before she left that compound once the quarantine was lifted, she had made her heart's commitment to follow Christ. That woman was my great-great-great-grandmother, and her conversion started my ancestors on the road to the Christian faith.[1]

So They Will Not Forget God's Glorious Works

One way to remind grandchildren of God's glorious works is in the daily fabric of life—here a little, there a little. Kristin Kriegbaum explains: "I enjoy taking my grandchildren hiking at places like Starved Rock, Lake Ellyn, Herrick Lake, and Honey Rock camp. This is a wonderful way to teach enjoyment of simple pleasures and God's creation. One of the finest hours was last fall, after my husband Ward and I hiked and then sat and read Psalm 19 together. I was smitten with the idea that day by day, the creation pours forth speech about the Creator. So the next day, I gathered up two grandchildren, took them hiking at the same place, sat on the same picnic bench, and read them the same Psalm. I also asked them to memorize a few of the verses. The memories of that experience are emblazoned on my mind, and I'm sure on theirs also."

So They Will Obey God

Obeying God is a matter of committing our hearts, minds, and bodies to God. At the heart level, it's a desire to please God. It's a response to seeing who He is and how He works. This is the kind of obedience we pray for in the lives of our

1. Ravi Zacharias, *Walking from East to West* (Grand Rapids, MI: Zondervan, 2006), 42–43.

children and grandchildren. A few years ago, my husband Jim and I received a letter from our oldest son, Chad, who was teaching at Vienna Christian School in Vienna, Austria. In his letter, he wrote, "A discussion in chapel the other day turned to reasons why we believe and follow God. In class right after that, a student asked me, 'Well, why do you believe?' I thought for a bit, and then answered that one of the biggest reasons I believe is because I have seen [the generations] before me live out their faith before God. They haven't served Him perfectly, but as they've sought to obey Him and live authentic Christian lives, they've given credence to the gospel that they acknowledge with their lips. That's a big reason why my faith has remained an important part of my life."

So They Will Learn from the Past and Not Repeat the Mistakes and Rebellions of Their Forefathers

For my husband, Jim, and me, telling our children about God's Word and wonders has included some great memories. We began with simple Bible stories and songs (on records!) when the boys were young and encouraged a growing love for God's Word as they matured. Being part of a Christ-centered church that preaches God's Word has made a huge contribution to their growth as well. We've rehearsed God's wonders in our lives—how God provided so we could purchase our first home on Pershing Street, how He supplied college money for our sons in unexpected ways, and how He guided them to excellent jobs when they graduated—working at an engineering firm, teaching at an international school, and working for Ravi Zacharias.

Telling our children about God's wonders in our lives has also included some difficult memories. During a season of pain in our marriage, our sons saw our struggles and experienced their own pain. Thanks to God's truth and grace and the help we received from family, close friends, pastors, and counselors, over time our sons also observed things like repentance, forgiveness, and healing. Jim and I haven't regretted talking with our sons about our journey of working through those difficulties, even though it felt awkward at first. Sometimes there were uncomfortable moments of silence, sometimes there were questions, and sometimes there were tears. As we've been honest with our children in a straightforward and respectful way, they've had opportunities to learn from our struggles and avoid repeating the same mistakes. Consequently, Jim and I assume that our sons will pass some important lessons on to their children and even grandchildren in days yet to come. We have come to understand that God's power to help us in our difficulties is not a secret to be kept. It's a hope to be shared.

Years back, during some of the dark days, Jim and I had moments when we wondered how anything good could ever come out of the pain we were experiencing. We're grateful, though, for the joy we feel over the good things God has accomplished and is accomplishing in our lives—in our family, our church, our work, and our opportunities to serve others. At about 7:45 most mornings, Jim and I stand in our kitchen, pray together, and say these verses:

> Satisfy us each morning with your unfailing love,
>   so we may sing for joy to the end of our lives.
> Give us gladness in proportion to our former misery!
>   Replace the evil years with good.
> Let us, your servants, see you work again;
>   let our children see your glory.
> And may the Lord our God show us his approval
>   and make our efforts successful.
> Yes, make our efforts successful!
>   (Ps. 90:14–17, NLT).

God's Word and God's Spirit have equipped and encouraged me for various stages and circumstances of my life to this point. I have walked with Him long enough to say with certainty, "You are the God who works wonders" (Ps. 77:14). If God blesses me with the role of being a grandma in the future, I'm confident that He will equip me for that privilege and responsibility, too. What I hope for each of you is what I hope for myself: That we'll leave a good legacy for future generations. That we'll remember God's Word and wonders in our lives, and rehearse those things with future generations.

For some of us, the role of grandma is yet to come. Others are buzzing in the center of the active zone. Due to circumstances or distances, some are influencing and relating to grandchildren mainly through prayers, phone calls, and e-mails. Regardless of whatever age or stage we're in—or the color of our hair—here's a good prayer for us all:

> Now that I am old and gray,
>   do not abandon me, O God.
> Let me proclaim your power to this new generation,
>   your mighty miracles to all who come after me.
>   (Ps. 71:18, NLT).

Two

Activities
and One-on-one Times

When I was a little girl, some of my favorite things to do with Grandma and Grandpa Banks were:

- Swinging on the porch of their two-flat in Chicago.
- Riding the carousel at Kiddy Land.
- Eating at the Choo-Choo (a bit of a greasy-spoon diner where kids sitting at the counter saw their burgers and fries delivered by a train).

But my absolute favorite thing was to stay at Grandma and Grandpa's house and have Grandma all to myself. In the summer, we'd ride the bus to Chicago and back. At Christmastime, we'd sit and look at the bubble lights on her little Christmas tree. Each time I visited her alone, she took me to the dime store and let me pick out one thing I wanted. It was there that she bought me my first bottle of nail polish. Oh, the undivided attention of a grandma!

Activities

Our grandsons, Lucas (5) and Micah (3), call us "Opa prik"—in English that's something like Grandpa prick, because he has a beard that's prickly—and "Oma Ham" because Ham's our last name. They live nearby, and every Tuesday I pick them up at twelve o'clock and we have lunch together. The boys are fond of frankfurters (I think that's what you call those little sausages). Every week I buy some frankfurters and some white rolls, and then we have a frankfurter party. One time, though, there was a big problem, because both grandsons wanted to serve the frankfurters. So we came up with the idea that one week Lucas would serve the frankfurters and Micah would serve the rolls, and the next week it would be the other way around. To make it special, we made two caps for the boys. On one cap we wrote: "Vandaag ben ik knakworsten directeur" (Today I am the frankfurters boss). On the other cap we wrote: "Vandaag ben ik bolletjes burgemeester" (Today I am the rolls mayor). We made a checklist so they can see who's on term for which task. That makes every Tuesday a happy day. *(Grandma, The Netherlands)*

My three grandchildren live locally, so I go to their home one day a week to help out and to give Mom a break. Each week, I take a special red bag that holds little treats for the children—usually something from the dollar store. Each time I come, they ask, "What's in the red bag, Grandma?" *(Grandma, USA)*

My mom is a quilter and a seamstress. She has been sewing all my life. But it's kind of a family joke that I didn't get the "crafty gene" because I can't stand that stuff. She has tried, over the years, to pass her love of sewing on to my girls. A couple of them have taken a real interest. So this winter, Mom planned a trip up here for a week. Before she came she ordered us a brand new sewing machine and had it delivered to our house. When she arrived, the girls and their grandma had a great time unpacking the machine, reading the directions, and learning how to wind a bobbin. I stood back and watched. When the sewing machine was up and ready, we took several trips to every quilt shop imaginable to get fabric for a project for each girl. In the end, Julia quilted a pillow, Caroline made pajama pants, and Kate started a quilt of her own. I was amazed that they had so much talent—and patience! The neatest part was that I had nothing to do with it. My mom took the initiative to order the sewing machine and to get the girls going on their projects. And the girls responded much better than I could have even imagined. If I had tried to teach them to sew, it would have been an absolute disaster, but with my mom they each had success and sweet memories to keep them going. *(Mom, USA)*

My husband and I try to do a few things with our grandchildren that we do only with them. Bubbles are a hit, whether we blow them outside, in the bathtub, or at the kitchen sink. We also sing songs with Grandpa's guitar or banjo—they each have their own song that Grandpa wrote for them, so that is a special and unique gift! They love to hear their own song, but have learned each other's song, too. We bought the kids a little fish, just for them. Whenever I know that they are coming over, I save the feeding time for the kids—the littlest grandchild wants to grab the fish and love it, but the older one knows just what to do! *(Grandma, USA)*

Every Grandma needs an attic! If you asked my granddaughter what her favorite room was when she came to visit, she would respond, "Grandma's attic." I saved several hats that I had made when I was younger as well as many pairs of high heeled shoes. My grandchildren

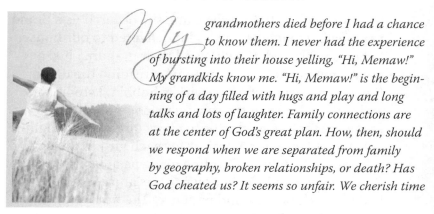

grandmothers died before I had a chance to know them. I never had the experience of bursting into their house yelling, "Hi, Memaw!" My grandkids know me. "Hi, Memaw!" is the beginning of a day filled with hugs and play and long talks and lots of laughter. Family connections are at the center of God's great plan. How, then, should we respond when we are separated from family by geography, broken relationships, or death? Has God cheated us? It seems so unfair. We cherish time

spent hours up there playing house. Their grandfather made a doll house, which was also fun to play with—and that stayed in the attic. *(Grandma, USA)*

We live about ten miles from a larger town where there are buses for public transportation. I was reading to some of my grandchildren about buses, when I decided to take the children on a bus ride. One day, I told all five of my grandchildren who live close to us that I had a surprise for them. We drove to the mall where there was a bus pickup, and we waited for the bus to arrive. They got so excited that they were going to ride a real bus. We rode around the entire bus route, and every time the bus driver put on the brake to pick up a rider, my youngest grandson who was about two at the time, said, "I'm not going to get off this bus." The bus route took about an hour and a half, and my grandchildren were thrilled. Their ages ranged from two to six years of age. We followed our bus ride with a visit to McDonald's, and it was a day of making memories. An added bonus was that the bus driver thought it was such a great idea that she wouldn't even charge for the children! *(Grandma, USA)*

Some springs, I plant a small garden that is just for the grandkids. *(Grandma, USA)*

with our loved ones. If this earth were all there is of time, then indeed, many of us have missed rich blessings. But our heavenly Father has greater things in store for those who have put their trust in him: eternal life. All those who love Jesus will spend eternity together—that's unlimited time for hugs and play and long talks and lots of laughter. So, I'm praying that my grandkids will love Jesus. My grandmothers loved Jesus. Someday, I'm going to meet them and say, "Hi, Memaw." —Nanci Alcorn

● I make two quilts for each grandchild. The first is a "good" quilt that is hand-quilted. The second is a "drag-around" quilt that often has to be repaired or altered. Granddaughter number 4, Caroline, came to me recently and asked if I would make hers larger; it didn't cover her toes because she had grown! Each of the girls has her own quilt box that holds the fabrics she has chosen as well as some works in progress. I found some tape measures that are a chicken with an egg, dog with a nose, and cow with a tail for the pulls, which have been fun. *(Grandma, USA)*

● When working in the yard or washing the cars, my husband and I sometimes call and ask if the grandchildren would like to help. Ours rarely refuse, as they love dirt and water. We use these opportunities to teach appreciation of things that have been created for us by our loving heavenly Father! *(Grandma, USA)*

● We are fortunate to be within walking distance of a game reserve. We hike over and look at the hippos, lions, leopards, and giraffes. We talk about the animals and what makes them special. *(Grandma, South Africa)*

I have a niece who is a really good golfer. For the past two summers, my parents (Paige's grandparents) have invited Paige to come stay with them for a week—just Paige; no parents. For the week that Paige is with them, my parents golf with her every day. My dad is a really good golfer, too, so he gives her pointers on her game, and Paige has some great memories of golfing with Grandma and Grandpa and even some of Grandpa's buddies! Also, every summer for the past several years Paige has golfed in a tournament in Texas (where she lives), and my dad has driven to Texas from Arizona to be her caddy in this tournament. Can you imagine your grandpa being your caddy? I know that doesn't have much to do with grandmothers, but it does say something about grandparenting in general. I think my parents have done a great job of connecting with my girls even though they live far away. They have found common interests and pursued them with each one. Even though they can't be together a lot, they are leaving each granddaughter with special memories of the times they are together. *(Mom, USA)*

My husband and I live on a farm, and we enjoy having the grandchildren come and visit. Grandpa takes us in the truck to see the cows. In the summer, we wade in the creek together. We like to catch minnows and crawfish, plus find pretty rocks and frogs. We also pick berries, especially gooseberries, and after we pick them, we stem them. Now that the girls are older, they like to drive the golf cart around the farm. *(Grandma, USA)*

My granddaughter and two-year-old grandson enjoy going fishing at a pond near our house. There are several sunfish in the pond. With Papa's help, the children fish with worms or corn as bait. They are also happy feeding the fish small pieces of bread. The fish seem to sense the "special people" as they come to eat the special treat. *(Grandma, USA)*

As able, I include my grandchildren in my daily life—things like a trip to the store, gardening, meal preparation and clean-up, baking, etc. There are all kinds of ways to share time together. *(Grandma, USA)*

I like it when Grandma gets up early in the morning and goes fishing with us. When we catch a fish, she puts on her rubber gloves and helps us get it off the hook. *(Grandchildren, USA, ages 8 and 10)*

One time, my granddaughter and I made a castle using cardboard boxes and tubes from paper towels. We added flat jewels that we had purchased at a craft store. *(Grandma, USA)*

As my grandchildren grew older, five and seven, we started spending a lot of time together. We began oil painting and learning how to sew on the sewing machine. Each grandchild had his or her own box of fabric for the quilts they were working on and another for their paintings. To this day, they are proud of their accomplishments. *(Grandma, USA)*

I love being a grandmother! I enjoy doing activities with my grandchildren that provide a variety of interactions that are fun and that teach them something. I take them places and do things with them that their parents don't have the time to do. Children love to stay busy and, of course, they love to talk. *(Grandma, USA)*

My boys love to draw, and my mother will often draw with them. She tries to draw pictures of activities that they have done together or places they have recently visited and writes a short caption on the picture and the date. Then she punches three holes in the paper and keeps them in a three-ring binder. The boys love to look through the binder at all the drawings and remember things that they have done with their Grandma. *(Mom, USA)*

- Some of my favorite memories are growing up helping Grandma and Grandpa in the big garden, stacking wood, and being allowed to do things that made me feel valued. I especially remember going out into the woods on my grandparents' land and just walking among those huge trees with my dad, brother, and Grandpa. Sometimes Grandpa would bring the metal detector along, and we would search for buried money. We never found anything very valuable, but the anticipation and excitement that were created by the beeps of the metal detector and the effort of digging and then guessing what those scraps of metal were was and is always a highlight of visiting Grandma and Grandpa. *(Grandchild, Austria, age 17)*

- My husband loves to go to the circus and couldn't wait until our first two grandsons were old enough to go. Ringling Bros. and Barnum & Bailey circus was coming to Peoria, and he wanted me to get the best tickets we could. We were fortunate enough

There are a few things I like to do at my grandma's house. First, I like to eat her homemade sugar cookies. They are soft from the inside out. They are small, but it's worth it! Second, I like to play card games with her—she is very good at Phase 10. I try my very best, but she is too good. Third, I like it when we go out to dinner. It is very nice when Grandma takes us to see our great-grandma, who is ninety-two years old. (Grandchild, USA, age 8)

to get ringside seats, which cost a lot of money. The circus hadn't been going very long when the boys said they wanted to leave. We informed them they were staying whether they wanted to or not. They were clearly bored. Finally they asked if we could leave and go to the Hardees restaurant with a playground. We made them stay until the end, but then we went to Hardees, and they had much more fun in the playground than they had at the circus. Moral of the story: don't try to force grandchildren to enjoy things. *(Grandma, USA)*

Every grandma needs to have a big basket or box full of older clothes, shoes, purses, hats, etc. for grandchildren to play dress-up. The little ones love to come parading out to show off their new outfits, and it's so much fun for the adults to see. *(Grandma, USA)*

The city we live in has lots of parks, so we try to visit them all. Some are more suited to one age group than to others. Some of our grandchildren like to play, while others prefer to sit on the bench and visit with us. Not all children have the same level of energy! *(Grandma, USA)*

Most of my favorite memories of my Grandma from recent years also involve my mom and me—the three generations—and boy, do we have fun together! One of our favorite things to do is spend an afternoon together at the Little Traveler, a smattering of quaint boutiques in Geneva, Illinois. We laugh, and eat, and shop, and laugh, and laugh, and laugh. I have been so fortunate to have taken several trips with just my grandma and mom—our friendship is unique and something I do not take for granted. I now live in North Carolina, too many miles away from these people I love, but that has not stopped our fun and special times together. Just last spring, my mom and grandma made a special springtime visit, and we are in the midst of planning another! Though circumstances have changed, our friendship has not. Our love for one another has only grown deeper. *(Adult Grandchild, USA)*

We go walking in the woods—one grandson calls them "the hundred acres woods"—which is always an adventure. My grandchildren love outings to an array of places: the pet store, a dollar store or toy store, Dairy Queen, a Christian bookstore, the mall, or to a park to play on the equipment. *(Grandma, USA)*

During the summer, we do finger painting outside, walk in the rain under an umbrella, and visit all the parks in my town. *(Grandma, USA)*

In a very materialistic society and with lots of toys and entertainment at our fingertips, my mother longs to share a contentment and fascination with the ordinary and simple and foster a great sense of imagination in her grandsons. In the course of their outside adventures together, my mother and my sons have gathered a collection of medium-sized (clean) stones that they use to build barns, construction sites, houses, castles, and roads. Sometimes they even use the stones and bang them together to make music and keep beat as they sing songs together or pound out rhythmic Bible verses. Other times they sort the stones into lines by size or color. These stones are kept in a special place and are taken out only when Grandma is with the boys. This makes them all the more special, and they look forward to being able to play with them. The stones have made several trips from the East Coast to the Midwest. They are a source of great enjoyment and enthrall my young sons' imagination for hours at a time. Whenever my sons see their grandmother, the first thing they want to do is play with the stones. *(Mom, USA)*

● Every now and then, I do a Domestic Day with my granddaughters; I teach them how to sew on a button or how to sew a hem, and then I take them out to tea. *(Grandma, USA)*

● One time when four granddaughters came to our lake house to visit for several days, I made a list of things that would keep them happy and occupied. I thought that one of the mornings they could decorate hats. I had straw hats and many silk flowers as well as ribbons and a glue gun (for me to use.) Somehow, what I had planned to take all morning turned out to take about one hour. My dilemma then was what to do with the rest of the morning! I learned that I couldn't plan their days for them, as they had lots of fun ideas of their own. So you see—we're never too old to learn. *(Grandma, USA)*

● When I was four years old, I went to my grandma's house for Christmas. She gave me so many presents. She gave me a remote control, Lego, and more. I liked that day because we sang together. The best part was sleeping at Grandma's house. After that day, I went to the beach and sat in the boat. We ate fish and rice. Then, I went back to Grandma's house and said thank you very much. That was my best day ever. *(Grandchild, Indonesia, age 10)*

● Last spring, I organized a party for St. Patrick's Day and made it our first training day for a local 5K run that is always held the first Saturday in June. Several times we trained together as a whole family for the run. I particularly worked with one ten-year-old grandson last spring. He was being homeschooled, so we trained together for his gym time. It was exciting the first time we ran for a whole mile without stopping. I took him different places to run to make it more interesting. Sometimes we went to an indoor track. We ran in several different parks. We used a college outdoor track that is in our area. It was a commitment on my part because he lives about twenty minutes from me, and I tried to pick him up three times per week for about eight weeks. I had my grandson ride my bike before we ran because it has a computer to measure miles. Then after we knew the correct distance, we would jog it together. Each year, I encourage the family to participate, and I pay for their registration fee because I think it is a great family event. *(Grandma, USA)*

When Grandma comes to visit, we wake up early and crawl in bed with her. We have special talks and play games while our parents sleep in. *(Grandchildren, USA, ages 8 and 10)*

Everywhere I went with my grandchildren, we talked on the way and sang on the way back home. They enjoyed choruses as well as camp songs. Their favorites were "Mr. Moon" and "The Laughing Song." The "Laughing Song" became a favorite at a family Christmas party when they were three and five. Puppets were the thing that year, and because the sofa sat in a prominent spot, the children lined up behind it, pretending that the puppets were singing the laughing song. They had all of us laughing! This past year, a granddaughter was graduating with her Bachelor of Science degree. We flew to California to attend. What a delight when she said, "I'll be back in Michigan for Christmas this year, and I want to give each of my cousins a CD of our 'Laughing Song.'" What fun there was with friends and family there laughing and singing along! *(Grandma, USA)*

Because my husband and I live close to our children, stroller walks give the parents a break and us time with our young grandchildren. *(Grandma, USA)*

● On a winter night when we have a fire burning in our fireplace, we sometimes sit in front of it with our grandchildren and ask them what they see in the fire. A castle? A horse? A dress? It's fun to see them use their imaginations. **(Grandma, USA)**

● My mother loves to share her passions with her grandsons as well as express a genuine interest in theirs. My boys are only two and three, so their passions are limited to trains, food, and a few other things. However, my mother always takes them on a train ride when she visits and reads them lots of books (her passion as well). My mom is an avid gardener and has taught my boys to love to work outside, to appreciate good soil and the miracle of watching a seed grow into a plant that bears fruit. They love to help her dig, plant, water, weed, and watch the plants grow, not to mention picking, tasting, and enjoying the fruit of their labor. Although we live far apart, my mother will even take pictures of a plant as it grows to show the boys how it has changed since they planted that tiny seed together. **(Mom, USA)**

I like that my grandma loves me and my family so much. I like that she loves to bake. I appreciate that she lets us help with anything. I'm glad that she likes to come and watch me play basketball and that she likes the piano. My grandma loves to have the cousins, aunts, and uncles over for a big lunch. At Easter we have a big Easter egg hunt. I call my grandma Nana Banana for a funny name. (Grandchild, USA, age 10)

● My granddaughter wanted to learn how to sew, so I helped her make a quilt for her doll. She even learned how to hand-stitch around the edge. *(Grandma, USA)*

● While riding in the car or walking, my grandchildren and I play word games like I Spy, rhyming words, and number games, or we look for cars of a certain color. Sometimes we tell silly jokes that don't even make sense. At home I have a button box that holds about one hundred buttons in all kinds of sizes and colors. Once in a while we pour out the buttons and sort them by color and count them. *(Grandma, USA)*

● My husband and I feared that trains would eventually go by the wayside and our grandchildren would not have the chance to ride a train. So, we decided as each child entered first grade we would take them on a train ride to Chicago. Since our grandchildren are very close in age, we decided to take the first two together. We purchased a large bag of Skittles for the two-and-a-half hour train ride. Two years later when we took the next two, the first two said, "Be sure to get a bag of Skittles." Consequently it became a tradition to ride the train to Chicago and eat Skittles on the way. On one trip the train was full, and my husband and I either stood or sat on the floor because we wanted the children to sit and look out the window and enjoy their train ride. *(Grandma, USA)*

● God has blessed us in Africa with wonderful sunny days and ample time for outside play. My grandchildren and I make memories by playing together in my garden, recognizing and enjoying the beauty of God's creation. *(Grandma, South Africa)*

● I have fond memories of quilting times with my granddaughters. I have a picture of my oldest granddaughter "quilting" while on a visit—she was about three and loved fussing with fabric, pins, colors, and other tactile objects. She has since made several quilts; they are priceless, and I'm thinking of framing them so she can have them forever. She reminds me that every quilt has to have "documentation" before we can say that it is finished. *(Grandma, USA)*

When I'm with my grandchildren, we do a variety of things:

- Read stories, play lots and lots of table games, do puzzles.
- Plant a garden, pick berries.
- Jump rope, fly kites, go to the playground.
- Go for a picnic, take a hike.
- Go to Giordano's for pizza or the Stupe for ice cream.
- Visit Kline Creek Farm, Cantigny, or the Morton Arboretum, watch a parade.
- Take in a Cougars baseball game, or basketball, or soccer.
- Visit the historical museum or Shedd Aquarium, view the windows at Marshall Field's (now Macy's), take an architectural boat tour, go to the zoo.
- See a movie, such as *Finding Nemo, The Nativity Story*, or an OmniMax feature. *(Grandma, USA)*

On summer nights before going to bed, my husband and I take our young grandchildren on walks when it's dark and look up at the stars. *(Grandma, USA)*

My mother is incredibly creative and will use ordinary things that she finds around her to create impressive crafts with the boys. The last time she visited us, she took them on a train ride. Because it was the dead of winter, they went to a nearby coffee shop to wait for the return train. At the coffee shop, they played with the wooden stir-sticks, making the shapes of letters and numbers and designs. When they arrived home, they decided to glue the sticks together to make unique snowflakes that they painted white and hung from our window. My mother-in-law desires to spend time with my children, but has a harder time knowing what to do with the boys to engage them and share a fun activity together. My husband and I have found it helpful to come up with activities ahead of time (before she visits) that we think she would be comfortable doing with the boys—things like taking a walk around the block while the boys ride their bikes, playing certain games, reading books, finger painting, playing with Play-Doh, going to a favorite place to eat, taking them to a nearby zoo— things that she can choose to do at her leisure during her visit so that she and the boys can enjoy each other's company. *(Mom, USA)*

The little girls love tea parties. We set the table with little dishes and small pretty napkins. If we have flowers outside, we pick a few for a small vase. Sometimes we put on a hat. Then we put little foods such as chocolate chips, oyster crackers, raisins, blueberries, etc., on little plates. We give them "tea names" such as biscuits, scones, and fruit nibbles. So far, I have been unsuccessful in teaching the girls to enjoy drinking real tea. So we have water and pretend that it is tea. Using water does have its advantages because it is no problem if someone spills a little. Pouring the tea is always a highlight. We always hold the cups with our little pinky finger up. *(Grandma, USA)*

My husband and I go to games and activities of all sorts to see our grandchildren: baseball, football, basketball, soccer, cheerleading, swimming, ballet, tae kwon do, piano recitals, concerts, plays, gymnastics, and a myriad of other things. We have taken photos of all of these things to preserve for a lifetime of great memories. The kids love when we come, and often ask their parents, "Who's coming to my game today?" They watch for us, and now the older ones just give us a tiny finger wave and a half smile that says, "I see that you're here for me and I love it, but I'm too cool to shout." That's OK—we did the same thing once. *(Grandma, USA)*

My husband and I love the outdoors, so we take our grandchildren on many walks to the playgrounds or parks. It's a neat way to be together. It gives the children an opportunity to run hard and play and provides wonderful moments for us to talk about God's creation. *(Grandma, USA)*

Sometimes I play pretend school with my young grandchildren, and I let them be the teacher! *(Grandma, USA)*

All of my grandchildren love to play board games—from the seven-year-old down to the three-year-olds. Our favorites are Junior Monopoly, Uno, Checkers, Candy Land, Chess, and tic-tac-toe. The old standbys of crayons, coloring books, and Play-Doh never seem to lose their appeal. *(Grandma, USA)*

When my daughters were in junior high, one of their grandmothers came and guided them through the process of making a dress. She was an excellent seamstress, so they learned from a pro. *(Grandma, USA)*

Sometimes we have a picnic and spread a blanket under the trees while I become part of my grandchildren's world for a few hours. *(Grandma, South Africa)*

I had a number of dress-up dresses, formals, long skirts, and ladies hats from long ago that I kept in a closet for my granddaughters to play with. They had so much fun with them. One summer day I told my two granddaughters that they could each invite two friends to come for the afternoon and play with the dress up clothing. They wanted to have tea. We got out a set of good dishes, and they dressed up, and I was the maid and served them tea and cookies. They talked with an English accent and enjoyed every minute of asking for more tea, more cookies, etc., and having the maid (Grandma) wait on them. *(Grandma, USA)*

When my mom comes to visit, she brings craft ideas from magazines and does special projects with the girls. The fun is in the process. *(Mom, USA)*

Last year my daughter arranged a fishing derby to be held at our retirement community fishing pond. Everyone had a chance to catch fish for prizes—one child in each family got a certificate and a gift card for ice cream to be shared. Afterward we went to my daughter's home for a cookout, and everyone played games in the yard. Although I have arthritis, I still manage to play hide-and-seek, golf, baseball, and I just enjoy being involved. The kids are most forgiving and show concern for me. I think this is a valuable lesson. *(Grandma, USA)*

I enjoy teaching my grandchildren how to skip, gallop, jump rope, and play games that we used to play, like SPUD. Sometimes my husband and I take them to the soccer field to kick the ball around or to the basketball court to shoot the basketball. It gets them good and tired and makes an easier evening for their parents. *(Grandma, USA)*

A game that I enjoy playing with my grandchildren is Careers. Other games that we like to play are Dutch Blitz, Cat's Eye, Uno, and Rummikub. In the car or while waiting, we play "Would You Rather?" I love hearing the children's responses! *(Grandma, USA)*

Each family gets a special weekend at our house every year, doing things that they choose—bowling, swimming, horseback riding, seeing a play, going to Great America, choosing meals, watching movies, playing board games, etc. *(Grandma, USA)*

I like to take walks with my grandchildren and look for birds. I'm trying to teach them the sounds of various birds. *(Grandma, USA)*

I bought a Lego racecar set on sale (with lots of pieces!), and the grandsons and I are working to put it together. *(Grandma, USA)*

My aim is not as much to educate my grandchildren as it is for us to enjoy each other through play. Playing ball, running, and playing cricket keeps me in shape, too. I thank the Lord for my good health. *(Grandma, South Africa)*

Both of my grandchildren enjoy taking a trip to the children's zoo near our home. There, they see farm animals, ducks, and several kinds of special birds in the exhibits. There is also a stationary caboose to climb into and pretend to take a ride. In the fall, there are mounds of pumpkins for sale. *(Grandma, USA)*

My mom loves to have outings with my kids. When she visits us, we go to the zoo, the park, children's plays, children's museums, etc. When we visit my parents in Florida, they take my kids to see the manatees at a local nature park, to visit a nearby fire engine manufacturing plant (a big hit with the three-year-old grandson), to the beach, to Downtown Disney, etc. When my parents first moved to Florida, they began researching good places to take the grandchildren when we would come to visit, and they're still discovering new kid-friendly attractions six years later. *(Mom, USA)*

For granddaughters who like ballet, I provide CDs with ballet music, long ribbons for the girls to twirl around, and tutus and ballet outfits that have been purchased at resale shops. *(Grandma, USA)*

My grandchildren and I enjoy taking the train for various events—sometimes into Chicago or a neighboring town for lunch or ice cream treats or to walk in a park. Of course, we sit in the upper deck of the train so we can see everything! *(Grandma, USA)*

One summer day I was keeping two of my grandchildren, and we were trying to think of something to do that was fun. Well, we decided to bake cookies—lots of cookies. I told all five of them that the next day they could invite their friends, and we would rent a moonwalk and have a party. The party sounded like a lot of fun so we hired a magician to come and entertain the kids. He wasn't very good, but he didn't cost very much, and the kids thought he was wonderful. We served the cookies that the kids and I had baked the day before and had lemonade. At one point there were about thirty-five to forty kids in our backyard all having so much fun. *(Grandma, USA)*

My grandmother and I live on different continents and visits are scarce. What I remember from our visits in the past is that she was always very welcoming and hospitable. Despite the lack of frequent contact, we tend to catch up during the summers when my family and I fly to America to visit relatives. (Grandchild, Austria, age 15)

My husband is a beekeeper. Once the children reach the age of seven, they may help grandpa in the beeyard one-on-one. The whole family participates in the harvest days. We start early in the morning and rotate the jobs. Even the young children help bottle the honey and, of course, we have plenty of opportunities to taste it. Several of the children have taken beekeeping clothes and equipment to school for science projects or show-and-tell. *(Grandma, USA)*

I have tried to give the kids different experiences than their own families would do. We have gone several times to the Lizzadro Museum of Lapidary Art in Elmhurst, Illinois. They can look at the exhibits, but their favorite part is buying rocks for their collections from the gift shop. *(Grandma, USA)*

I'm not a birder, however I do enjoy the flashes of color around our home and confess to having spent a few dollars on (eight) bluebird houses. (Did you know that you need two of them close to each other—one for the flickers, sparrows, or swallows who arrive first and quickly jump in and one for the blue beauty?) I spent even more dollars on black-oiled sunflower seeds for my all-time favorite bird, the regal scarlet cardinal. Of course, being a grandma, all that information can't be hoarded but must be shared with my little ones. So we fill birdfeeders, put slinky toys on the feeder poles to confound the squirrels, and listen for familiar birdcalls, especially in the springtime, all in hopes of gaining anything closer than a bird's-eye view. *(Grandma, USA)*

When we retired in Florida, we sold one car and bought a four-seater golf cart so we could drive our grandchildren around our community when they visited. My father was a golfer and always had an extra golf cart on the property when we visited him and my mother in New

Hampshire—my children loved to ride up and down the hills with my mother as a driver! My grandchildren, Hannah and Carter, call our golf cart Grammy's jeep! *(Grandma, USA)*

- I have gotten my grandchildren to enjoy theater a lot. I don't mean expensive theater, though at times we have paid up to twenty-one dollars for a great performance locally. It started when I took a two-year-old grandson to *Annie* at a local high school. The performance was over two hours long, and he never took his eyes off the stage. *(Grandma, USA)*

- Grandma teaches first grade at a Christian school, and for the last two summers has made sure that she's taught a summer school class that Hannah can attend with her. *(Mom, USA)*

- One thing my grandchildren like about visiting my husband and me is that we have a big backyard. There is a lot of space to run around, and we also have a tire swing. They love getting underneath dogs! When they were here last winter, we had quite a nice time sledding down our backyard hill together. It made for some great pictures! *(Grandma, USA)*

- When my grandchildren were very young, I went to Half Price Books and found several indoor and outdoor activity books for children. Those books have given me many, many ideas for creative play in all seasons and all kinds of weather. *(Grandma, USA)*

- When the grandchildren were young and driving a little jeep around the yard, driveway, and sidewalks, I made up individual driver's licenses for each of them with a picture and details similar to our own license:

Caleb Denver Cochrum
Height: So Big
License ID Number: JUS-2-CUTE
(Grandma, USA)

- We love taking our grandkids to White Sox ballgames. Grandpa has season tickets, so we try to take each of the children to at least one game during the season. We take them to other special events as we hear of them. Just a few weeks ago we took three grandchildren to the Chicago Boat and RV Show. Every now and then we call them and invite them to a new children's movie. *(Grandma, USA)*

- With cold weather being the norm in Chicago, I some-times plan a winter picnic with my grandchildren. We pack a picnic basket, line up for a pretend train ride through the house, and finally arrive in the woods (the family room) where we spread a plastic tablecloth on the floor. We tell funny stories, or I read a story. We take the same train back to the kitchen after everyone helps clean up the picnic sight. *(Grandma, USA)*

- I subscribe to the *Daily Herald* newspaper; local papers give us all kinds of activities that we stumble upon by reading daily. I have a constant stream of things going on with the kids through this local information and then through our affiliation with the wonderful resource of Wheaton College. *(Grandma, USA)*

- On a rainy day, spread a sheet or a plastic tablecloth on the floor and put the electric popcorn maker in the center. Let a child pour in the popcorn kernels, but don't put the lid on. Sit back several feet and watch the corn fly in all directions. Finally, eat the popcorn off the sheet! *(Grandma, USA)*

We have taken our grandchildren to the arboretum—hiking the trails, looking for the gigantic rock, and enjoying the little bridges over the ponds and river. Our own kids used to complain about this as being kind of boring, but years later Jonathan took Elizabeth there to propose marriage, because it was a special place. Now that we live elsewhere, we take the boys on the nature trails near us. We once enjoyed seeing a beaver dam and some of the branches the beavers had chewed. *(Grandma, USA)*

Grandma periodically takes the grandsons to lunch. No parents or girls allowed! It has been good for the boys to get to know one another better and to spend time with Grandma. And of course, they enjoy eating great food—a boys' love language! *(Mom, USA)*

Last spring, I sent some Rubbermaid containers full of arts-and-crafts materials to my daughter. She stores them in the kitchen for quick access when she's cooking and needs to keep her kids busy. At other times, she uses them for a little art project. I used gallon-sized Ziplocs to store many different kinds of materials. Some things I included were construction paper, cardboard, newsprint, pads of paper, precut circles, squares, triangles, glue sticks, Scotch tape, Elmer's glue, blunt-end scissors, tissue paper, crepe paper, stickers, foam shapes, pipe cleaners, water colors, markers, crayons, colored pencils, seasonal items, plastic aprons, and strong refrigerator magnets to display the children's masterpieces. *(Grandma, USA)*

A soft sock battle in our family room was something our grandchildren tried to save their dirty socks for whenever they came to Grandma and Grandpa's house. I must say that the parents frowned a little and rolled their eyes on this idea. A few socks sometimes came up missing. *(Grandma, USA)*

We play a lot of games with our grandchildren and laugh a lot. When I read a good joke that is appropriate to their age, I share it with them. They seem to enjoy it. *(Grandma, USA)*

I enjoy getting yearly membership passes to the children's museum, the zoo, and the arboretum. Some days when the children do not have school, my daughters-in-law and I take the cousins on outings to these places. *(Grandma, USA)*

One year when the grandkids came to visit, we made placemats for each of them by cutting out magazine pictures of various people as well as cutting up photos of the kids. We used the magazine bodies in combination with the children's heads to get them doing a variety of things. We pasted the combinations on placemat-sized colored paper and laminated them. It is four years later, and the grandkids are still using them! *(Grandma, USA)*

Although we do try to do special things once a year with the grandchildren, when they visit we like to do simple, everyday sorts of things with them—going to the park, going to the library, going for walks, playing board games, coloring or doing crafts, reading books together, baking or cooking, watching old movies. It allows for a natural setting for our relationships to grow and for meaningful conversation to take place. *(Grandma, USA)*

For more than six years I have been taking my grandkids all over the western suburbs of Chicago to see theater. Then I also became involved in community theater. After performing several times, I invited a granddaughter to be in a summer musical with me. She did, and we were together the entire summer, and the whole family came out to see us. (A little aside, Ward brings all the little grandchildren to a dress rehearsal so they can squirm and fall asleep, but they never do—they don't want to leave.) I am always on the prowl for theater for the kids and often find things through posters in downtown windows. *(Grandma, USA)*

Grandma has taken the grandkids on day trips to the arboretum and Klein Creek Farm. Grandma grew up on a farm, so she shares many memories as they walk along. *(Mom, USA)*

Most children enjoy taking a walk with grandparents. I like to point out special things such as an unusual building, a particular tree, or a bird. I often take along a snack or plan to stop at a candy store on the way back. Sometimes, we go bowling with our grandchildren—afternoons are great because there are special rates and fewer people. It's a good rainy day activity. *(Grandma, USA)*

One-on-One Times

I like to spend time with each grandchild individually (ages nine months to four years). This way we build a special relationship, and I get to know their likes and dislikes. *(Grandma, South Africa)*

My favorite thing to do with Oma is to play hide and seek. One time when we were playing hide and seek at my house, I hid in the closet. My grandma looked in there about ten times, but she still couldn't find me! Finally, I had to come out. We laughed so hard! I love my grandma, and she loves me, too. She is the best grandma in the whole world! *(Grandchild, USA, age 11)*

● My mother is a wonderful grandmother to our children. She is genuinely interested in them and in their interests. I'm sure there have been times she's done things with them that aren't of interest to her, but because it is meaningful to them, she enters into their excitement. She is happy to be part of any event that is important to them. When they were little, she got down on the floor to play with them. Now that they are older, she enjoys talking with them about their lives and interests. She knows them—their likes and dislikes—and always cooks their favorite foods! *(Mom, USA)*

● My husband and I do one-on-ones with all of our grandchildren. I watch the school calendar and make arrangements with the parents for dates that work for them. They come to spend the night and do what they want—quilt, watch videos complete with soda and popcorn and lots of snuggling under quilts, fish, bake cookies or

I have always enjoyed my grandma. I remember when I was about four years old, I loved to go to her house. She would always have a lot of candy, and the kind I enjoyed most was Skittles. We would always play games or do puzzles. And she always had a bunch of little toys for me to play with. She made the best food I had ever had, and when I would go out and play with my cousins she would look out of the window every once in a while to check up on me. (Grandchild, Sweden, age 14)

55

breads, cook pancakes, go out for lunch, or set up the train set. *(Grandma, USA)*

When my grandchildren are young, I have all-day dates with them. When one of them is four or five, I give him one day a year that we spend together, and he is in charge of planning the day. With my grandchildren who live in another state, this means that I spend the night at their house the night before. The child chooses what we eat for breakfast, lunch, and dinner (my only requirement is that there is enough healthy food involved that we don't feel sick before the day is half over). A lot of pancakes and ice cream have been consumed. They choose where we go and what we do all day, until after dinner. One grandson wanted to spend an entire morning looking at coins at a local coin store. One grandson just wanted to spend the day at a pizza place with lots of video games. *(Grandma, USA)*

I love to have tea parties with my grandma. We pick out which teapot to use, and we drink our tea out of teacups complete with milk and sugar. Grandma also serves some sort of treat, too! *(Grandchild, USA, age 8)*

My granddaughter (eight) comes to our house after school two or three times a week. We like to relax together after a big day, and routinely after afternoon tea, cuddle up together on the couch to watch *Play School*. OK, we know we're both too old for *Play School*, but we don't care! We pretend we are watching it more analytically, and it's a very special time together. *(Grandma, Australia)*

I invite grandchildren over to bake or work at a favorite craft or art project. It's a good opportunity to teach them art skills or color charts or how-to's. Kenedy has her own apron hanging next to mine for our art projects and for our baking times. She already understands primary and secondary colors and how yeast must be activated by very warm water and must sit and soak for a few minutes before we add the rest of the ingredients. *(Grandma, USA)*

Probably the best thing my husband and I have done with our grandkids is to have time individually with each child—with no sibling rivalry and the chance to cook special foods and do things that child wants to do. We give them choices of major excursions: going to see Thomas the Train, the butterflies at the zoo, a museum, the local river walk, going out for pizza, the climbing wall, swimming, etc. *(Grandma, USA)*

I've planted gardens with my grandchildren. One year, Ryan and I went to the stone quarry office and bought some flat rocks to make a path through the flower garden. It was a lot of work, and he was very pleased with his efforts. *(Grandma, USA)*

I like to sew with my grandma. My grandma and I are making a quilt. I also love to knit with her. We knitted a hat and a bag. *(Grandchild, USA, age 8)*

Once a year, my husband and I take the grandchildren separately (there are nine of them) to stay the weekend with us, and they choose one special thing to do. The top activities have been going to a play, going to a Christian rock concert (a real stretch for Jim and me), horseback riding, bowling, swimming, going to an arcade, or going to the arboretum. *(Grandma, USA)*

Micah likes to play hide-and-seek. When he finds me hiding under the table or behind a door, he laughs and enjoys me. To make him laugh, I sometimes wear a clown mask and he in turn wears the same mask to make me laugh. His laughter keeps him healthy and me happy. *(Grandma, India)*

● A favorite outing for me is a visit to the local coffee shop. My little grandson calls each year before my birthday to ask me to Starbucks on his dollar (a scrunched-up fistful of bills). He orders the strawberry frappuccino, and I order the mocha. We sit at the window and watch the traffic while discussing all the important things of life, like his last vacation trip, what he'll do this summer, and what he's currently reading. *(Grandma, USA)*

● I think it's important that each grandchild have personal time with each grandparent. I sometimes take a grandchild out to lunch or to a local zoo, museum, etc., by themselves, so that they have time with me alone, not always with a group of people or with their siblings. My husband has taken each grandchild fishing in a small boat. We think that fishing is not only about catching fish, but about being out in God's beautiful creation and building thankfulness and relationships. Catching fish is a fun sideline. *(Grandma, USA)*

● Our family has always played games together with the adults. A particular family game was Killer Uno, a rapid-fire game. Our older grandson began to play by five or six but the younger children could only watch. So when we asked our granddaughter what she wanted to do during her week with us one year, she said "I want to learn to play Killer Uno so I can surprise James." She did learn. We played over and over, and she was so proud. *(Grandma, USA)*

● Being able to spend time with a grandchild one-on-one is the most satisfying way to build a relationship. The grandparent is able to see and get acquainted with the child without siblings or parents to distract or compete with. *(Grandma, USA)*

When my granddaughter comes, she likes to sew. One time we made a pretty pillow and blankets for her doll's cradle. Last time, we made cool pajamas for her doll. *(Grandma, USA)*

When our grandchildren were very young, we invited them to visit us one at a time. Most of them lived in another state, so this was always a fun time they anticipated. We read, played with them, visited museums, and took them to the zoo or a children's play. I often took the girls shopping for something new to wear. *(Grandma, USA)*

It is sometimes overwhelming for grandparents to step into a kinetic household and just take over, but to be able to whisk one child away for an outing or an overnight changes the group dynamics at home for the better as well. One less child is always easier! Also, that child will often open up and chat more than if they remained in their birth order environment. *(Mom, USA)*

Baby and Child Equipment

When our young family of five visited my parents, my mom was a step ahead of us in what we might need for our children. When our kids were infants, Mom prepared a room for young moms to nurse in, bought a crib for babies' naps, and stocked whatever kind of milk or juice our kids preferred. During the toddler stage, tricycles and little swimming pools appeared in her backyard. No matter what the age of our children, Grandma's kitchen overflowed with kid-friendly foods and snacks—especially the children's favorites.

I'm grateful that my parents saved many of our childhood toys and games, because our sons as well as our nieces and nephews spent hours of fun down in my folks' basement playing with those items. Our youngest son, Jordan, says, "When I was a kid growing up, my favorite room at Grandma and Grandpa's house was their basement!"

● My mother was always good at giving us practical things for the boys. She didn't spend lots of money, but every weekend (unless she was caring for the boys) she would visit "boot sales" (probably garage sales are the closest

United States' equivalent) and pick up quality clothes and toys for them. She also gathered so many little scooters and ride-on toys (as well as books and other toys) that I was able to set up and run a local toddler group in our village hall on behalf of the church. Almost fifteen years later, one of the mothers in our village gave me a big hug and said, "I never thanked you before—did you know that many of my friends in the village now are the ones I made at the group you ran?" So my mother's help went far beyond my own family. *(Mom, England)*

- Following in the footsteps of my mother-in-law, I have a kid's room in my house. It is a bright and happy room with a futon (where the kids can sleep for naps or overnights), toy chest (full of toys), a bookshelf (with many books and lots of photos—especially of their out-of-town aunts and uncles), and a little desk with paper and crayons and markers. They love this room (we all do!), and I think it makes them feel extra-special. *(Grandma, USA)*

- One practical thing that both moms have done is to have supplies at their house for us. We have to travel a distance to see both sets of grandparents, and they try to help us limit what we need to take. They stock diapers, wipes, food, a feeding seat, and toys in addition to having

Once my family was driving, and my grandma was driving in the car next to us. My Dad swerved in front of her, and she yelled, "Watch out, you clumsy driver!" My Dad just laughed, and so did I. She finally noticed it was us, and she looked embarrassed. That is a story we like to tell when my grandma comes to visit. (Grandchild, Austria, age 9)

places for Noah to sleep (which is getting more complicated, due to his disabilities). My mom even bought a stroller to have at her house. *(Mom, USA)*

We have a drawer in our bathroom just for our grandchildren that contains a clean change of clothes, jammies, diapers, etc. That way we can offer to give them a bath at our house when they come to visit. We also have baby shampoo and bath soap on hand for their specific needs. *(Grandma, USA)*

There is a bookshelf in my home that contains only books for my grandchildren. I also have a box with *their* videos. And a large bin to hold *their* toys. When our grandchildren were small, we set up a kids' tree at Christmas, complete with lights and unbreakable orna-

My favorite story about my grandma and grandpa is the one about my mom's glasses. When my mom was in third grade, she got new glasses. She was cartwheeling in the yard, waiting for her parents and her brother (they were planning on going to see the movie Benji*). Since my mom didn't want her glasses to fall off while she was doing cartwheels, she took them off and put them on the roof of the car. When the family was ready, they all got in the car and left for the movie. About two blocks later, my mom remembered her glasses. Her family never made it to the movie, because my grandma and grandpa found my mom's glasses smashed on the road. They weren't very happy about it! (Grandchild, USA, age 6)*

ments that they could touch and play with. We never had a problem with them touching the tree and would, in fact, take them to the big tree and sit with them and let them touch some of the good ones. I think that taught them respect for other's possessions. *(Grandma, USA)*

One of the most wonderful helps mom has offered is that she has invested in baby and child equipment so that her house is a convenient place for us to come. She keeps a high chair, crib, and swing handy at all times. She has diapers, wipes, baby blankets, Sippy cups, child-sized eating utensils, etc.—all things that make it easy for us to come over and have an enjoyable experience. She has made these investments cheerfully and intentionally and has never made us feel like we're causing trouble. She delights in this part of being a grammy and loves to make us welcome. *(Mom, USA)*

I have a low kitchen drawer that houses a myriad of plastic plates, cups, and silverware, and the children love to select their own for mealtimes or snacks. Many of the cups were from special places where we had

My favorite story about my grandma is the time my mom locked my grandma out of the house. My grandma was working in the garden. My mom was inside the house and locked the doors. Then she went to sleep. My mother was a sound sleeper, so when my grandma banged on the window, my mom didn't hear. My grandma called the neighbor, who broke the door down with a broom. They had to get a new door. (Grandchild, USA, age 8)

lunch together, so the memories bring smiles and stories. *(Grandma, USA)*

We have a crib and high chair and extra crib mattress and used to have a car seat here for our grandchildren and the grandchildren of all of our neighbors. We saved many of our children's favorite books and toys for our grandchildren. We have a tent and tunnel that occupies our living room when our grandchildren are present. We bring out additional toys at each visit so that they are age-appropriate, and keep ones with small pieces in our bedroom for the older grandchildren. We invite the children to stay in our bedroom for slumber parties when they visit us. We always go visit all Grammy's lady friends in my jeep—most of them have sort of adopted my grandchildren and have goodies and/or treats ready for our visits. *(Grandma, USA)*

I am glad that I kept quite a few of my own children's toys. I have also purchased a few new toys to keep at our home. It is great to have toys available for the children when they come. I have several shelves in the basement reserved just for them. The children know right where to go to find them—even the little ones. At one time, I had two high chairs and four boosters for the table. I also had a stroller and three car seats. *(Grandma, USA)*

When our first grandchild was born, a dear friend gave us a sturdy wooden child's chair. It has been the perfect size to sit in front of a low table in our family room. Through the years, it has been

My grandma is ninety-one years old, and still acts no older than seventy. My grandma is still going strong, and I think she has got a few more years left in her. (Grandchild, UK, age 13)

64

used (with several other chairs added) for crafts, puzzles, snacks, meals, etc. A large tin of crayons, markers, coloring books, paper to draw and paint on and cut out, watercolors, and Play-Doh provide endless fun. A simple length of ribbon tied between door handles, with clothespins ready, is a great way to hang and dry water color paintings. The children love it. *(Grandma, USA)*

We have a drawer in our kitchen that is Kenedy and Kade's filled with things just for them, and they go right to it when they first arrive. Right now it has in it a few pieces of chocolate, a few gummy worms made with real fruit juice, sugarless gum, a little mini book on Noah's Ark, colored pencils and a coloring book, a mini soft car from All State Insurance, Scotch tape, a glue stick, stickers, mini note pads, an old cell phone, old keys on a keychain, and their mother's flutaphone in it's original felt bag that she needed for an education class (I rescued it from her garage sale). *(Grandma, USA)*

When I prepared for visits from my grandchildren, I often went to garage sales and found some treasures: a battery-operated jeep (Big Jake—a huge favorite and worth the price many times over), a four-wheeled lime green scooter, a bike with training wheels, and some books. Add to that a Pak 'n Play, a bouncer, high chair, booster chair, bed guard, car seat, stroller, and various sizes of diapers, and we felt ready for the arrival. *(Grandma, USA)*

Our grandchildren tend to like the simple things when visiting. We saved all of Jonathan's action figures, Legos, Lincoln Logs, etc., and those are the things the kids like to pull out. One grandson likes to play with inexpensive plastic links, dropping them down from our loft and fishing for the small toys Cal attaches at the bottom. I don't get rid of children's books, puppets, etc., because they will always be used by the grandkids. *(Grandma, USA)*

Wood puzzles last from one generation to the next, as well as toy soldiers and Legos. One set of wood blocks can be used endlessly to create all kinds of wonderful castles, forts, and structures, whether by a thee-year-old or a nine-year-old. *(Grandma, USA)*

The toys we have in our house for our grandchildren range from a dollhouse, dolls, dishes, and Polly Pockets to trucks, balls, stuffed animals, many table games, and a Game Cube (their favorite right now and our least favorite because of lack of interaction). At bedtime, they often choose one of the bean bag animals to sleep with—each child seems to have his or her favorite! *(Grandma, USA)*

Four

The Bible

All Christian grandmas," wrote Rebecca Lutzer, "can do spiritual mentoring without a theology degree. Simply put, it is imparting biblical truth to grandchildren of all ages in a variety of ways. From the earliest age, we can tell them about Jesus and His love for them, sing songs about Jesus, and pray simple prayers with them. We can talk about God—from the creation to the cross. So many daily activities become teaching opportunities. We can help them memorize Scripture verses that teach obedience, sharing, and God's love and help. We can give them age appropriate books and videos or DVDs that teach about God/Jesus for birthdays, Christmas, Easter, or anytime. We can be the one to give them their first Bible. When they have learned how to read, we can give devotional books, and then ask them once in a while how they're doing. It's always good to remind them that we're praying for them."

On the mantel of our (Ellen and Jim's) living room fire-place sits a favorite picture of our three sons taken in front of the Chicago skyline. On the other side of the double-faced frame is a verse from the Bible, printed in calligraphy: "I have no greater joy than to hear that my children are walking in the truth" 3 John 1:4. As parents, that's what we want for our children—that they love and obey God's Word. Our hearts are delighted when they do and disappointed if they don't—similar, I'm sure, to the way God feels about us. Nothing makes me happier than knowing that my children want to obey God's Word, so I pray for that daily. I'm grateful we can pray that for future generations, too.

- When each of my children was born, the first gift my mom gave them was a children's Bible. She wanted to establish a spiritual relationship with them early on, and make sure that they had God's Word available to them. *(Mom, USA)*

- A Bible study teacher I once had encouraged underlining and writing margin notes in our Bibles. She said it could someday be an inspiration to grandchildren after we're gone. *(Grandma, USA)*

- Visiting Grandma is always fun for our kids. Grandma often seizes the opportunity of the visit to teach them how God loves us. In my culture, a good Grandma *always* welcomes her grandchildren affectionately— even when the child is in trouble with Mom or Dad. This places her in a better position to explain to the children how God always welcomes us and gives us peace and security when we are in trouble. *(Mom, Burkina Faso)*

- My grandmother gave each of her grandchildren a bonded leather Bible with some study helps when we turned ten. Later in life, I realized that the Bible was having a big impact on one of my cousins at the age of fifty. This motivated my husband and me to buy a Bible for each of our grandchildren, with their names imprinted. We asked them to memorize a chosen passage of Scripture before they received their Bible. *(Grandma, USA)*

For Christmas 2007, my husband and I put together a legacy DVD. Making the DVD was quite a learning curve for me, and it took a while since we have seventeen grandchildren. My goal was to commission them with a sense of responsibility to live for Christ, feel a sense of community in the family of Christ, and carry the message of Christ. I chose to include the message with Hebrew music coordinated with pictures of the Holy Land and promises given to us in Scripture, like Jeremiah 29:11: "For I know the plans I have for you," says the Lord. "They are plans for good and not for disaster, to give you a future and a hope" (NLT). I didn't want the DVD to seem morbid, but I wanted the grandchildren to have the message that Kris and I, their parents, and hopefully they will pass on. I wanted to remind them that they are receiving a torch to carry and to pass to their children and others. We want that for them. Once our Christmas dinner was over, and we still had plenty of energy, we all sat down to watch the DVD together. Each child was captivated, watching for their pictures and taking in the message. There were lots of laughs at funny pictures of the kids or Grandpa with the squirrels. There were pictures of stained glass projects, times we sewed aprons together, birthday celebrations, and vaca-

My grandma's name is Diane. What I like about her is that she loves God, and me. One of her children is my step-dad. What I like about going to her house is that she has a big backyard, and I get to see her. I like going to her house for Christmas because my cousins come over and we make cookies. My grandma makes the best pumpkin pie. I love my grandma. (Grandchild, USA, age 10)

tions. We even included pictures of a great-grandfather as a little boy in his buckskin outfit. After the viewing, it was easy to affirm our desires for each of them to follow Christ—to be an offering and to carry the torch, generation to generation. My strongest desire is for my grandchildren to know Christ. *(Grandma, USA)*

My grandkids are so open to listening as I share Bible stories. They are also eager to spend time in prayer. Reading God's Word to them from an early age makes it easy for me to talk to them about God. *(Grandma, South Africa)*

Many occasions of life lend themselves to spiritual mentoring. We can ask our grandchildren lots of questions to find out what they're thinking and what they know. We can explain the plan of salvation to them simply, guiding them gently into understanding that all of us are sinners and need Jesus to forgive our wrongdoing (sins), and help us to obey. *(Grandma, USA)*

When we lived in Minnesota, and each visit meant a trip, we often kept each older grandchild for a few days at a time. One summer, we took a short chapter of the Bible and memorized two verses a day (using any possible method, singing, or a bit of a bribe), so that when the grandchildren returned home, they recited the entire chapter to their pleased parents. *(Grandma, USA)*

I traveled by Amtrak to attend a birthday party for my daughter-in-law. At the birthday luncheon, I said how thankful I was that she and our son were consistently teaching their girls, our granddaughters, about the Lord. Then I read Psalm 78:1–8, which reads, in part, "We will tell the next generation the praiseworthy deeds of the LORD . . . so the next generation would know them, even the children yet to be born, and they in turn would tell their children. Then they would put their trust in God" (NIV). ***(Grandma, USA)***

● The prophet Joel said, "Tell it to your children, and let your children tell it to their children, and their children to the next generation" (Joel 1:3, NIV). ***(Grandma, India)***

● When we were babysitting two of our granddaughters who are sisters, then being two-and-a-half years old and one year old, we decided to take them to the mall to walk around, as the weather was not good that day outside. We used our son and daughter-in-law's van because it had the needed two car seats. Our two-and-a-half-year-old granddaughter asked if we would turn on the "Jesus tapes" so she could hear them. We pushed the loaded cassette on, and were amazed at the little voice coming out of the backseat—she knew every word of the sweet Christian song, and she sang every note right on key! My husband and I glanced at each another and were almost afraid to break the magical moment by turning around and looking at the little person in the backseat who was singing angelically! We'll never forget it. It was also a reminder of how much our grandchildren are impacted by the music their parents play in the home and in the car. "Jesus tapes" taught our granddaughter many wonderful truths of Scripture through singing that would be much harder to learn in other ways. ***(Grandma, USA)***

● Being available to talk, spending time with our grandchildren, being willing to listen, being vulnerable in sharing, and knowing and applying God's Word in our lives have reaped great rewards. Sometimes, what Grandma says carries more weight than what parents say. The Word of God, prayer, and holy living have to be paramount and obvious in Grandma's life before it can be copied by them. It is the greatest gift we can give. And it lasts long into their adult years. *(Grandma, USA)*

On extended visits, it has been my joy and delight to read bedtime Bible stories to our granddaughter. Sometimes she requests specific stories that are her favorites, such as Esther and of course, baby Jesus. *(Grandma, USA)*

My granddaughter likes me to put her to bed when I am visiting. One evening, I was reading her the story of the very first Passover from her children's Bible. She interrupted me:

Alisha: "Did all the firstborns die?"

Nani: "Yes, Alisha."

Alisha: "Did little children and little animals also die?"

Nani: "Yes."

Alisha: "Why?"

Nani: "Pharaoh was a wicked king and he disobeyed God."

Alisha (with trembling lips and eyes filled with tears): "But only Pharaoh was wicked. The children and little animals did not do any wrong!"

It is very difficult to answer questions like that. *(Grandma, Singapore)*

> *On Sundays—which is Grandma's favorite day—we go to church, and she always falls asleep. But as soon as someone calls her name, she immediately wakes up. (Grandchild, Taiwan, age 16)*

When grandchildren stay overnight before a school day, I have special opportunities to talk with them at bedtime, share stories, and pray together. At breakfast, I sometimes read a Bible verse while they are eating and then pray for their day. *(Grandma, USA)*

I pay my grandchildren to memorize God's Word. They must learn one whole computer page of Scripture, which I choose. That length is not too long for a nine-year-old to master, but it's long enough that they really have to work at it and go over and over it to learn it—that's the point! I do make exceptions. I have a six-year-old grandson who wants so badly to be a part of this; I pay him by the verse. I also have one with a significant learning disability who struggles with any memorization. He also has been getting paid by the verse. This year I had the tearful, joyful experience of hearing him recite the first nine verses of Isaiah 53—his idea, I didn't assign it. A moment of triumph! Incentive is everything. When the older grandchildren need money for camp, mission trips, special events, they come to me to learn Scripture. The money's good, and it's one of the best investments I make. The value is eternal. *(Grandma, USA)*

Grandma is a good storyteller, and my children like stories. She connects evening storytelling to Bible verses to memorize. She usually keeps a surprise or a reward for the best listeners, and this helps children to give full attention to the story. *(Mom, Burkina Faso)*

After praying for help, the Lord gives me ideas for devotions to share when our extended family is together. This year, I gave each grandchild wooly lamb figurines with Psalm 23, hoping that they will always remember that the Lord is their Good Shepherd, and that we are His sheep. *(Grandma, USA)*

Our granddaughter is curious about little things, such as insects of all kinds. She and our daughter collected a couple of caterpillars last summer and placed them in a bug cage. Over several days, they fed the caterpillars the leafy plant they found it eating until they each spun a chrysalis on a twig. Our daughter took a photo-journal

My grandmother Chapman suffered *from severe arthritis. Earlier she raised five children, but by the time I came along she was already unable to walk. Someone had to move her from her bed to her chair. That was the circle of her life. She died when I was about five years old, but I remember*

of the process and let our granddaughter take it to kindergarten to share with her class. Our granddaughter patiently watched until beautiful butterflies emerged. It certainly provided a great lesson in the transformation we make when we become a Christian and also illustrated the transformation of Jesus after His death on the cross for our sins—His transformation into heaven. *(Grandma, USA)*

My key verse for grandparenting is Deuteronomy 4:9–10: "Be very careful never to forget what you have seen God doing for you. May His miracles have a deep and permanent effect upon your lives. Tell your children and your grandchildren about the glorious miracles He did. . . . I will instruct them, so that they will learn always to reverence Me, and so that they can teach my laws to their children" (TLB). *(Grandma, USA)*

As the grandchildren grow older and have different issues, they know that grandmummy has a ready, listening ear and plenty of advice based on the Bible, as well as prayer points galore. The grandchildren literally have to be dragged away from grandmummy's house whenever it is time to leave. May God bless and keep grandmummy always and renew her strength. She has been and continues to be a source of wisdom, love, and

that when I went to see her she would always tell me a Bible story. I remember sitting on the floor, looking up at her, and listening intently. She had little energy, but she used it to talk about what was important to her. It is a memory that I treasure. —Gary D. Chapman

joy to all who meet and know her, especially her grand-children. *(Mom, Nigeria)*

- Opportunities to share my love for God happen in the daily rhythms of life. Sometimes a special opportunity presents itself. Recently, I was helping my five-year-old grandson with his shoelaces, and he told me that I did it really well! I told him that was because I had been doing it for so many years. He then asked, "Did you accept Jesus into your life?" I said, "Yes, did you?" He said "Yes," too. Then, his four-year-old sister, who was working nearby, said, "Grandma, are you excited to go to heaven?" We had some wonderful conversation about going to heaven! *(Grandma, USA)*

- I enjoy reading God's Word with Hannah and Carter. I especially enjoy telling them what I have read that morning during my personal devotional time. I read to them straight from my Bible instead of from a Bible story book when I do that. I do read Bible stories during their bedtime routine, but I like them to hear God's Word in "grown-up" talk also. *(Grandma, USA)*

- I use God's Word as much as I can in gift-giving to my grandchildren. When I send a little love gift to my college granddaughter, I always connect a Bible verse in calligraphy to the package. I use soccer games for my high school grandson as an excuse to write a note of

I lived with my grandmother from the time I was a few months old till I was about six. Every night my grandmother would read to me from a picture Bible. We would sit in bed and talk for hours about how things would be ten years from then. I remember her going through my baby clothes once. She said that she would show them to my husband so he could laugh at how dumb they looked. She never will get the chance to meet my husband or my children, though. My grandmother died five years after I moved to New York City with my mother. Sometimes I wonder if I had still lived with her if I could have taken care of her and she would still be here today. (Grandchild, Namibia, age 15)

encouragement or congratulations and enclose a special verse of Scripture. *(Grandma, USA)*

When the grandchildren reached middle school they needed a lot of money for trips to The Netherlands, France, and Spain. Instead of just giving it to them, I decided to ask them if they would like to copy twenty-five chapters of Scripture, stating the verse in each chapter that was the most meaningful to them; when done I would give them five hundred dollars. Needless to say they were excited. My youngest grandchild did hers at age nineteen. She had just gotten out of drug rehab and wanted to make it on her own, and she needed big bucks! The part I think is really neat is that she sent me the twenty-five chapters all handwritten and said she had decided to find all the Bible stories she had learned in Sunday school. Now that must have taken a lot of looking! Praise the Lord! *(Grandma, USA)*

I have learned that while telling Bible stories we need to be careful not to give undue importance to the people who fought against God. Once after seeing a video of the story of David and Goliath, my grandson Micah started saying, "I want to be a Goliath." He seemed to think that Goliath was being presented as a great hero. I always try to tell Micah about the gracious things God did through His people and avoid telling stories in such a way that will create bitterness in his heart. I tell him about Zacchaeus becoming a friend of Jesus, the feeding of the five thousand, the miracle of Jesus turning water into wine, etc. *(Grandma, India)*

Christmas and birthdays offer opportunities to do something special with verses or passages of Scripture—a collage, an illuminated calligraphy, a drawing illustrating a particular verse or passage added to the gifts I give them. *(Grandma, USA)*

> *My nana is a kind, loving person. She loves a lot of stuff, like tennis, Grandpa, grandchildren, cooking, Badgers, Packers, and God. Those are just a few of the things she loves. (Grandchild, USA, age 10)*

When our two grandsons were of preschool and kindergarten age, they spent every Thursday morning with us. Along with other activities and lunch, we spent time helping them memorize the section of Scripture dealing with the great commandment: Matthew 22:36–40. We felt that a disciplined individual is one who obeys God's great commandment—to love God and to love his neighbor as himself. *(Grandma, USA)*

When I was eight years old, we moved far away from my grandparents who had always lived nearby. Grandma started sending birthday cards, and she always included a Bible verse. At that young age, I did not find them significant. But in my early teens I rededicated my life to the Lord and began to read the Bible for myself every day. At that point I began to genuinely appreciate those verses that Grandma sent until she wasn't able to send out cards anymore. Since I've had grandchildren of my own, I have also put Bible verses in cards and letters even to my very young great-grandchildren. I pray that someday the Lord will reach their hearts and His Word will be as meaningful to them as it has been to me. *(Grandma, USA)*

My mom realizes how important it is to give my boys a good foundation in knowing the Word of God. She is well aware that these early years provide a prime and fleeting window of opportunity to learn and memorize Bible verses, providing a foundation on which to build for the rest of their lives. Although I know this to be true, too, I am often busy with the mundane tasks of being a mom and sometimes don't put as much time or effort into organizing methods of instilling Scripture into my sons. My boys love having their grandmother by their side as they play, and my mother will frequently quote memory verses to them during the quiet lulls in their playing or while driving in the car or while they fall asleep at night. The boys love to have my mother put them to bed because instead of just tucking them in and leaving, she sits in their room at night quoting verses until they are asleep.

They enjoy this so much that my mother started to make CDs for the boys of her going over verses they are learning together. My boys listen to the CD at night and hear their grandmother saying the Word of God as they drift to sleep, even when she is not visiting. My mom also goes over memory verses on the phone with the boys; as they learn a verse by memory they love to call her and recite it to her. So what Bible verses do they learn? My mother came up with several alphabets of verses. The alphabet is the organizer to help keep track of the verses and it is a memorization aid. She started with the book of John and came up with short but meaningful verses that start or have a key word for each letter of the alphabet. She has now done an alphabet for several books of the Bible and one on the character of God as well. My mother has also been teaching my sons hymns, and together they have worked on memorizing short catechism questions and answers. My boys love doing the catechism questions with my mother because they love being able to answer questions. It gives them great satisfaction and a sense of accomplishment. They beg my mom to ask them another question. It's a big game for them and they are, at the same time, gaining a deeper knowledge and understanding of the Christian faith. Although the way my mother shares her faith with the boys will certainly change as my boys get older, my sons are not only grateful for their grandmother's efforts on their behalf, but they also immensely enjoy the process of learning important things together. *(Mom, USA)*

If I were asked to share one thought, one piece of advice, one idea as a grandmother, it would be this: stay so connected and so intimate with our Lord, so as to develop a higher level of discernment. I want God's love and His light to be revealed to my grandchildren and their parents through me, their grandmother. I want to stay so close to our Lord to be able to give sound answers and wise counsel with gracious speech, for that all comes from Him. *(Grandma, USA)*

Through God's grace, I am a grandmother (Buni—an abbreviation of the word *Bunica*, which translated means "the good one") of nine grandchildren. This is a reason to thank God and be filled with gratitude for the way He has worked in my life. My husband Nick and I were very blessed to have been born and raised by God-fearing parents who served as models for our Christian walk. It was in such a home and atmosphere that we raised our own three children. We are very thankful for their decision to follow the Lord and allow Him to reign in their homes. Even though they were all raised before Communism fell in Romania, we took a stand for the Lord by attending church and praying. I can still remember the spoken threats of their teachers as they were warning us that we were making a mistake to influence our children in following Jesus. I, nonetheless, knew what it meant to walk with the Lord and lose your job, so I desired nothing less in their lives than to see Jesus glorified, no matter the consequences. In all those years of hardships, we had the support of other friends and families from the church who were facing the same temptations and challenges. We all decided to stand together, to get to know the Lord better every day, and hope and pray for Him to

> *My grandma is the best in the world, but I call her Mama. She lives in Puerto Rico. Mama has a wonderful house. She grows bananas, grapefruit, and sugar canes. The best thing is that she is a Christian. Her husband is a pastor. Mama is loving, caring, and compassionate. Mama will do anything to help me. She has a huge backyard full of lizards. (Grandchild, USA, age 10)*

show His mercy on our situation. Presently, three of our grandchildren live nearby, and we see each other almost daily. My prayer is that I would have a godly influence on them and on their character, helping them stay close to the teachings of God's Word, the only Word that can give wisdom and salvation, through faith in Jesus Christ (2 Tim. 3:15–17). There are several Bible passages that have become very dear to me throughout my entire life, and these I would like my grandchildren to know and appreciate as much as I do (Deut. 6:1–6; Pss. 1; 15; 37; 43; 119:11; and 121). Every day, I pray Moses' prayer from Numbers 6 for all of my grandchildren, asking the Lord to bless them, make His face shine upon them, be gracious to them, turn His face toward them, and give them peace (Num. 6:24–26). ***(Grandma, Romania)***

Five

Books

My mother-in-law, Connie Elwell, loved to read. When I was pregnant with our first child, she gave me a copy of the book *Honey for a Child's Heart*, by Gladys Hunt. In that fine resource, parents are encouraged to read their children books that are full of truth and excellence. Although Jim's Mom has already gone to heaven, the input she gave me early on about selecting books for children lives on in her grandchildren today. It was part of the good legacy that Mom Elwell left for the next generation.

Since I had the luxury of reading the ideas people sent me for this book as I received them, I've already acted on some. Gloria Leff wrote that she collects children's books for her grandchildren from cities and countries wherever she travels. So when my husband and I traveled to Amsterdam this past year, I purchased *Katje, the Windmill Cat* (Gretchen Woelfle) and read it on the bus between Amsterdam and our hotel. When we went to London, I purchased the book *Paddington* (Michael Bond) and read it out loud to my husband while riding on a double-decker bus. (I really did. I was enthused and Jim was amused.) When we returned home, I added the books to a growing collection that I'm saving for grandchildren in a basket next to our fireplace.

● My favorite chair is "Grandma's reading chair"—an overstuffed chair-and-a-half. My grandchildren select several of their favorite "Grandma's house" books from a bookcase full of children's books, and we snuggle in for a good, long read. At bedtime, it's Bible story time. They love to hear the Bible book stories I read to their moms when they were small—Gilbert Beers's *Under the Tagalong Tree* or *Castles in the Clouds*; or one of Ella Lindvall's *Read Along Bible Story* books. I try to select books that have become classics—books by well-loved authors or illustrators or books that teach important truths. Gladys Hunt's *Honey for a Child's Heart*, Elizabeth Wilson's *Books Children Love*, and Elaine McEwan's *How to Raise a Reader* have been helpful in making selections. The older children are now into chapter books, mystery series, junior classics, and the Bobbs and Merrill Childhood of Famous Americans series. *(Grandma, USA)*

My grandmom spends time with me telling Aesop stories, true stories, other stories, and reading books with me. I help her to cook sometimes. She showed me how to kill a snake, but I've never tried to kill a snake. She spends most of her time praying. (Grandchild, India, age 10)

● Books have always been my passion. When I was still living in Finland and my three sons had families in the United States, I tried to bring books for my grandchildren every Christmas. At that time it was mainly Swedish children's books or songbooks. Now that I live closer to them, it is easier to share my love for books with my grandchil-

My grandchildren don't have to do anything for me to adore them. I long to be with them. Watch them. Hear their sweet voices. Hold them in my arms. Receive their spontaneous hugs and kisses. They give unconditional love and joy.

What do I love about my grandchildren?
- *Their laughs and giggles.*
- *Sitting on my lap to hear me read a story.*
- *Their excitement and joy when they see me.*

dren. Even though children and teenagers today often use the Internet as a source of knowledge when they do their projects in school or when they need information about something, I think they still appreciate a book every now and then. I spend many hours in bookstores every May and November to find summer readings and Advent reading for twenty kids (some of my grandchildren's friends have become like my own grandchildren). By giving them Advent readings, I want to remind them what Advent means and what happened during Advent. They usually get their books on the first Sunday of Advent and the last weekend in May. As the children grow older, it gets more challenging to find suitable books for them. I want the books to capture their interest and at the same time have a Christian message. **(Grandma, Finland and USA)**

My grandmother was always interested in my life. She asked questions about what I was reading (we both loved to read), what I was studying, or what I was making. Every

I like that Grandma buys storybooks for me from places she visits. (Grandchild, USA, age 3)

- *Watching them take part in a program or sports event.*
- *Wanting to sit by me at mealtime.*
- *Telling me about an experience they've had.*
- *Their reaction to a new experience such as a power outage—they loved lighting candles and using flashlights, and getting ready for bed in semi-darkness.*

I love being a grandmother! —Rebecca Lutzer

birthday as far back as I can remember she gave me a book to read. **(Adult Grandchild, USA)**

I subscribe to two magazines for each family, one for the younger ones and one for the older ones. This gives them something to look forward to; every month there are special stories and things to do. The children like getting something in the mail with their name on it. **(Grandma, USA)**

Whatever I give my grandchildren for Christmas, I have always used the opportunity to include an appropriate Christian book. In some of their homes, it might be the only ones they ever get and the only input of Christianity in their lives. **(Grandma, Australia)**

When my mother was diagnosed with terminal brain cancer, I was pregnant with my third child. We both knew the baby would not remember his grandmother (she died when my baby was ten weeks old). So I asked my mom to read some of our favorite books on tape for our new baby. She also talked to him at the beginning of the tape. I know this will be a priceless possession for my son. **(Mom, USA)**

● Each Christmas I buy a new children's Christmas book. I love Christmas and I love books. It is so fun to sit and read with the children! *(Grandma, USA)*

● I have two books that I've found valuable. The first is *The Long Distance Grandmother: How to Stay Close to Distant Grandchildren* by Selma Wassermann. I encountered the first edition when Marisa was born eleven years ago and recently bought the new edition. It has great ideas no matter how close or far we are from our grandchildren. The second is *A Grandmother's Guide to Babysitting* by Ruth Meyer Brown. It has good practical information and suggestions whether we are babysitting for a day or a month. *(Grandma, USA)*

● As each of my grandchildren prepares for kindergarten, I give them the Dr. Suess book *My Book about Me* to fill in during their first year of school. *(Grandma, USA)*

● When grandchildren stay overnight, I love reading them bedtime stories. Naturally, to put off "lights out" they choose several books. My eldest granddaughter loved me to read to her even when she was twelve, though she could, of course, read quite adequately by then. I was happy to oblige. *(Grandma, Australia)*

> *I like it when my grandma reads me a bedtime story. I like the stories she picks. I like it when she plays with me. We put puzzles together. I like it when my grandma takes me to the lake. We search for snails together. (Grandchild, USA, age 8)*

One of my favorite activities with my grandchildren has been reading books together. Bedtime is a favorite time, though I enjoy reading together with a grandchild on my lap anytime. Reading time is a good time to snuggle! *(Grandma, USA)*

I liked when Grandma took me to see C. S. Lewis's old desk, then to the antiques store, and to Hugo's Frog Bar to eat frog legs for my birthday. (Grandchild, USA, 10)

I have so many favorite children's books that I cannot begin to name them all. Here are a few of my favorites:

- *Read Aloud Bible Stories*, volumes 1–4 by Ella Lindvall and H. Kent Puckett
- *Where's Waldo?* by Martin Hanford
- *Stories Jesus Told* by Nick Butterworth and Mick Inkpen (I love the illustrations.)
- Sandra Boynton books for small children, especially *Oops* and *Blue Hat, Green Hat*
- *The Beeman* by Laurie Krebs
- *The Kids' Fun-Filled Question & Answer Book* by Jane Parker Resnick and Tony Tallarico
- Most of the old familiar books such as *The Three Bears* and *The Gingerbread Man* (be careful what version you get; some are much better than others)
- Many of the Dr. Seuss books, especially *Green Eggs and Ham, One Fish, Two Fish, Red Fish, Blue Fish,* and *Horton Hatches the Egg.*
- I cannot leave out Richard Scarry's books and Franklin books and The Berenstain Bears books. Oh my, there are so many children's books that I love! *(Grandma, USA)*

When my husband and I visited England, I brought back children's books that are easy to read with a British air, because of the choice of words and sentence structure. We had a jolly good time reading them. I also brought them a book from Oregon about a girl who found a blue glass ball on the ocean shore and a few books from Hawaii, such as *The Goodnight Gecko* and *Baby Hanu*. There's a whole world of new adventures waiting for us in local bookstores! *(Grandma, USA)*

Reading to my grandchildren has always been a priority. One book in particular has made a great impression. It is *The Big Picture Bible Story Bible* by David Helm, published by Crossway Books. One time I read it in one sitting to three grandsons who were ages eight to twelve. They were captivated. Later, when I read it to their younger sister, the two younger boys wanted to listen again. One of my grandsons was so excited he could not keep from telling his sister what was going to happen next in the story. *(Grandma, USA)*

When I was small, my grandma would read me stories when I was in my bed. That is one thing I really liked about my grandma. (Grandchild, Austria, age 14)

I like to read my grandchildren the Beatrix Potter books because all the animals in her books can be seen outside the windows of my home. *(Grandma, USA)*

There are many good books that have helped me develop my philosophy and approach to parenting and have given me ideas about how to deal with specific concerns or issues with my kids. Whenever I read a really good book or article, I tell the grandmothers about it, and they try to read it, too. My mother has more time to read than I do, and she often shares good parenting resources with me. My husband and I have found it helpful to share these resources with others (the grandparents, aunts and uncles) because it helps us to be on the same page in our approach to raising our kids. Although we don't always agree on every little thing, it helps the grandparents understand why we are doing what we are doing in raising our kids. Thankfully, we come from families that love to read. Even though we all live far away from each other, we can have significant discussions over the phone about books that we've all read. *(Mom, USA)*

Six

Childcare

My parents lived only forty minutes away from my husband and me when our children were young, and they were great about watching our kids. The first time that our oldest son, Chad, stayed overnight with Grandma and Grandpa was when he was two, and I was in the hospital giving birth to our second son, Nate. Chad's stay at my parent's house was wonderful—until he asked my parents to read him the Dr. Suess book, *Are You My Mother?* They tried to talk him out of it, fearing it would make him homesick, but he wouldn't be convinced. Sure enough, when they started reading, Chad started crying, "I want my mom!" After my folks called me at the hospital and let Chad talk for a few minutes, he was fine. Apparently, hearing my voice was all he needed, and he scampered off to play with Grandpa in the basement. Sitting in the hospital bed nursing Nate, I held myself together pretty well until Chad got off the phone. Then it was my turn to cry. I missed him, too.

What I appreciated most about the times my parents watched our boys was that I trusted them. I trusted them to care for the boys physically. But it was more than that. I also trusted that my parents would care for the boys' hearts. They did then, and they still do. What a huge blessing that continues to be.

● The babysitter par excellence in my culture is Grandma. She devotes her time to watching over the kids so that their parents can have more time for their activities. Grandma carries a grandchild on her back (traditional style) for several hours, and a child on Grandma's back usually falls asleep within a quarter hour. It gives the child a sense of peace and safety while Mom is gone or busy. Other times, especially at harvest, Grandma stays at home with younger kids all day long so that the parents can work in the field. **(Mom, Burkina Faso)**

● I have a dear friend whose mother has always given my friend and her husband a week every year. My friend's mom takes all three of her children for a week so that my friend and her husband can take a vacation and reconnect. I think this is such a wonderful idea. And if my friend hasn't planned her vacation with her husband, her mom will call her on it, prompting her to make that time alone with her husband a priority. What a gift! I can't imagine anything better than for a parent to recognize how important the husband/wife relationship is and to give her own child that time alone with her spouse. The added benefit is that Grandma gets her grandkids alone, all to herself, for a week. She loves that! **(Mom, USA)**

My granny is nice. She makes nice food and plays snap with me. She always cuddles me when I watch TV. (Grandchild, Australia, age 8)

When I was homeschooled, Grandma sometimes took over the schooling when Dad and Mom went away. It was fun to have a different teacher during those times. ***(Grandchild, USA, age 8)***

Our son, Noah, has a lot of complicated medical equipment (feeding pump, oxygen concentrator, pulse oximeter, etc.). My husband and I are grateful that both of our moms are willing to learn to use the equipment and provide care for Noah so that we can get a break. We feel so confident in their ability to care for him and their understanding of him that we have taken several trips on our own while one or both moms have stayed home with Noah. (This is a huge blessing since it is getting harder and harder to find people who can watch him, even for an evening, because of all of his issues.) ***(Mom, USA)***

My mom decided to shop for toys at garage sales and secondhand shops so that she has her own collection of toys for her grandchildren: Mimi's box. When she comes to visit or babysit, she brings her toys: classic toys such as Roy Rogers, the Lone Ranger complete with horses, and Lincoln Logs. The kids look forward to seeing what she will bring next. As they get older, she continues to add to her collection. ***(Mom, USA)***

Martin's parents took care of our children while we were in captivity . . . and they did an excellent job! My mother-in-law is the one I call on, even today, when I am going to be out of town speaking and the kids are going to need something. For the most part, my kids (teenagers) like to be on their own while I'm gone—but they will often end up over at Grandma and Grandpa's to hang out or have

● I have a surprise drawer in my kitchen that contains things like Play-Doh, scissors, crayons and coloring books, paper dolls, stickers, stencils, and Scotch tape. From time to time, I refresh it with new things. I like it to continue to be a surprise! *(Grandma, USA)*

● Because my mom lived one-and-a-half hours away when my children were little, she would come to our home one or two days a month. On those days, I would make doctor or dental appointments, get a haircut, or go grocery shopping *without* children. Sometimes, when I didn't have any pressing errands, we would all go to the mall, shop, and eat lunch at the food court. This was a treat for my girls—eating under the umbrella with Grandma! My mom loved to help out in any way she could, and taking care of my girls was something she absolutely adored. Not only did she help us, but she was able to spend quality time with her granddaughters. Dad helped too . . . but you know how that goes; Mom would always tell him *how* he could help. How I have missed that over the years (my mom died when my girls were very young). I know Mom would have always been available if she were still alive. *(Mom, USA)*

a nice meal. I never have to worry about the kids while I am gone. Martin's folks have made it clear that they are there to help me with anything, whether it is taking the car for an oil change or running to pick up a gallon of milk. Grandma is a very gifted person, and the kids often hand off sewing projects to her since their mom can't help them. They have been such a blessing for this single mom, and I'm so thankful for them! —Gracia Burnham

I used to drop off my four-year-old granddaughter at preschool and take her younger two-year-old sister with us, then either drive home or have an outing. One day, I was feeling unusually stressed and anxious as I drove. Suddenly from the booster seat in the back of the car came Laura's clear, tuneful voice singing "Jesus Loves Me." Bless her! *(Grandma, Australia)*

I babysit often but also reserve the right to say no. I am retired, so can often adjust my time. The children grow so quickly, and I want to have lots of memories. We have stayed with the children or had them with us for long periods of time and have no regrets. We always make sure we have rules and boundaries, and the children know we will do our best. *(Grandma, USA)*

I appreciate the willingness both sets of grandparents have shown in watching our children so that my husband and I could get away on a trip for just the two of us. We haven't gotten to do this as much as we would like, but I am grateful for their willingness to support our marriage and free us to get away. When we would leave, it was great to know that our children were in good hands, and it allowed us to relax all the more. In addition, the fact that both sets of grandparents live out of town makes these opportunities even more special. *(Mom, USA)*

When I exercise by walking or running, I sometimes ask to take the grandchildren along in the jogging stroller. It gives my children an hour for themselves. *(Grandma, USA)*

Grandmas have the honor of caring for the older child or children when a brother or sister is born, and what excitement there is for the older ones when they see their mother and the new baby through the viewing window. We said prayers at bedtime for mommy and daddy and baby, and I often rocked the littlest one to sleep while I sang Jesus Loves Me. What a pleasure and privilege it was to be there and help with the new baby at home and to build a special new relationship with a daughter or daughter-in-law. Grandmas have such fond memories of those times with the new mothers and fathers and grandchildren. *(Grandma, USA)*

Perhaps one of the best things a grandma can do for her grandchildren is to support and encourage her children in their marriages. As a mother of seven, I realize that it's sometimes hard to keep my relationship with my husband a priority over caring for my children; however, I do think the best thing I can do for my kids is love my spouse. Since our wedding day, my mother-in-law has always encouraged my husband to demonstrate his love for me through affection, quality time, encouraging words, service, and gifts (she's even helped him pick out some beautiful pieces of jewelry to give me over the years). One of the kindest things she has done for us is to stay with our children while my husband and I go away for a vacation. Although taking care of seven children for an extended period of time is not an easy job, she is happy to do it. She loves spending time with the kids and knows that she is investing in our marriage as well. *(Mom, USA)*

Our children have been very thoughtful about asking us ahead of time to care for the grandchildren, if needed. It is a joy for us to be with them, and we agree if at all possible. They have never expected us to fill in all of their childcare needs. We do encourage our children and their spouses to get away on a short vacation from time to time, especially around their anniversary, and we care for the grandchildren during that time. It is a way we can help them get some much-needed R&R—a chance to get a fresh perspective and keep their marriages healthy and happy. *(Grandma, USA)*

Whenever George and I visit Janna and Greg, we try to plan some mornings where I can take sole care of the children so that Janna can sleep in and get some much needed rest. *(Grandma, USA)*

When my two boys were small (aged two and three) my mother made an enormous contribution to the health of my marriage by having both of them to stay for the whole weekend once a month. This not only gave my husband and me quality time together but enabled us to do some work on our house, which really made our home a joint labor of love. Every time I walk on the floor we sanded and varnished together, it takes me back to that special time. Our breaks from the boys also helped us to appreciate them all the more! From my mother's point of view she was able to really enjoy them without worrying about whether I felt she was trying to take over. (I wouldn't have. Any parenting skills I have came from her—my mother is the original Grandma from heaven!) She took our two little ones to her church on Sunday morning, and they were made to feel part of another church family as well as their local one. I really feel that their being welcomed in this church as well as their own was a great

My grandma always helps me with my home-work. Sometimes I have hard math problems, and she likes helping me with them. I always get my homework done faster when she's helping me. She gives me money. I always put it in the bank. She comes to my sport games, and she always cheers me on. I always see her there. (Grandchild, USA, age 8)

expression of the church as family wherever we are. *(Mom, England)*

- Babysitting can be quite a challenge when you have six grandchildren age six and under at one time. Sometimes in the afternoon I put on kids' music, and we all dance together in the living room. Reading stories together is always popular, especially before bedtime to try to get everyone calmed down before hitting the beds. Praying together is wonderful, especially as I hear the little ones thank God for many everyday things that we sometimes tend to take for granted. *(Grandma, USA)*

My grandma always makes us breakfast. She makes us pancakes, donuts, and eggs. She also lets us climb trees and sit in them. (Grandchild, USA, age 8)

- Grandma is always willing to watch the kids so we can get away for a quick overnight or a long weekend. *(Mom, USA)*

- Although we enjoy babysitting the grandchildren for special occasions, such as parents' anniversaries or birthdays, we do not usually babysit on weekends. Since my husband is not retired and travels often, the two of us like to be able to eat dinner out with friends or go to a movie on the weekends. We like to babysit whenever we can during the week, but we enjoy having our weekends free. We encourage our children to find other babysitters for their weekend outings. *(Grandma, USA)*

- Mom constantly makes herself available to watch my children. This is such a help to me, especially when emergencies come up. Sometimes, she'll offer to babysit so that my husband and I can go on a date. Mom's close relationship with my children gives them a great sense of ease and security when my husband and I are gone. *(Mom, USA)*

I recently heard a grandmother say that she refuses to babysit or to change diapers because she had her days of doing that. She says that her job now is just to play with them when she has time or when she wants to. I sadly thought that she would not know the gift of hearing, "I want my Mimi to give me my bath." Or to know that wonderful feeling of having your arms full of a sighing, comforted toddler who just needs his Mimi's arms after a long day. *(Grandma, USA)*

Our grandson Micah used to spend a lot of time with me as his parents were busy in the evenings with Christian activities. Sometimes when they were recording songs, Micah was with me the whole night. It was a joy to be with him and take care of him. I always accepted it as a God-given privilege. Babysitting my grandson has been a joy and never an obligation or a bother. *(Grandma, India)*

Every time I visit my grandma, there is this closet in her house full of stuff from my grandpa, such as his uniform during World War II. Every time my grandma sees me looking at it, she tells me about the war. My grandpa, who passed away a long time ago, used to be a leader in World War II. My grandma got kidnapped during the war. My Grandma told me how her husband saved her. It was an amazing story. (Grandchild, Indonesia, age 16)

● Taking care of older children when Mom and Dad were away for a long weekend often proved to be a challenge: the children sometimes challenged directions from Grandma. "That isn't what Mom would do!" It was also difficult for me when, after preparing a good healthy dinner, the children wouldn't eat the veggies or, even with coaxing, taste the food. When staying with teen-aged grandchildren, the challenges often came because of sibling rivalry, disagreements, arguments, heated words, etc. One or the other would not be satisfied with Grandma's decisions. Often the older sibling wanted to take charge or control. He would feel he knew what his mom or dad would say or do, which would be better than what Grandma would say or do. It was also difficult for me when I slept overnight with grandchildren old enough to be out on their own when they didn't come home at the specified time or didn't let me know why. I wondered whether that behavior should be reported to the parents. I also wondered if I should agree to take that responsibility again and be subjected to the worry and concern over their welfare. *(Grandma, USA)*

● There is no greater gift that anyone could give me as a mother with several small children than time to myself. It is easy for me to call my mom and ask her to take my children when I have a doctor's appointment or special event, but the offer to take my kids just to allow me to have some time to run to the mall and shop or to clean my house or get my Bible study done would be a dream come true! I guess this is where the rub is. I desire my mother to offer, and she expects me to ask if I need help. Obviously some of us need a little help with communication skills! *(Mom, USA)*

● My grandchildren were all born within several years of each other. The moms appreciated me picking up the toddlers—one at a time—and giving the moms time to be alone with their babies. Of course that gave me time alone with a toddler. We fed the ducks, had Mickey Mouse pancakes at restaurants, watched the airplanes, and especially watched the windsocks blow. *(Grandma, USA)*

Recently, we cared for four of our grandchildren while their parents took a little anniversary trip. Our ten-year-old grandson is busy with so many things that it is more difficult to be one-on-one with him these days. However, he had two special creative projects due that week that I helped him with. One was to create a new cereal and the box to put it in. Another was to rewrite a cartoon and create a cartoon. We had a great time working together, and he was excited about his projects. *(Grandma, USA)*

When Peter was fifteen months old, he became sick while we were at my parents' farm. His little body was feverish. He wanted to be with Grandma! All evening his grandma sat on the sofa with Peter snuggled up to her. Then she checked on him twice during the night, praying over him, giving him water, and checking his fever, which was gone the next morning. *(Grandma, USA)*

Seven

Communication

*C*ommunication between grandmas and grandchildren happens on many different levels.

Sometimes, communication includes written words. My parents continue to send monthly letters (with money for Taco Bell tucked inside) to their college-age grandchildren. In their notes, they enclose reminders to the grandchild that he or she is loved and prayed for.

Sometimes, communication includes spoken words. "One day my phone rang," wrote Carol Genet, "but since there was a lull on the other end, I thought it might be a marketing call. Soon I heard, "Grandma, I—I—I got big boy pants today." His mother had taken him shopping to celebrate this milestone. He wanted to share the good news. His younger sister likes to call also: "Grandma, I'm Gabrielle." Sometimes I understand the subject and sometimes I need help. The important thing is that we are communicating."

Sometimes, communication goes beyond words. In serious circumstances, the comfort of presence is just as important—maybe even more fitting—than words. One grandma reflects on how everything she had ever learned about communication was called on one rainy Friday night in October, 2006. Kajsa-Lena Nyblom wrote: "I received a phone call from the hospital with the news that my granddaughters had been in a car accident. I cannot even put into words how it felt to come to the emergency room, where in one room lay my six-year-old granddaughter sedated and with a neck brace, and in another room was my sixteen-year-old granddaughter with a neck brace. And then, to find out that one of my granddaughters had died—my heart was ripped apart! It was incomprehensible that our Moriah, eleven years old, had gone to be with Jesus. Even though it was one of the darkest moments in my life, my role that night at the hospital became to comfort the rest of the family, especially Moriah's siblings. Mia had to go through neck surgery, and Hannah needed intensive care for a couple of days for a pelvic fracture. Today they are both doing well physically, but the pain in their hearts will last a lifetime. It is extremely painful to lose a grandchild. Moriah left an empty hole in my heart, my home, and our family. Even though nothing can ever fill that emptiness, I have realized that my job now is to focus on the grandchildren that I still have. I feel it is important that I talk with my other grandchildren about Moriah and her death. I know that they think about her, the accident, her death, and the funeral. By discussing these things with them, I want to give them an opportunity to express their feelings about all of it. The only comfort I have is knowing that Moriah went to be with her Jesus she so dearly loved."

Whatever it is that we want or need to communicate with our families, I'm thankful that God shares His wisdom with us when we ask. "Wise words satisfy like a good meal; the right words bring satisfaction" (Prov. 18:20, NLT)

● Teatime is our special time together. We take out the tea service for any occasion. This is a memory I share with them from my childhood. Countless prayers are sent over a cup of tea. This is a custom I have shared with my husband and our children, our families and friends, and now my grandchildren. My hope is that this will become a special way for us to communicate as they grow into adulthood and that they will look forward to teatime with Grandma. *(Grandma, South Africa)*

The greatest memory of me and my grandma is how she was and still is so caring. I love it when my grandma wants to know how I am and spend time talking with me. I don't get to see her that often, because she lives in the States, and I live in Austria. But when I do get to see her, she is so nice, always asking how I'm doing. I feel that I can also really trust my grandma. When I lived in the States, we would visit my grandparents in Texas, and we would go fishing or just hang out. I miss hanging out with my grandma. She is there when I need her, and she is willing to do whatever it takes to make me happy and to make it a good time for the both of us. *(Grandchild, USA, age 16)*

My mother will often send my boys postcards in the mail. Although she doesn't travel too often, she finds different postcards with animals or special places in the area that she has been to with my sons or places she plans on taking them. She will usually write to them about the picture or write about a memory they have shared. We keep these postcards in a special box, and my sons like to take the postcards out and look at all the pictures and re-read some of them. *(Mom, USA)*

The stories Grandma told gave me a deep appreciation for my heritage. She told how my great-great-grandparents wanted to come to America from the Ukraine and how my great-grandparents met in Cuba where they had come to work, hoping eventually to live their parents' dream. I heard how Grandpa, a farm boy from Indiana, met Grandma in Cuba when he was stationed at the Naval base in Key West, Florida and how he proposed in a letter, sending her the engagement ring. This was my history. **(Adult Grandchild, USA)**

My step-grandson e-mails me to update me on his chickens and ducks—and to remind me that his supply of my chocolate chip cookies has run out. **(Grandma, Australia)**

One spring day when Ben was about five, I saw him sitting on top of the far corner of his family's picket fence looking out into the marsh behind their house. When he came in, I casually asked him about his vigil. He said, "Oh, I just go there to think, Grandma." About a week later, he came running into the house, saying, "Come follow me, I have something to show you." We ran to the thinking spot, and peering over the fence, I saw one blue iris in all its splendor. Tears came to my eyes as I shared with him the essence of that lone beauty. When my mother (an avid gardener) needed to leave our beloved Michigan homestead and go to live with my sister (my mother has since gone to her heavenly home), we gleaned some of our favorite perennials and bulbs to keep. Our

When I was little, I would often ask my grandma to tell me a story. Sometimes she would start, "I'll tell you a story about Jack O'Nory and now my story's begun. I'll tell you another about his brother, and now my story is done." But if I was lucky and Grandma had time, she would tell me wonderful stories about her childhood and how she grew up on a farm in Cuba. She would tell me about the many chickens they had and how one insisted on laying her eggs in a tree. I never tired of hearing these. (Adult Grandchild, USA)

daughters were given some, and this bulb was an extra to be tossed over the back fence. For the next few years the two of us, Ben and me, shared a common vigil each springtime, watching for the lovely blue iris in our secret garden—his for the fun of the discovery and mine for the inseparable picture of my dear mother's face with it. *(Grandma, USA)*

Many people are amazed at the relationship that my grandma and I have—we are best friends! We talk weekly and laugh together, cry together, and share secrets. Like any close friend, she is always interested in what is happening in my life, and she offers well-tested advice so that I can learn vicariously. I am sure that Grandma and I would not be this close if she did not make it a priority to be actively involved in all twenty-four years of my life. When my family moved from Illinois to Florida, Grandma lived with my parents for the first six months of my life. She was a spectator of my early milestones, which helped to form an indelible bond between the two of us. Never living more than an hour away, Grandma has had the opportunity to be available in my life, be it for recitals, graduations, or other important events. She was my favorite babysitter, and now her house is the best place to visit for a respite from graduate school. Having Grandma has provided me with confidence as well as a chance to view events from a different perspective. She is a wonderful comfort, and I could not wish for a closer friend! *(Adult Grandchild, USA)*

My oldest grandchildren live in another state. When they were very little, still unable to read, I wanted them to know that mail I sent them was from me. So, on every note or valentine or birthday card I drew a little lopsided heart above my return address. They learned very quickly that a heart on the envelope meant something for them from Mama. *(Grandma, USA)*

When my grandparents got older, they came to our house for Sunday dinner every week. This was before the days of dishwashers, so we spent hours drying dishes listening to grownups talk. I loved to listen and still do. I think we need to be aware that children do listen, and they want to hear what grandparents think and feel. I am sure there were life-lessons I learned in those conversations that were intentional, even though I was not aware of it at the time. *(Adult Grandchild, USA)*

When my granddaughter, Alisha, was not even three, she looked at my gold chain, which has a cross for a pendant, and said, "Jesus died on the cross and rose again. I don't have to die because He died!" *(Grandma, Singapore)*

My son thinks his grandmother knows just about everything. She answers all his tough questions such as "What is a scenario?" or "What does reinforcement mean?" Whenever Mom and Dad don't know, just call Mimi. *(Mom, USA)*

As I grew into my young adult years, Grandma shared with me about Grandpa's past. She told of things that were too hard for Grandpa to tell: his difficult upbringing as the second youngest of six boys who were raised by their widowed father and his years as a prisoner of war in a Japanese prison camp in the Philippines. Learning about his past made me proud that he was my grandpa. *(Adult Grandchild, USA)*

Because of the demands of my busy job, I don't have long slots of time with my grandchildren. Every morning I call my two-year-old granddaughter on the phone on my way to work. I have a silly theme song that I always sing to her. She loves to dance along with my singing (so her mom reports). When I am with her, I sing more silly songs, nursery rhymes, Sunday school songs, and old simple hymns. She associates me with music, fun, and laughter in these early years of her life. *(Grandma, USA)*

Living near my grandchildren and being able to spend a lot of time with them has been a great blessing, but I began to notice that I was taking them a little bit for granted and not giving them the undivided attention they craved. I had to re-learn some valuable techniques I had learned as a parent, such as getting down on their level and looking in their eyes when listening and talking to them (of course, I used to be able to get back up again!); repeating what they say so they know that I really heard them; and giving them lots and lots of hugs and affirmations of love. I suppose I assumed that great love makes a great grandmother, but I have learned that just like any other relationship, the one between grandparent and grandchild has to be carefully nurtured in order to thrive and be healthy. *(Grandma, USA)*

I have learned that in communicating with my grandchildren, it is a great advantage to share the same language. For me, it has been emotionally difficult not to share the same language with my grandchildren. The cute "small talk" with children is easier in my native language. Normally a grandma knows and can share with her grandkids songs and rhymes she learned when she was a child or when her kids were growing up. I had to start from the beginning and learn the English songs and rhymes with my grandkids and from my grandkids. I would have wanted to read books for my grandkids when they were little, but because I did not feel confident in my English pronunciation I did not read much to them. But I have also learned that there are many other ways to communicate love to my grandchildren. A

My parents were Dutch immigrants to western Canada, and my wife Cindy [Morgan] grew up in the east hills of Tennessee, so our childhoods were vastly different. As a result, I'm fascinated by the true life "hillbilly" stories that emerge at Cindy's family reunions. Our young daughters love the stories, too—so foreign to lives of an Internet generation. Grandma Lola, Cindy's mother, sits with them for hours to tell and retell those stories in her soft southern accent. Most of the stories involve Cindy's father, Cova, who

hug and a kiss can speak more than a thousand words. *(Grandma, Finland)*

- Even though my daughters don't see my parents more than a couple of times a year, my girls e-mail my mom all the time. In fact, just the other day Julia said to me, "Boy, I haven't had an e-mail from Grandma in a while." So I suggested she initiate another round of e-mails. I know my mom was thrilled to get one! *(Mom, USA)*

- God bless the man who invented the Internet because it is such a wonderful way to keep connected with grandkids. When they're in college, care packages sent frequently are most appreciated. *(Grandma, USA)*

- When Grandma comes to visit, she sometimes hides funny notes under our plates at dinnertime and has us read them during dinner. *(Grandchildren, USA, ages 8 and 10)*

- One time I was visiting a friend of mine, Joan Lopez. When her grandson came in the room, she said, "Tell Mrs. McDonell who I am." He immediately responded, "This is my beautiful grandma, Mrs. Lopez." Joan

passed away before our daughters were born. Through those stories, so patiently told, Lola establishes a beautiful bond with the girls. Through these stories, our girls have learned to cherish a great man and to cherish the values that were important to him. Through these stories, I'm seeing clearly that what you do truly does affect the next generation, and I pray that I'll be able to follow in Cova's footsteps so that my daughters will someday be able to tell stories about me with the same respect and affection. —Sigmund Brouwer

laughed and said, "I taught him to introduce me that way." *(Grandma, USA)*

- I try to remind my daughters to share their triumphs and despairs with their granny. She is to be the first person they see when they come home from holidays, camps, or school excursions so she can share in their experiences. They are to share their exam results—good and bad—and she always gets to read their reports. Grannies don't get cross—they just encourage grandchildren to do their best. *(Mom, Australia)*

- At one time my mother told me that "mothers are the curators in the museum of memories." My grandmother took the time to make her memories living history for me. *(Adult Grandchild, USA)*

- My mother is the most wonderful cheerleader in my children's lives. Living only four blocks away, it is her habit to stop by during her walk to see how they all are doing and to hear their latest musical pieces. "Would you please play for me? I would love to hear what you are working on!" she exclaims enthusiastically. She then sits down on the couch with her full attention directed to them. If they happen to play a particularly lively piece that is not in her taste she will say, "That's not my favorite." But the next piece she will say, "Oh! I love that! What was that? Oh, my! You sound like Mr. Singley (our wonderful church organist and pianist). Just gorgeous!" Well, needless to say, my sons love playing for their grandmother. My youngest even asks for grandmother to come over and hear his latest favorite piece. They also enjoy playing for her over the telephone. Her enthusiasm is such a rich investment in their lives and skill-development, not to mention providing great motivation in practicing. *(Mom, USA)*

- My grandma is one of the people who understands me and has the same hobbies as me. *(Grandchild, Korea, age 16)*

- My daughter Cindy and grandchildren Caleb and Tori spent a few days in Florida with us when the rest of their family was in Russia on a missions trip. When they were ready to leave our condo, we could not find Tori's favorite stuffed toy, Presto. We all searched high and low, but it was nowhere to be found. Tori

Grandma never talked much, but when she talked, it was wonderful. I don't exactly remember how she sounded because she had a stroke that affected her right hand and her mouth. She can't talk properly, but when we sing hymns, she immediately catches the song and sings with us. What I think is really amazing is that my grandma can write "mirror image" in Chinese. We can only read it when we put a mirror on the paper because she writes with her left hand. (Grandchild, Taiwan, age 16)

was quite upset. Several days after they left, however, Grandpa located Presto. Before we sent Presto home to Tori in the mail, we wrote a story about Presto's adventure. I sent the story along with Presto in a comfy package. It was a nice surprise for her. Cindy said that Tori laughed and laughed! *(Grandma, USA)*

My father, who was ninety-three, passed away while I was helping Preeti after the birth of her second baby. My conversation with big sister Alisha went something like this:

Alisha: "Why did big Grandpa die?"
Nani: "He was very old. . . ."

(Six months later)

Alisha: "Nani, how old are you?"
Nani: "I'm very old, Alisha."

(A week later)

Alisha: "Nani, you are very old, and you haven't died yet?"

All I could do was laugh and marvel at her logic!
(Grandma, Singapore)

My grammy was known for her ministry of encouragement through letters. She wrote me letters almost weekly from the time I was small. She absolutely lavished me with mail. The letters contained nothing "special" (just the details of her everyday life from what errands she'd run that week to what wild animals she'd seen in the woods around her house), but any child knows that personal mail in itself is special. As I grew up and went away to summer camp, college, an out-of-state summer job, and my first apartment, she always had a letter waiting for me upon my arrival at my new residence. I remember my first summer on staff at a dude ranch in Colorado. I was overwhelmed and wondering what I'd done in deciding to come here by myself for three whole months, but all my doubts dissipated when I was shown to the staff mailboxes and I already had a letter from Grammy. My co-workers quickly came to know me as the girl who got all of the mail, for my grammy's stream of letters came as regularly as always. *(Adult Grandchild, USA)*

Whether our grandchildren live nearby or in another state or country, communication is essential. There are so many ways to stay in touch and to let them know that we are thinking about them. This makes them feel special and important, especially when they are far away and don't see us often. I utilize all forms of communication: phone calls, e-mails, cards, and notes. Occasionally, I send them an e-card (they're free) from DaySpring or Hallmark to their mom's e-mail. This is a quick way to get a word of encouragement or congratulations to them. They love getting these. From their first birthday on I always send a card with the corresponding amount of money. As they get older, they really like this. *(Grandma, USA)*

I am learning to ask questions instead of making statements. I am learning to ask forgiveness for mistakes I have made, and have had to do this a number of times! *(Grandma, USA)*

The word faithful describes my grandma wonderfully, not only in the way she prays and seeks God but also in the way that she loves her family and friends. She is a remarkable letter writer; it is a unique gift that the Spirit has given her that bears much fruit—much of the time it is fruit she never sees. She writes letters faithfully to those whom she loves and to those who need encouragement. I have been the blessed recipient of hundreds of these letters over my almost twenty-four years. *(Adult Grandchild, USA)*

I remember laughter being a key part of visits with my grandparents. Usually my grandma or grandpa had read a funny joke, or they would reminisce about a funny story of long ago. I loved the reminiscing. They made stories of when they were children so interesting and so fun! I think the art of telling a good story is a precious treasure to children. *(Adult Grandchild, USA)*

I sent valentines (some of them handmade) to each grandchild every year. I included appropriate Scripture verses in most. When the grandkids got into their teens, I wondered if I should keep sending them. My youngest daughter told me to keep it up because her three sons treasured and saved those valentines. *(Grandma, USA)*

One of my grandmothers lives overseas, and she sends regular e-mails to see what's

My grandma used to play the piano very well when she was young. But then for some strange reason I do not know, she had to quit playing. Now, every time I play the piano, she comes and sits by me. I can see tears falling down from her cheeks. She cries every time I play. Then after I finish playing, she dries her tears and tells me the story of how she used to have a very good talent in playing, but she never managed to achieve her goal of becoming very good at it. She says that every time I play, I remind her of herself and make her feel that her dream is finally coming true. (Grandchild, Iran, age 13)

new in my life and how things are going for me. *(Grandchild, Australia, age 13)*

● Be a good listener—some tales go on forever!
(Grandma, USA)

● I sometimes send my out-of-town grandchildren a care package with appropriate treats or small, inexpensive gifts. For those nearby, I give a treat or inexpensive gift each time I see them. This communicates to them that they are special and that I am thinking about them.
(Grandma, USA)

● One night when our two granddaughters stayed over, I went in to say goodnight. One of my granddaughters asked about the lady in the photo on the wall. "That lady was *my* grandmother," I told the girls. "I saw her only once when I was ten years old, and that was when she was in her casket." That was the beginning of a good talk with my granddaughters. *(Grandma, USA)*

● Mom loves to tell the grandchildren stories of when their parents were young. The grandchildren are absolutely captivated by these stories, and it's a wonderful way to communicate truth to them in a winsome way.
(Mom, USA)

● My grandmother loved to use proverbs such as "your sins will find you out," and "you shall reap what you sow." I heard these many times—in a loving manner—so I did not resent her telling me these bits of wisdom.
(Grandma, USA)

● I love to spend time talking and listening to my grandchildren. Children, young and old, love to talk. They will tell us things they won't tell anyone else. And we can tell them things no one else may have the time to tell them. I've heard more than one older grandchild say, "My grandma tells me like it is, and I'll listen to her." What a privilege we have to guide, bless, and influence these precious lives! *(Grandma, USA)*

● I give my grandchildren books and take them to movies that I feel will help form their lives. Then we talk about what we read or saw. I think it's also important not to push a dialogue on them when they do not want to talk. *(Grandma, USA)*

● My grandma and I don't have the closest relationship, to be quite honest. So when I heard that she was coming to Vienna all the way from Chennai in India, of course I was kind of freaking out! Our family waited for her at the airport, and we immediately recognized her. She came out with this big, traditional Indian sari, a bindi, and sandals—not something that you normally see people wearing in Europe. Right then, I felt embarrassed of my own grandmother. Why couldn't I just be happy to see her and the beautiful Indian clothes she was wearing? After getting back to our apartment, I took her for a tour of our small rooms. It was nothing great to me, but her face showed so much happiness, which made me feel good. The next day we took the train to Melk. Melk is a place outside of Vienna, and it's pretty cold there. So we all went with huge jackets on, and even though my grandma was also wearing one, guess what she wore underneath? That blue and red sari! I never knew I would have the coolest time, but I really did. My grandma and I connected, and we tried building long conversations. Now I regret what I had thought of her

> *My grandma always cares how I am and can tell if something is wrong. (Grandchild, USA, age 13)*

before, because you would want to know her. She really is *that* cool. **(Grandchild, India, age 13)**

I look for opportunities to visit with my grandchildren. One of the best is riding in the car together. There are times when I have been uncomfortable with teenage moods. Communicating at such times can be difficult. I tell myself not to force communication (trying to say what I think they might want to hear), but just be myself and remain cheerful. Eventually, their moods change. **(Grandma, USA)**

Grandma tells us funny stories about her colleagues at work. **(Grandchildren, USA, ages 8 and 10)**

I try to speak with my grandchildren on the phone every week or two (although it's sometimes like pulling teeth to get them to reply). Just this week I told my sixteen-year-old that sometimes talking to him was like trying to get blood out of a turnip. He told me turnips don't have blood in them and I said, "Precisely! I want to talk to you every week, but please don't make your poor old grandma work so hard. Please think of something and tell me without my having to pry it out of you!" **(Grandma, USA)**

I send short letters or postcards to the grandchildren at least once a month. We have ordered several age-appropriate magazine subscriptions for them so that they get mail regularly that way also. **(Grandma, USA)**

With the older grandchildren, I e-mail them about their activities and interests and remind them of special times like Random Acts of Kindness Week in February. **(Grandma, USA)**

When I call my grandchildren and chat about their activities, I always close with "I love you and am praying for you." **(Grandma, USA)**

When my mom was sick and dying, we had her and Dad answer questions for us on tape. (This was back in the '80s; we recently just burned a CD from our cassette tape.) The purpose of the tape was to provide children and grandchildren in our family with some knowledge of family history and an opportunity to get to know Grandma and Grandpa better. Some of the questions we included were:

- Where did you go to school as a young girl/boy?
- Who were your childhood friends?
- Where did you grow up?
- What was your favorite subject in school?
- What was your elementary school?
- Did you have a favorite teacher?
- Did you have hobbies? What were they?
- Did you play any sports?
- Did you play a musical instrument?
- What church did you go to as a child? Or did you attend church?
- How did you become a Christian?
- Where did you go to college?
- How did you meet Grandpa/Grandma?

With both my mom and my dad gone now, I'm so glad we have that. (I think there are books at the Christian bookstore in which grandmas and grandpas can record thoughts and ideas for their grandkids, but a tape or CD is neat because it's nice to hear their voices.) *(Mom, USA)*

Eight

Cousins

On the dedication page of this book, my nephew Brent wrote, "Grandma has a way of making each of her grandkids feel like they are her favorite." My mom has been great about that. She strives to be fair with her children and her grandchildren. That goes a long way in promoting good relations between siblings and cousins.

Sherri Litfin told me that one day after some of her grandchildren had been playing hide-and-seek in Granddaddy's library, they ran to Sherri at the dinner table. Almost in unison they asked, "Grammy, who do you love best? I'm you're favorite, right?" At that moment, Sherri knew that saying she loved them equally and didn't have a favorite would seem unsatisfying to them and might actually prolong the rivalry. So she shocked them by saying, "As a matter of fact, I *do* have a favorite!" Her grandchildren's eyes got really big as they waited for her to go on. Sherri quietly told them that whoever she was looking at—at that particular moment—was her favorite. Then she looked around the circle, staring at them one at a time, saying, "You're my favorite . . . you're my favorite . . . you're my favorite . . . you're my favorite . . . you're my favorite." When she finished, they broke into cheers and ran off, fully satisfied with her response. Sherri heard them saying to each other, "I *told* you I was the favorite—she loves me best!"

● My home has become a place where cousins meet for dinners and other events. I especially remember when my little granddaughters from all three families used to come over and play together. They used my old nurse uniforms and dressed up and played hospital together. They pretended to be nurses, doctors, and patients. They also played school and Sunday school. I had to be prepared for this, and I made sure I had enough notebooks and school supplies. *(Grandma, Finland)*

● When we visit our grandma, who lives in another state, she takes our cousin and us out to breakfast. We usually get Mickey Mouse pancakes and sometimes eat more than we should. No parents allowed! *(Grandchildren, USA, ages 8 and 10)*

● One of the thrills of having nine grandchildren in the area is watching the grandchildren play together as friends and cousins. All are close in age, with the oldest of the nine being not quite five years old.

My grandma has taken care of all her grandsons since they were born. I am not the oldest grandchild, but she has seven grandsons in total. Every day, she picked us up from school, took us to her house (imagine seven kids in her house), and prepared meals for all of us. We used to stay there all evening. Our parents have a lot of work, and they never have holidays, so Grandma takes us to a beach that is near the city—all of us! I really like spending time with her because she is like a mother to me. (Grandchild, Mexico, age 15)

Two of our daughters-in-law are especially good friends, so they get together frequently during the week. Their children, therefore, are becoming wonderful friends, though they are a mixture of girls and boys. Just last night we were at the home of one of our sons for dinner along with another son and his wife and children. The two families had been in different parts of Florida for over two weeks, so the little cousins had not seen one another during that time. I was privileged to be at the front door when our almost-four-year-old grandson spotted his cousin's car turning into the driveway. He announced loudly to his little brother, now two years old, that Holly and Ally had just arrived! It was a thrill to see them tear out to the car and embrace their little girl cousins like it was the highlight of the week. Cousins, I can see, can be even better than best friends. *(Grandma, USA)*

> *My grandma makes us good dinners, like chili and spaghetti. When we're finished eating, we play games like Mastermind and Stratego. (Grandchild, USA, age 8)*

Mom has been intentional about having family gatherings and meals (Sunday lunch, Friday nights, etc.) at her house so that the grown children and grandchildren can share time together and build memories as an extended family. *(Mom, USA)*

When our grandchildren were growing up, my husband and I hosted eight grandchildren from three families for six to eight weeks of cousin camp at our Florida home. In our van, we picked up the grandchildren from various locations along two interstate highways. Our purpose was to get to know the children, allow them to get to know their cousins, and give the moms and dads some alone time while we made memories and had fun. My husband and I set up our seven-room, two-bath home with enclosed porch and pool to have one room for the boys and one for the girls. We ate meals on the porch, had night pool parties, and observed one hour of quiet each afternoon—no talking allowed. (The older kids drew, painted, wrote letters, or read while the younger ones napped.) We took day trips to the state forest, beach, prairie, or Dollar Store. We caught butterflies, frogs, and lizards, and went fishing together. Every night, we had Bible reading before lights out. On Sunday afternoon, we invited special missionary guests for lunch. The departure was usually staggered, but the kids always made reservations for the next year. *(Grandma, USA)*

Cousins' time usually includes the whole family at our house, and we try hard to make that happen often. Any excuse is a good one for us: birthdays (God gave them to our family nine out of the twelve months), holidays (we alternate the big ones with the other grandparents), programs, summer, or whenever they're in town. *(Grandma, USA)*

I am a tennis player and have worked with each grandchild to get a game going and have also given private lessons through another pro tennis player as a Christmas gift. I have given these lessons so cousins can be together as another added highlight. *(Grandma, USA)*

Because all twelve grandchildren live within twelve minutes of my house, we are able to have structured as well as unstructured time at my house. For the last seven years, we have had Cousins' Day at my house every Tuesday afternoon from 3:30–6:30. Typically, the children have a snack when they arrive, followed by a craft around a large table. I've learned that the success of the craft is not in what is taken home, but rather in the process; doing things together is what they enjoy. My college grandchild often stops by to see what's going on and sometimes to help. The crafts have included such activities as clay sculpture, face (and body) painting, origami, collages, sand painting, papier-mâché, bead work, sculptures out of found objects, painting T-shirts, sidewalk chalk art, making soap, collecting fall leaves and laminating them, and silly races on an open field with equally silly prizes. After the planned activity, the children split up into their various groups or pairs and play together. Cousins' Day always includes supper together, which they love. The conversations are sometimes hysterical. There is usually more talking than eating. *(Grandma, USA)*

When our oldest grandson was about six, I started doing something I called Mama Camp (my grandchildren call me Mama). They slept in sleeping bags on the floor of my bedroom. They had input on the meals we ate. Since this spanned four or five days, I didn't let them choose *all* the food. They chose where we went and what we did. If I had more than one child, I had them take turns choosing activities. We visited a wildlife shelter, a children's museum, a major aquarium, and several large museums.

We were all there at her graveside. Nine grandchildren. Grandma had lived to be ninety-three. She had lost Grandpa forty-three years earlier and was preceded in death by her own adult children by too many years. Her principal legacy in life was in that small congregation of cousins. We took turns speaking from the depth of our loss about what that remarkable woman had meant to us. Later that afternoon, I was reflecting on the comments my cousins and I had shared as we celebrated the life and love of our grandmother. I was struck by the realization that in each of our stories, there was this common theme. Every one of my cous-

We have made pizza, baked cookies, watched movies, listened to music, shared funny stories about our family (they especially like ones about when their mother was little), decorated T-shirts, taken pictures of our activities, and written journals. *(Grandma, USA)*

We frequently vacationed with my parents, and they were so good at finding ways to spend time with the grandchildren individually. Since my brother and his wife had children about the same ages as mine, my parents took the kids on outings in pairs; they liked the divide-and-conquer approach. One vacation they had a six-and-sixty club. They took the six-year-olds with them to the pool, and the younger ones understood they weren't included because they weren't six. Then the next set—the four-year-olds—were in the Harris Teeter Club, and they were allowed to go to the Harris Teeter grocery store with the grandparents. *(Mom, USA)*

I found it fun to have two grandchildren from different families who were the same age and sex come to visit

ins had indirectly attested to the same truth: "I know Grandma loves all of us, but I'm sure I was her favorite!" Somehow in Grandma's interactions with all of us, she loved us each with such singular focus and purpose that we each became convinced that "Grandma loved me best." It was never a contest, but rather a quiet reality that we each came to believe and accept. Who loves like that? Who loves with that kind of singular interest and commitment? I've heard it said that God loves each one of us as if there were only one of us. My grandmother's life makes that phrase believable. Because I've experienced it, I can believe. I want to be like Grandma. —Bruce Howard

at the same time. I discovered they not only enjoyed playing together, but they also learned things from each other—like trying new foods. On one occasion I had two small grandsons sitting side by side in booster seats eating lunch. I knew one of them liked kiwi, and I tried to coax the other one to try some. At first he didn't want to, but as he watched his cousin enjoying it he announced, "I want some *wee wee*." *(Grandma, USA)*

My husband and I used to host a week-long Cousin Camp, which included anywhere from four to nine grandchildren at one time (all of them girls!). For a number of years Grandpa and I did this together, but since his death in 2003, I have carried on alone. Each year we choose a spiritual/biblical theme for the week. For example, one summer we studied the Lord's Prayer. I gave each girl a blank book to create prayer journals. Each day, for maybe a half hour or so, we took a phrase or sentence or thought of the Lord's Prayer (which I had typed out ahead of time) and glued it on one page. Then we talked about what it meant and tried to put it in kids' language. I had stickers, colored pencils, pictures, and pens they could use to illustrate and write down ideas. We used songs, dramas, and anything to make it come alive. In the process we also memorized the prayer. By the end of the week, each girl had her own unique journal to encourage her to pray. As part of Cousin Camp, I planned a tea for the girls. Some years it was a special tea at a restaurant with fancy petite sandwiches. Sometimes we did our own tea and invited great-grandma. That involved planning, making the goodies, and helping a guest to feel special. The girls loved to fix up a fancy table and make individual place cards. One year we had reservations at a dress-up shop where they could choose long dresses to wear and then have tea with cookies. *(Grandma, USA)*

I have lots of memories of my grandma because she took care of me when my mom was gone for her job. Once when I had to go to my cousin's wedding, someone accidentally burned my clothes while ironing them. So my grandma took me out immediately to shop and bought me exactly what I needed. Another memory I have of my grandma is her cooking—I loved my grandma's chicken curry! Most of all, we shared everything with each other and tried to help each other out with different problems. I love my grandma a lot, but she isn't here anymore.

(Grandchild, Pakistan, age 15)

It has become a tradition each year to have a sale of miscellaneous objects that the cousins can purchase with coupons they have made. It's kind of like a giant garage sale geared to kids. All year long, I pick up little items on final sales' tables or thrift shops. I also include gifts I've bought for specific occasions that I haven't used. Items include toys, clothes, household items (for mom), food, games, CDs, etc. The cousins are given an equal amount of coupons to exchange for items they want. Certain items are identified as one-per-person or one-per-family. The kids go home happy, and it's up to the moms to decide what to do with the stuff I just cleared out of my house. ***(Grandma, USA)***

I grew up in Maine within five miles of both grandparents. What fun we had when all the cousins came in! As farmers, both sets of grandparents had big rambling farmhouses. We were allowed to sleep over one night when the cousins came in. All the girls were in one room and all the boys in another. We talked and giggled all night—what fun memories we made. *(Grandma, USA)*

One Cousins' Day, I bought a painter's cap from the hardware store for each child with the instruction to paint it any way they wanted. The kids did a great job painting their caps, left them to dry, and went off to play. Noticing that the caps weren't drying very fast and wanting them to be dry enough for the children to take home, I decided that the solution would be to warm them on the racks of two ovens. Fine—except I didn't notice that one cap had slid halfway off the rack and was touching the coils. Suddenly I realized we had an oven fire. I extinguished it immediately (and excitedly to the delight of the children) and spared the caps . . . . almost. Every single cap had been burned at least a little, but none completely burned. I was horrified to have ruined their good work, but they thought it was hysterical. They laughed until they were sick. We have a wonderful photo with all ten of them wearing their burned caps. *(Grandma, USA)*

"Can I go to Grandma's house?" If you came to my house you would hear that a lot, because my grandma is the best! What I really love about my grandma is that she always treats the grandkids equal and handles bad situations well. I love when I get to go to Grandma Kay's house when it's just me, because I have three brothers and it's nice to get away from them sometimes. (Grandchild, USA, age 10)

Nine

Family Relationships and Challenges

Although we sometimes face challenges in life that don't involve family relationships (cleaning out an attic, losing ten pounds, or learning how to use a computer), I doubt we'll ever find a family relationship that doesn't include a challenge.

In these pages, you'll read how other extended families deal with the usual challenges of in-law relationships, family visits, and how much to say—or not to say—to children and grandchildren. You'll also read poignant reflections of grandmas, moms, and grandchildren who are facing major challenges such as disabilities, divorce, and death. Whatever the size or scope of the challenge, Christian grandmas don't face their challenges alone. "The LORD is a stronghold for the oppressed, a stronghold in times of trouble. And those who know your name put their trust in you, for you, O LORD, have not forsaken those who seek you" (Ps. 9:9–10).

When we have lovingly invested ourselves in our grandkids' lives from birth to adulthood, the result is a relationship that goes very deep. Our words and wisdom are heard and appreciated, and we have the enormous joy of having been helpful in the formative years. Godly, caring, and involved grandparenting is a win-win thing! Any investment of time, energy, effort, and love, coupled with modeling spiritual truths and biblical concepts and teaching pays rich dividends. *(Grandma, USA)*

My husband and I are as non-interfering as can be with our children and their families. This keeps our relationship robust. We are there for them when they need us, and we pray for them regularly, but we have decided that as parents we should give unconditionally and not have any expectations. I have seen relationships grow sour in several families because of interference from grandparents and their expectations. It is good to let children make their own decisions and learn through their mistakes. Providing a solid Christian foundation is a must along with all the security that parental care can give. Once parents have done their bit, it is good to remember that our children and grandchildren belong to the Lord and He is their keeper. My prayer is that no matter what happens, righteousness and godliness should continue in our family for generations to come. *(Grandma, Singapore)*

I like to stay in touch with the in-laws. I call them periodically, send a box of candy at Christmas, send cards every so often, and keep building the bridges. *(Grandma, USA)*

Just before my husband and I married, my parents-in-law told me that they would really like it if I called them Mom and Dad since they felt that they were gaining a daughter. It was a special privilege for me to do so, since I loved them, greatly respected them, and enjoyed being with them. Over the years we have grown very close, and I do feel that they love me as their own daughter. Likewise, my husband has always shown great respect for and kindness to my parents and also calls them Mom and Dad. They love him as if he were their own son. My husband and I endeavored to build good relationships with our parents to ensure that our children would be close to their grandparents. *(Mom, USA)*

● There are all kinds of disabilities: physical and mental, severe and less apparent. One of our grandsons has NLD—nonverbal learning disability. It's not always easy to get a diagnosis, and it can be quite a struggle for our children when they are not taken seriously when they suspect something is wrong with their child. As grandmas, we can support our children, encouraging them to find help for their child. We can encourage them that most of the time a mother is right when she senses that there is a problem. And of course, we pray. We pray for strength and wisdom for the special task God has given our children in raising their special child, our special grandchild. When we have a grandchild with a disability, especially one that is hard for someone else to perceive and understand, we sometimes meet with incomprehension: people think we are exaggerating. That can be hard to handle. Our children and grandchildren need our support, and they need to know that we take things seriously. *(Grandma, The Netherlands)*

● One of the things I appreciate the most about my mother-in-law is the way she serves me when she comes for a visit. She takes over doing my laundry and does all the ironing—which I hate to do. She also does the dishes af-

> *Like a lot of grandmas, my grandma is very forgetful. She forgets her keys, her purse, and a lot of other things. When I find her missing things, she laughs about it. Grandma laughs at her own little mistakes.* (Grandchild, Taiwan, age 16)

My dad and mom retired from the pastorate during our year of captivity [in the Philippines] so they could work on our release in any way possible. Once I was home and chose to settle in Kansas, my parents agreed to move from Arkansas and live next door to me at my request. More than once I have called my mom in a panic when I get a call that a television crew is on their way to my house. She and Daddy always drop what they are doing and come over and run the vacuum and straighten the kitchen while I go change and get makeup on for the interview. If Mom sees me stressed

ter meals and tackles cleaning projects that I often don't do during my weekly cleaning (such as cleaning my microwave). Since going back to work full-time, I appreciate even more her expression of love. She doesn't do these projects to make me feel guilty or to make me feel like an inept housekeeper. For her, it is a way to serve me and to lighten my load. *(Mom, USA)*

When I was a child, my father's mother lived nearby. I spent a lot of time with my grandmother and loved her dearly. I now know that she and my mother had some "issues," but as a child I never once realized this. It would have been so easy for either of them to have made belittling remarks or to have sniped about one another. Allowing me to love without divided loyalties was a treasured gift that I try to pass on to my own grandchildren by being respectful of their parents (and the other grandparents) even when I don't always agree with them. *(Grandma, USA)*

The kids always like going out with Grandma or inviting friends over to play. But this is frequently a time of disagreements and sometimes fights. While Grandma

out—which happens more than I care to admit—she'll quietly come over and start doing laundry, sweeping floors, or doing dishes. She never makes a fuss, never asks for thanks, just cheerfully serves, and just as quietly goes back home. Daddy knows that Monday is trash day, and often, before I even think about it, he has taken the trash can from the garage out to the curb so I don't have to. My mom's classic line is, "Honey, you are doing a good job!" That encourages me to keep going even when I know in my heart that I'm not doing a good job. What would I do without those two? —Gracia Burnham

helps maintain peace, she also explains to the kids how getting along is a learning process. She reminds them that they would never have disagreed if they did not get together, so friendship means learning to share and to forgive. Grandma uses this time to teach respect of self and others as well as the importance of good company, love for God, and love for others. *(Mom, Burkina Faso)*

- For families in which grandchildren are experiencing serious health issues, as has been the case in ours, I suggest prayer, taking things a day at a time, reading up on whatever the challenges are, providing childcare, providing meals, doing laundry, and being willing to accept the situation but not blow it out of proportion. It's important for grandmas to remember that our children have to live with the situation. When they're struggling, I try not to fix things or make suggestions. I help, and I say, "I'm sorry." *(Grandma, USA)*

- Mom is always ready to discuss parenting advice, being careful to speak positively of me and my husband and my children. She provides a lot of parenting wisdom by her

131

example of how she interacts with my children. I regularly learn from her as I watch her with my kids. *(Mom, USA)*

- Challenges:

  - Having the same energy with later grandchildren in the park and garden today as I had with the earlier grandchildren when I was younger and fitter.
  - Being fair and equal in attention, time, and particularly gift-giving to all grandchildren.
  - Treating grandchildren and step-grandchildren equally.
  - Praying appropriately for my grandchildren constantly.
  - Accepting defeat in board games with older grandchildren!
  - Trying to keep up-to-date with new technology the grandchildren are using. *(Grandma, Australia)*

- When my mother comes to visit us, she comes with the motivation to serve. I know she enjoys spending time with her grandchildren (and her children), but she comes with the intention of giving her grandchildren some undivided attention and giving us, the parents, a break. When my mom is here, she plays with the kids all day, giving me the opportunity to do the things I haven't had time to do. Especially in the evenings or on the weekends when my husband is home, my mother offers her free babysitting services so that my husband and I can spend time together and get out alone together as much as possible. She knows that the best thing for her grandchildren is to have happily married parents! Although we wish we lived closer together, the fact that we live so far apart makes her visits all the more intense. She could never give my children several days of undivided attention if she were in her own home and environment with all of her work and distractions and responsibilities. Although we wish we could be together more often, I think we all have begun to see how we can make the most of our living far away from each other. Visiting frequently is a big priority for us. My mother tries not to go more than six weeks without seeing her grandchildren, and when we are together she puts her entire focus on them (and us). *(Mom, USA)*

I take special care to let a struggling child know that I am in his corner. We have had a child and a grandchild with huge and serious challenges and struggles. Grandmas are not parents, so what we can do is limited. But we can make sure they know that we are there for them, care deeply about their problems, are praying fervently and constantly, and that we will be their advocate and cheer-leader and encourager. Bad behavior cannot be tolerated, but often I've found that if we expect better of them and say so, we'll see them do better. *(Grandma, USA)*

Because my first grandchild is on the way, I have been seeking out the "one piece of advice" from women I con-sider excellent grandmas. Never would I have guessed the most common response: "Just because you can say something, doesn't mean you have to." I have already be-gun to follow the suggestion with my pregnant daughter. There is so much I *could* tell her about what's ahead and what to watch for and what to pray about and what could be looming ahead. But I hold my tongue unless, of course, an issue could be truly dangerous or if she asks me about something. My daughter will come upon her own fears, doubts, and questions soon enough. Then I will be there for whatever she needs me for. *(Grandma, USA)*

I think the best piece of advice I've heard is that I shouldn't give advice unless it is asked for. My mother promised to do that for me when I got married, and it was greatly appreciated. So, I did that for each of our kids when they got married. Sometimes it is hard to do, but for the sake of preserving a good relationship, it is important to try. I try to talk to each of my in-law kids on the phone regularly. I let them know that I want to hear their voice (not just my own child's voice) and know how they are doing. I think it makes them feel special, and it has been a joy for me. The other thing I do is pray often for our kids and their families, and I tell them so. I sometimes share a specific verse that I am praying for them. I try to encourage my daughter-in-law with compliments about what a good wife and mother she is. I look for specific things to mention, and she seems to appreciate the thought. *(Grandma, USA)*

I don't know what I would do if I didn't have people to call and ask questions—when my child is sick, what to do about discipline issues, and when I need general wisdom about parenting. It makes sense that if grandmas know their grandchildren well and have their best interest at heart, they are ideal people to impart this wisdom. The catch comes when the line is crossed between giving suggestions or ideas and expecting that things be done a certain way or later criticizing because the suggestion wasn't implemented.

Because I am the mom, God has given me the responsibility to raise my children however my husband and I think is best. I love to and need to ask questions. It is helpful to have a sounding board to help me think through difficult situations. For mothers-in-law, it is wonderful when the relationship is close enough that daughters-in-law feel free to call and ask and think out loud. After listening, I would hope that I would be allowed the freedom to make decisions as I see fit. *(Mom, USA)*

When our children were very small, my mother prayed for them, showed them affection, took care of them, and helped them by giving baths and changing cloths. Though my mother-in-law was away from us, she loved us and our children and expressed it practically. Our parents were like friends to our children. They set a model for me to be a good grandmother. Love and affection were the key words. *(Grandma, India)*

I try to make my children's jobs a bit easier by making homemade frozen entrees and heart-healthy muffins for them when I see them. This helps their budget and their workload. Also, John and I do not put pressure on them to visit us or come for holidays, weddings, large family picnics, etc. We do not place guilt on them. We always invite them, but respect their decisions. We tell them, "We'd love to have you come, but we know it's a ten-hour round trip." As little Noah and future grandchildren grow up, hopefully they will recognize that Grandpa and Grandma Johnson are easy to get along with and do not cause stress in their family. *(Grandma, USA)*

I am blessed in that all four of our daughters-in-law are very special women. God picked out the very best for our sons. They are wonderful Christian wives, mothers, homemakers, and career women. I wish that they could call me *Mom*, as it is such an affectionate name. All of them call me by my first name. They feel like it would be disloyal to their own mothers. I sometimes feel jealous when I hear other mothers-in-law referred to by their daughters-in-law as *Mom*. I am also sad that two of them seldom call or e-mail me as they believe that is their husband's responsibility. I know that they do love me, and they are most kind and gracious to me and allow me to have wonderful times with their children. I must admit, though, that I still yearn for a daughter who would share with me regularly about her life. I think I will ask God about that desire, which I have had since childhood, when I get to heaven. *(Grandma, USA)*

I have always tried to be helpful to my mother-in-law (and of course, my own mother, who, in fact, probably

I was a very shy guy when I was in middle school. I didn't want my friends to see my grandmother or my parents. I felt embarrassed. One day I saw my grandmother and my mother waiting for me at the school gate. Our class got off the bus, and as we entered the school, my grandmother came running toward me and gave me a big hug, which I tried to ignore. All of my friends were looking at me, and I felt like I was a baby boy. I pretended like I didn't know her. When I think about that situation right now, I don't know why I did that to her. I want a big hug from her now, but I realize that it is too late. (Grandchild, South Korea, age 17)

taught me to do this in the first place), helping to clean up from a meal or offering to help in any way to get a meal ready, set the table, etc. Over the years, my mom, Mom B, and I have had many fun times and meaningful conversations in either their kitchens or mine while preparing meals or cleaning up together. This has certainly helped to build a great daughter-in-law/mother-in-law relationship. *(Mom, USA)*

Four of my grandchildren live in another state. One lives in the same town and one lives in my house. When my grandchildren who live far away come for a visit, I greet them with open arms and a big smiley welcome. I decided that the grandchildren I see frequently should be greeted with just as much enthusiasm. When our grandson who lives in our house comes home from daycare, I try to have a big smile on my face so he knows I am just as happy to see him as I am to see his cousins. *(Grandma, USA)*

My husband and I do a lot of babysitting for our grand-children, since all nine of them live in the area. It is easy to see that though there can be fun and play amongst the siblings, the old nature of competition is very much alive as well. Grandparents can do a lot to help ease that tension. I like to be purposeful in calming fears and af-firming the value of each of them as individuals. This includes being sensitive to presents purchased so that all have a similar budget, and no one grandchild is the re-cipient of an unusually wonderful present that shows fa-voritism (like Joseph in the Bible, with his coat of many colors). In the same way, it's a great idea to affirm each child for things they do right, seeking to build them up positively. It is easy to enjoy being around the most lov-ing and well-behaved grandchildren, but the reality is that many times the ones who are "leading the charge" and are more dominant or loud have great potential as adults some day to be leaders for the Lord in ways we do not now see. Affirming them, while setting some re-alistic behavioral boundaries, is a goal for grandparents. Who knows how much impact the love and affirmation of a grandparent can make on an otherwise insecure or competitive grandchild? *(Grandma, USA)*

One of the greatest gifts we can give to our grandchil-dren is to see that they love their mom and dad and grow in a close relationship with them. *(Grandma, India)*

I think it is important for moms to work hard at includ-ing the grandparents in school programs, birthdays, an occasional meal together, or even a trip downtown on the train or to the zoo. Life is a two-way street. The healthier our relationships are, the more the kids ben-efit. I am blessed with a wonderful mother-in-law. She is nonjudgmental, helpful, and kind. She almost never offers her opinion on parenting issues and never flat-out sides with my husband. *(Mom, USA)*

Our grandson came to us as a gift. Our daughter married a wonderful man who has a son from a previous marriage. So, when Matt became part of our family, so did his son, Stephen, and God put us together in an incredible and loving way. As those who are in this same situation may know, holidays are not always a time when our grandchildren can be with us due to the scheduling of visits. At our house we have learned to celebrate at all different times and days . . . never forgetting the holiday and Stephen. So, we aim to be flexible and accepting of the situation. *(Grandma, USA)*

We have three adopted grandchildren. I do for them just as I do for the others. I tell them often how much I love them and am glad that they are part of the family. *(Grandma, USA)*

My husband and I love that our moms have made our son, Noah, one of their priorities. Noah is severely disabled. Although we don't have an official diagnosis, we know that he is profoundly mentally retarded with physical impairments. Our moms are always interested in hearing about Noah and his latest accomplishments—rejoicing with us in every little step. They are also willing to listen to complicated medical information when we need to talk and have even done their own research online to try to better understand all of Noah's issues. I know that they grieve just as much as we do over him, but they have jumped in with both feet to try to understand him and reach him at his level, rather than getting stuck in all of their lost dreams for grandparenting. Both of our moms have also been willing to be involved in the practical details of his care. During the first few years of Noah's life, my mom traveled down to visit us about once a month, scheduling her visits so they coincided with important doctor's appointments, since there was no way my husband could go to all of them with me. She spent a lot of hours in the car, doctors' offices, and therapies as a support to me. My mother-in-law came at the last minute to stay with us during a hospitalization so that she and I could take turns being at Noah's bedside. When our families visit they are always interested in coming along to our weekly therapy visits so they can see what Noah is doing and know what his life is like. *(Mom, USA)*

● I can be opinionated and speak without thinking (though God has been working on me), so I have said and done some things that I should not have. I can remember three specific incidents since Hannah was born in which God nudged me to make things right with my son-in-law; once I e-mailed him an apology; once I called him on the phone and apologized; and the other time I apologized to his face. Each time he has accepted my apology and things have been set aright. I am thankful for a God who nudges us to make things right before hurt feelings get out of proportion. *(Grandma, USA)*

I like going to my grandma's house for many reasons. First, she always helps me with my homework. When I don't understand something, she helps me. Second, she gets me out of trouble. When I had a messy worksheet, she talked to my mom. Third, I like to help her, too. I want to go to her house right now! (Grandchild, USA, age 8)

● One thing I taped on my video camera was my father sharing memories of his childhood and describing how he was saved. My mother was deceased by the time I got a camera. We taped my husband's mother in the same way, asking about various relatives that she could still remember. Someday, I hope this will be meaningful to our grandchildren. *(Grandma, USA)*

My husband is in a healthcare facility, so I try to encourage my grandchildren to visit him. Not only does this bring my husband love and cheer, but it is good for my grandchildren. It teaches them to show love and concern for the elderly and infirm. *(Grandma, USA)*

Divorce in the family is a very sad time. With many tears and much prayer, we determined to keep two granddaughters connected to our larger family as their parents severed their marriage. It is not an easy journey. I have no words of wisdom, except to pray and pray and try to stay in touch, especially with the children. We included the children in every family event possible; they continued to come to Cousin Camp. We wrote letters, called them, sent e-mail, and visited. The teen years were traumatic. Now in their early twenties, each one is finding her own way, and, thankfully, we still have a loving relationship with them. I don't know of any easy path through the process; only God's grace is sufficient. *(Grandma, USA)*

For a time, my husband and I provided a home for a grandson who was having difficulty with his family. Another time we provided childcare for the baby of an unmarried grandchild. *(Grandma, USA)*

I think it is important for grandmas to affirm both the grandkids and the parents in what they are doing right. Everyone does something right. *(Mom, USA)*

I always check with parents regarding TV shows and videos. *(Grandma, USA)*

My husband and I try to be supportive, loving, respectful, and inclusive of the other grandparents in our grandchildren's lives. At holidays, we let our adult children know that we'd love to have them and their children with us, but whatever they work out is just fine with us. *(Grandma, USA)*

One of my sons informed us during his second year of marriage that from that time forward all holidays would be spent with his wife's family. Those are the traditions that they have decided that they want to have for their children. We have not had those children or grandchildren for a holiday visit since that time some years ago. They do come in the summer and invite us often to visit them at other times in the year. They live a thousand miles away from us. We have a wonderful time when we are with them, and they are a darling, dedicated family. We miss them at holidays, but we know that we must adjust to their decision. We know that if we complain about it when we are around them, they will not want to have us on other occasions. They have taught their children to love us, and the kids are always so excited when we visit. They bless us, and yet sometimes we are still sad. *(Grandma, USA)*

My mother often tells me that her most important role as a grandmother is to encourage and support my husband and me. I am grateful for this because I think it's the foundation to a close family relationship among three generations. My mom shows her support to me in so many ways. Primarily she makes visiting us a priority. My parents live on the East Coast and we live in the Midwest, and they understand that we cannot afford to visit as frequently as we'd like. So they make it a priority to visit us. My parents are heavily involved in ministry, so it is a financial sacrifice and a time sacrifice for them. When they visit us they are very sensitive not to interrupt our family time and routines. When my mother visits alone and for a more extended time, she will often leave our house shortly before my husband arrives home from work each day and go to a library or coffee shop for several hours. She frequently packs a dinner to eat while she is gone as well. This is not because she doesn't want to see my husband, but because she wants my boys to be excited to see their father and to spend time with him. When my mother is around, the boys are not interested in anything or anyone else! This allows them to take full advantage of the time they spend each day with their dad and gives us time to be alone as a family for dinner. (We have to really beg her to join us occasionally!) *(Mom, USA)*

I have the most unbelievable son-in-law in the world, whom I cherish. He allows me to stay with them whenever I can. He allows me to take over reading to his children at bedtime when I'm visiting. He puts up with my constant presence during those visits, as well as my way of folding and putting away laundry, putting away utensils in the kitchen, and taking over their bathroom. He is a dear Christian father and husband and is very, very good to my daughter. *(Grandma, USA)*

I try to be available to my daughter when she needs help. I realize that building a good relationship with her and her husband also allows me to build a good relationship with my grandchildren. I try to stand by the values and discipline methods of the parents; they need to know that I value their child-rearing methods. *(Grandma, USA)*

When my granddaughter was about three, she sometimes called me to complain about some supposed injustice her parents committed against her. I always backed up her parents with a statement such as, "God gave you to your parents to raise you to love and serve Him. You need to listen to your parents and do what they ask because they love you very much." After several of those calls from her, she realized that I was never going to give her advice that was contrary to her parents. *(Grandma, USA)*

Grandma leaves parenting to my husband and me, which I think is wise. *(Mom, USA)*

I think it is important to find something I can compliment my son-in-law or daughter-in-law about in the presence of my grandchildren. *(Grandma, USA)*

During my husband's last week here on earth, he was at home on hospice care. Our three children, their spouses, and their children all came to our home. Never have I experienced such love and tender care—from the youngest child of eighteen months to the ninety-three-year-old great-grandma. His bed was in the center of a household of people, activity, and love. We spent many hours reading and singing hymns to him. He received beard and hair-combings from granddaughters, backrubs from children, and had many good conversations with friends and family members. We shed tears and relived many joyful memories. We talked about heaven and death. We helped the children create little memory boxes to fill with things that would remind them of Grandpa. I believe all the good times we had together in Cousin Camps helped us to share this most difficult part of our life journey—saying goodbye to a dear loved one. My granddaughter Abby's poem reminds me of the unique time my family shared that week:

> When someone you love dies
>   You feel like you're dying.
>   Your soul cries out,
>   "Oh why, oh why?"
>   And drops of water (called tears)
>   Fly down your cheeks
>   Again and again.
>   You feel like screaming,
>   And your body shrieks.
>   Yet between your tears
>   You somehow feel,

It's all right. It's all right.
That voice inside you is Jesus.
—Abigail Joy Maas *(Grandma, USA)*

We have been fortunate to have two great-grandmas living close by. Each summer we have included them in some appropriate event, like tea or lunch. We make a point of asking them about what it was like when they were young girls. They can tell us great stories about the early cars and living with no television or how they first heard about Jesus. They help bring history alive for us, with tales of the Depression years or people they have met or places they have visited. *(Grandma, USA)*

The December after my sons were married, one of my daughters-in-law mentioned that I had more pictures displayed of one couple than of any of the other family members. I apologized for that. After the holiday when everyone had gone home, I carefully went through all of the pictures in the house. I made sure that I had the same number of each grandchild and child displayed. I still am very conscious of the pictures that I display and try to keep them equal in number. I know that it was important not only to that daughter-in-law, but others noticed too. One of the men (whom I thought would be the least likely to care) said as he came in the kitchen on the next visit, "Well, I see you finally have a picture of me on your refrigerator!" *(Grandma, USA)*

We are blessed to have wonderful relationships with both my parents and my in-laws, and the two sets of grandparents with each other, too. We have been fortunate to never have to deal with feuding grandparents over who gets which kids for which holidays. My parents come to St. Louis for Thanksgiving every year, and we all have Thanksgiving dinner at my in-laws' home. We occasionally seek out the wisdom of their years of parenting to help us with major decisions of parenthood, while still remembering that the decisions are ultimately ours to make. *(Mom, USA)*

● I find it's best not to give opinions unless asked and then to voice them in gentle terms. I once asked a friend whose kids were older than mine how to handle this. Her response was that they always waited for the kids to come to them. "Advice that's not requested is seldom heeded." *(Grandma, USA)*

● I have come to understand how important the mother/baby (and the father, too) bonding is to a child's lifetime emotional health. All of our daughters have chosen to stay at home with their babies and to breastfeed, which are probably two of the most important ingredients to mother/child bonding (or as mothers have done in other cultures, working with their babies attached to them). One of our daughters has gotten into "attachment parenting"—going to groups, the family bed for baby, baby wearing, longer-term nursing, meeting needs immediately rather than letting baby cry it out, and more. I am thankful for what our daughters and their husbands are doing now for our grandbabies to help prepare them for life in this world. *(Grandma, USA)*

● If my husband and I have concerns, we try hard to pray about them instead of voicing them. We know that God has a plan for each part of our lives, and we pray in faith believing in His answers in His time. *(Grandma, USA)*

● We are fortunate to have good relationships with all four parents. Even though it may have a good deal to do with their personalities (they are easy people to love and be with), I think it also has to do with treating both sides of the family the same. We have tried to be careful to spend equal time with both sets of parents. We also alternate our family Christmastime with each side of the family. This has been important since they both live a long distance from us. *(Mom, USA)*

We never knew how wonderful sons were until our sons-in-law joined our family. God handpicked each of them for our girls, and we make sure they know that. They know they could ask me for just about anything, and I would oblige. One daughter used to smile and say, "I think you love my husband more than you do me." They are great dads who are good providers and helpful at home as well, so we have truly been blessed. It is not hard to be a good mother-in-law to them. *(Grandma, USA)*

Love covers a multitude of things in relationships with grandchildren of any age: acceptance, interest in what they are doing, who they are becoming, what their dreams and plans are. Some will share with a grandparent what they would not feel free to share with a parent. *(Grandma, USA)*

We try to treat each grandchild the same, never playing favorites. As with our own children, we love each of them for who they are, and each is truly incomparable. I love being a grandma and all that it involves. I love to watch what God is doing in each of their lives. They are each so unique, and a joy to grandparent. *(Grandma, USA)*

My grandma takes naps and snaps her fingers. She likes to wiggle her fingers and wiggle her toes. What I like most is that she loves me and I love her, too. She likes to have fun. She is short and old but I still love her. At bedtime she covers me up and says, "Goodnight, don't let the bed bugs bite." (Grandchild, USA, age 7)

From a young mom's point of view, a grandmother's job is not to spoil the grandchildren. (This was difficult when we first had our kids. My mom heard other grandmothers say, "Remember, your job is to spoil them.") After talking these things through, my mom and I agreed that a grandmother's job is to support her children in their childrearing task (Deuteronomy 6). *(Mom, USA)*

We have a great relationship with our children and in-law children. Discipline has never been a big challenge, since our children are raising their children similar to the way we raised them. In fact, we counted it as a huge compliment when our kids told us that they wanted to raise their children the same because they thought what we did was right. So, if a child is misbehaving, a parent is usually on top of it. And if we see the behavior, we have permission to deal with it as we see fit. (Although I will admit that we seem to be a little more lenient in our old age.) *(Grandma, USA)*

We are often tempted to provide free grandmotherly advice or criticism to our grown children on how to raise our grandchildren. It's easy to forget how challenging and physically demanding it is to be parents of young children. Our memories haze over the rough spots of those times with our own children. That's why I think it is important to encourage our children in their parenting. Often I tell my daughter and son-in-law what a wonderful job they are doing (and this is no lie!) in raising their two children. I tell them how proud I am that they are following God's principles for raising up children. *(Grandma, USA)*

I try to take every opportunity to tell my son-in-law what a good father he is. *(Grandma, USA)*

My daughter and her son moved in with us recently. Some things I am learning about having a grandchild living with me: Sometimes I need to keep my mouth shut—I am *not* the mother. Let my daughter have some time with just her son to be a family. Don't subvert what my daughter says. If she says no, I don't say yes. *(Grandma, USA)*

As a grandmother, I try to know what Micah likes and what his mother wants him to have so that there are no competitions or contradictions. A close relationship with my daughter-in-law—to understand what she wants her son to have—is important. Grandmothers are wise not to seek undue attention that can cause unnecessary problems in relationships. *(Grandma, India)*

"A good man leaves an inheritance to his children's children" (Prov. 13:22). We will all leave an inheritance to our grandchildren. I want to think about what I will be remembered for when I die and make sure I give my grandchildren a lasting legacy of spiritual influence. I agonized over going into foreign missions; our oldest daughter and her husband had just announced they were expecting our first grandchild, and I couldn't imagine being out of the country. As I bemoaned my dilemma with my friend, she wisely pointed out that I would be leaving a lasting legacy of a life of sacrifice and service. My experiences in the Dominican Republic have given me a treasure trove of stories as God worked though my fears and inadequacies: driving through fog and rain at night on winding mountain roads without guardrails, living in a country with a different language and culture, and working in poor barrios and seeing abject poverty. The way we live our lives—even in our retirement years—is part of the lasting legacy we leave for our families. *(Grandma, USA)*

Ten

Food

When it comes to common denominators between grandmas and grandchildren, food seems to top the list! The majority of kids contributing to this book mentioned favorite foods that their grandmas made.

One time when I was about seven and stayed overnight with Grandma and Grandpa Banks, Grandma asked me if I'd like to bake something. After flipping through her Betty Crocker cookie book (I still love that thing!) I chose the pinwheel cookies. I remember the look on Grandma's face. "Oh, my," she said. "Those will take a long time. Are you sure you wouldn't like to choose something a little simpler?" Because my seven-year-old mind was thinking more about the picture of the cookies than about convenience, I still wanted to bake the pinwheels—so pinwheels it was. Although the cookies were complex and time-consuming, to this day I remember how much fun I had baking them with Grandma. If I close my eyes and think back to her two-flat on Nordica, I can still taste the chocolate.

Some of my children's fond memories revolve around my mom's cooking—her roast beef, mashed potatoes and gravy, lime-pear-cream cheese Jello, Green Giant corn, and Oreo ice cream dessert. Even today, every time we sit around her table, my dad offers thanks for the food and the loved ones present and always ends with a phrase that warms my heart: "We'll give you the thanks and praise in Jesus' name, Amen." What great times of family solidarity these meals provide for us. I think back to times in our extended family when one or another of us were experiencing difficult times, and our children benefited greatly from the security of an extended family gathering at Grandma and Grandpa's house.

Is Grandmummy in? That's the first question asked when the grandchildren get to her house. Her presence lights up her home and the children's faces, and the grandchildren know that there is always one treat or the other to be had in Grandmummy's fridge. She makes lots of tasty food, and the grandchildren often eat till they are about to burst. They especially like her Jollof Rice, eaten with stewed chicken and fried plantain. Another favorite is pounded yam eaten with okra stew that includes meat, dried fish, and crab. And no matter what time of day it is or even if they have just had a good meal, Grandmummy won't say no to a bowl of the children's favorite cereal or snack. (*Mom, Nigeria*)

Although many grandmas are special, my nana is the best. She makes the best food and the best cookies. She makes the best ham. It always tastes yummy. She makes the best cake, too. It melts in my mouth, and I eat a lot of it. She loves everyone in my family. She loves Jesus, too. (Grandchild, USA, age 8)

My grandmother makes the best spaghetti and meatballs anywhere in the world. For every spaghetti dinner, family and friends come from miles to eat and spend time with my grandmother. We sit around a large table in the dining room and watch in anticipation as she brings the large bowl of spaghetti before us. They ask for her recipe and though she has given it a thousand times, no one can equal her greatness. Whenever visiting my grandmother, we call her miles down the road to tell her we can already smell the meatballs and tomato sauce cooking. Most of my memories of my grandmother revolve around the kitchen. It is the center and heart of her house. It is where you know you can always find her if you need a hug or someone to talk to. I think the special ingredient my grandmother puts into her spaghetti is the love and warmth that only a grandmother can have. *(Grandchild, Italy, age 17)*

My older two kids are fairly picky eaters, and Grandma makes sure that her fridge and pantry always contain something they'll eat in case we come over to visit. *(Mom, USA)*

My grandma's homemade jams, pies, cookies, and canned peaches are the best. I have fond memories of going to Grandma's and being handed a gigantic pretzel. They were good. *(Grandchild, Austria, age 17)*

November 23, 2004

Dear Fammo,
You have done so many things for me to be thankful for, and I don't think I can even name them all. I am thankful for the many great meals I have enjoyed that you have made for all of us. Whenever we kids hear that we are going to your house to eat, we are all thrilled because we know that there will be a delicious meal waiting for us there. I absolutely love your Reese Boodoah and Bannuguachua!

(I have no idea how to spell them.) [Her Grandma says that the Finnish words are *riisipuuroa* (rice pudding) and *pannukakkua* (pancake).] My friends who have come over to eat at your house always say how much they enjoyed them and wish they could eat them again. You are the greatest cook in the whole world, and I am so glad that I have you as my Grandma so I can eat all of your cooking!
Love, Mia *(Grandchild, USA, age 18)*

Every Sunday night after church we stopped at my grandparents' house; we always beat them there. Miraculously, there were always peanuts, a box of chocolates, and sometimes a cake and pie sitting on the table. I thought it was so great and so much fun to eat all we wanted. When my grandma arrived, the first thing she always said was, "Oh, I hope you kids found all the food!" *(Grandma, USA)*

My boys love pasta; it's their favorite food. My mother has taken their enjoyment of pasta to the highest level by getting a noodle maker and mixing up noodle dough with the boys. Together, they crank it through the machine and make long ribbons or shoe-string pasta that they plunge into boiling water to cook before consuming together with great gusto. *(Mom, USA)*

My grandma makes the best rabbit pie in the whole world. My mother and I take her to the butcher's, where she picks out a fat, juicy rabbit. When we get back to her house, we leave her to cook. She brings the pie on Christmas day, but my dad and I are the only ones that like rabbit, apart from my grandma, of course. *(Grandchild, UK, age 13)*

Living in Michigan, we had lots of berries. With all the fruit in Michigan, it was fun to take the grandchildren to the orchards where they probably ate as much fruit as they picked. Picking fruit together made for good memories! From some of that fruit, we made strawberry freezer jam. The grandchildren knew they'd always have their favorite jam for breakfast when they came to our house. *(Grandma, USA)*

One of my grandsons, James, had a special love for his grandad—and for a biscuit called Mallowpuffs. Mallowpuffs are plain cookies topped with marshmallow and covered in chocolate.

My grandma cooks for her whole family on every holiday. This is how I know that my grandma is nurturing and loving. (Grandchild, USA, age 10)

James's grandad had a love of the same biscuit. James lives about a three hour drive from us, and my husband always took Mallowpuffs when we went to visit. James started to do the same when he and his family visited us. It wasn't very long before James and his brother started to call their grandad Mallowpuff. The name stuck. When it was James's eighth birthday, my husband decided to send James's present with a special card. He bought some of the favorite biscuits and asked me to ice each one with letters that made up the word Mallowpuff. Then we wrapped them in foil and placed them on top of the gift. James's mother told him to open the foil packages first to work out who had sent him the gift. Imagine our surprise when late on the night of his birthday we had a phone call from my daughter asking what the biscuits spelled, as it was way past James's bedtime. He had figured out some of the letters, but what did the others stand for? We had a good laugh at the time and even after so many years (James is now fourteen) the

Mallowpuff story is still a family favorite. *(Grandma, New Zealand)*

During the Christmas holidays, the grandchildren would come over for cookie day. Stacy would cut out the cookies and then put sprinkles on them (also on the counter and the floor). Eric's favorite was the cookie gun cookies. He would often put the first ones in the middle of the cookie sheet. We made many batches of cookie gun cookies. Sprinkles went on some of them, too—also on the cabinets and on the floor. What a fun memory. *(Grandma, USA)*

One family tradition that has come down from my late mother-in-law is that I take some fresh grapefruit and selected oranges, cut them in half, and section cut each half of the fruit, putting it into a good-sized bowl and squeezing each piece of fruit to get all the juice possible in the bowl. Then I cut up maraschino cherries, add in a good amount of mini marshmallows, and mix them in with the fruit. I use a generous amount of the cherry juice to sweeten and add color. We like to serve this chilled, in a cup, early in the meal. Usually it becomes so popular that it doesn't last too long, so make plenty. Note: it does take time! Best if it sits overnight to marinate. *(Grandma, USA)*

My grandmother always makes me breakfast when I am at her house. *(Grandchild, UK, age 14)*

When the children come to our home for lunch, I like making some foods especially for them—simple things like finger Jello, pancakes with faces, individual pizzas, tacos in a bag, etc. *(Grandma, USA)*

My grandma makes good potato salad and good boiled eggs. The biggest reason I love my grandma, though, is because she loves me. *(Grandchild, USA, age 10)*

When my grandchildren stay overnight, breakfast is usually our favorite meal to make together (by lunchtime my energy is already waning!). We make chocolate chip Mickey Mouse pancakes, Grandma's special French toast, always sausages and sometimes bacon, sometimes scrambled eggs just because they like to watch me whip the eggs with a fork, and always juice in my grandmother's tiny painted cherry juice glasses. We always take orders, sometimes over the swinging Dutch half-door between our kitchen and the dining room. *(Grandma, USA)*

My grandma lived in a retirement home. I don't remember Grandma cooking very much, but when we visited her (and Grandpa, of course) she always made her famous delicious vanilla pudding and served it to us on her beautiful wood polished table. We always had a good time. *(Grandchild, Taiwan, age 16)*

When I married in 1978, I gained three stepdaughters, all married with children, ages two-and-a-half to six. Eventually there were five boys and three girls. That meant we had to find a way to care for all the little tykes when we ate together. I remember one celebration when we seated the four or five youngest in a row on a sheet (over the carpeting) in front of our living room picture window and put their food on the floor in front of them, almost like a row of puppies. It turned out to be very practical. They thought it was fun. They didn't spill since they were already on the floor and their moms and I were able to sit at the table in the nearby dining area and enjoy the meal, too. *(Grandma, USA)*

When our daughter and her family come for a visit over a weekend, I make a point of making a favorite coffee cake. "Grammy, no nuts, please," my granddaughter requests. We also spend time together making other favorite recipes like snickerdoodle cookies or cutout sugar cookies. Our granddaughter loves to help in the prep work for a meal. She stands on a sturdy chair so she can reach the counter better. She really enjoys making a tossed salad. *(Grandma, USA)*

When I visited my grandmother, she taught me how to cook Japanese food. She had a lot of old utensils that she used when we cooked. I love her cooking. *(Grandchild, Japan, age 15)*

Each time I come over to my grandma's house, she gives me a sweet. I love sweets, but my mom and dad do not let me have many sweets. *(Grandchild, USA, age 8)*

What I like about my grandma is how she always cooks for me. Every time I go over to her house or sleep over she always cooks something really good. The food is always ready for me to eat. This just really shows how thoughtful my grandma is. I'm a spoiled child. (Grandchild, Austria, age 15)

Occasionally I make a family recipe of buttermilk pancakes for breakfast, perhaps for Christmas morning. They're as light as a feather and enjoyed by all. *(Grandma, USA)*

I have had a number of tea parties with my granddaughters, complete with cucumber sandwiches, dainty cookies, good china, etc. We pretend that we are very sophisticated during the tea party (holding our pinkies while drinking hot tea or hot apple juice, and being extremely polite to each other.) You wouldn't believe how a four-year-old likes eating cucumber sandwiches when she has had a part in making them herself. We have great fun! *(Grandma, USA)*

- One thing I realize about grandmas is that they always make the most delicious food and are always ready to cook for us. I love it when my grandmas come over for Christmas or Thanksgiving because I always get to help cook the old family recipes. I try to remember them so I'll be able to show my kids how to make them someday. Also, whenever I am hungry, my grandmas make food for me, even if they are watching something on TV, reading, or anything. *(Grandchild, USA, age 14)*

- We sometimes go apple picking at an orchard by our daughter's home in Indiana. The children and adults enjoy this experience and the assortment of apples. They also enjoy the apple pie I later make for dinner. *(Grandma, USA)*

- What I like about my grandma is that on Christmas Eve, she makes lots of lobster. *(Grandchild, USA, age 9)*

- I have learned from my mother-in-law how to cook an ethnic meal (she was from Poland). I plan to teach my grandchildren how to do the same. It helps us to remember our roots. *(Grandma, USA)*

- When Grandma visits our house, she bakes apple pies with us. *(Grandchildren, USA, ages 8 and 10)*

- Use frozen or scratch dough to make quick bread items such as teddy bears or, as older children suggest, birds, snakes, or other animals.

My grandma is very nice; one thing that I really like about her is that she makes an apfelstrudel, which I think is much better than the ones you can buy at the stores. (Grandchild, Austria, age 14)

A good snack is rolling out a frozen loaf of bread and pricking it with a fork to make flat bread. Bake and serve it immediately with peanut butter and jam. You can use the same dough for quick pizzas also. Kids love to play with the dough, so be prepared to have some goof-off time and some waste of dough. If the dough is played with too long, it will not rise. *(Grandma, USA)*

Grandma shows her love by cooking delicious food for us when we go to visit. *(Grandchildren, USA, ages 8 and 10)*

When my grandson comes over, his favorite breakfast at my house is pancakes and monkey bread. *(Grandma, USA)*

We love to bake with Grams. She makes the best cinnamon bread. She lets us crack the eggs, measure the flour, sprinkle the cinnamon-sugar mixture, and punch down the dough. *(Grandchildren, USA, ages 11 and 8)*

I like making cutout cookies with my grandchildren at holiday times. I work with two or three children at a time. They like to be creative, and they add gobs of sprinkles to the cookies. The sprinkles hit the floor, chairs, and table. My motto is: be prepared and be patient! *(Grandma, USA)*

My husband's grandmother sent a box or tin of cookies to each of her grandchildren every month throughout their college and graduate school days for as long as she was able. (She made it through four-and-a-half of her six grandchildren's college/graduate school careers before she couldn't do it anymore.) She kept track of each grandchild's favorite cookies and then figured out how to make and pack them for shipment—even overseas for one of them for a semester. *(Adult Grandchild, USA)*

● At Easter time, we invite all four of our son's families over for Easter dinner and a traditional Easter egg hunt. One of the challenges grandparents face in this day and age is various food restrictions that each grandchild may have, depending on his or her health and the parents' personal preferences. This is a dilemma when it comes to treats, such as those found in Easter eggs. One of the helpful hints that came to us over time was to assign a specific color of egg to each grandchild. That adds to the fun of helping them learn colors. For example, all of Johnny's eggs are blue this year. Then the treats that are found in each of the eggs meets the food restrictions (or non-restrictions) of the parents, and it can make it all the more fun! *(Grandma, USA)*

● My grandma cooks for her whole family on every holiday. This is how I know my grandma is very nurturing and loving. *(Grandchild, USA, age 11)*

● Whenever my grandchildren come to visit, I take them to what they call "the good old Jewel" (grocery store), and let them pick out the food they want—cereal, fruit, bread, etc. *(Grandma, USA)*

● Grandma Claira loved cooking. She probably loved it because she was good at it. She always invited us over for breakfast. She probably cooked the best out of anyone I know. She was a great woman. *(Grandchild, USA, age 10)*

● My parents always had candy. They thought all kids needed candy on a regular basis. No wonder the kids loved them. When we lived in Charlotte, North Carolina, Grandpa and Grandma would send them a surprise package every so often with little cars, plastic guns that shot yellow pellets all over the house (thank you very much), and of course, lots of candy. It was like Christmas when those packages came. *(Mom, USA)*

My grandma always makes me schnitzel or Bustabensuppe. *(Grandchild, Austria, age 8)*

My grandchildren love to visit me on vacation, and the reunion is always warm. I like making them the traditional meals of our country. In this part of Nigeria, we eat pepper soup with yams and plantain in the morning. Other meals are bangor soup and agbono soup. They like to swallow it with garri, which is called Eba. My grandchildren look forward to these family traditions. *(Grandma, Nigeria)*

I like my grandma because she loves me and she lets me help make breakfast. *(Grandchild, USA, age 8)*

Eleven

Gifts

few months before our son, Nate, married Brit, I
flew to Bismarck, North Dakota, for one of Brit's bridal showers. The party was given at the home of Marilyn Strutz, a friend
of Brit's family. I appreciated what Marilyn had to say about
being a grandma, so when it came time for me to gather ideas
for this book, I asked her if she'd contribute. I'm delighted that
she agreed. She sent me a unique story about gifts. "It's fun to
give gifts to our grandkids," Marilyn wrote, "but we also want
to teach them to be cheerful givers. For the development of
their character, they need to know the satisfaction of giving.
For a few years we have been giving each grandchild ten dollars early in November with the instructions to give this gift to
someone who has a need and will not return a favor or gift to
them. This year my heart soared when I received an e-mail from
my college grandson sharing that he had given his money to a
homeless man at a service station. He ended the message like
this: 'I want to thank you for the part you played in this happening. Each Christmas for the longest time, you have given
us grandkids ten dollars to share. This is an example of how
it has rubbed off on me and affected my day-to-day life. Oh

yeah, I know we're not to spread the word of our good deeds just 'cause it helps keep our motives pure, but I wanted you and Granddaddy to hear this story, for you two are one.'"

● My grammy is someone whom I see in almost mythic proportions because I loved her so much. Everything my grammy gave me, no matter how small, was blanketed in love, which made even a bag of homemade Chex mix mailed across the miles seem like a mighty treasure. She loved to quilt and to knit. I had numerous hand-made sweaters and quilts from her over the years. My guestroom bed is even now covered with the quilt she made for me to take to college; it won Best of Show at her county fair. My grammy died eleven months before Greg and I were married. She never got to meet Greg or her great-grandchildren—something I sorely regret. Although she never met these four important people in my life, I know that she loved who they would be in my life one day. Shortly before Hannah was born, about two years after Grammy's death, a box arrived in the mail from my grandpa. In that box were several baby sweat-ers and a pink quilt that my Grammy had made more than a decade before she died and had stored in a box in her cedar closet for my children to have one day. Han-nah sleeps with that pink quilt and often comments on the fact that her great-grammy made it for her before she was even born because she loved her so much. Also in that box was a note from Grammy detailing when she'd made these things and how she made them just for my children to enjoy and use one day; what a treasure that little note in her handwriting is. The final contents of the box were things that my grammy had saved from my childhood for my children—a storybook, a Straw-berry Shortcake quilt, and some melamine dishes.
(Adult Grandchild, USA)

My mom gives our two daughters the gift of her time. She was always delighted to babysit for them when they were little, to have them for sleepovers as they grew older, or to take them out for a day of shopping and lunch when they reached an age where a "girl's day out" would be considered fun. One thing that she did for me, a homeschooling mom of seventeen years, was a week of Grandma Camp every summer. Our girls benefited from the extra time with their grandparents—basking in their unconditional love—and I had the blessing of uninterrupted time to plan for the coming school year. *(Mom, USA)*

While window shopping in Phoenix, Arizona, my husband and I came across a cute ceramic camel. Upon closer examination, I realized it was actually a bank, the perfect way to save money for our grandchildren who live in North Africa, the land of the camels. Now, all of our loose change goes into the camel bank. When it is full, we empty it and take the money down to the bank, where we opened an account for our grandchildren. It has been a fun and painless way to save hundreds of dollars for them. *(Grandma, USA)*

At Christmas, I base gifts for my young grandchildren around a theme. One year it was penguins. I bought penguin wrapping paper, gave them a National Geographic book about penguins, bought a penguin Beanie Baby, and gave them a CD of a penguin movie. Did you know that there are seventeen different kinds of penguins? *(Grandma, USA)*

When Grandpa and Grandma came to Vienna from Taiwan, they were able to celebrate my birthday with me. They gave me a little colorful bag with a Bible verse card, dotted socks, and money. It was all very cute and sweet. Every time we have a family reunion, Grandma gives each one of us money. So that means she has to

give thirty people money for Christmas and New Year!
(Grandchild, Taiwan, age 16)

We enjoy giving gifts on birthdays and special days. We are sometimes tempted to feel badly that we cannot provide expensive gifts as some grandparents do. But it was a compliment to read on my granddaughter's Christmas wish list a request for Grandma's homemade pickles and jam. Another granddaughter wanted Grandma's pumpkin bread and zucchini bread. *(Grandma, USA)*

One thing I have done for my grandchildren is to make them each a crib size quilt. When I made the first one seven years ago, I didn't think about how many I would have to make in the future, but now that I have set a precedent, I intend to follow through. I'm happy to say that I'm up to date right now, although we are expecting two more grandchildren this year, making a total of eleven. I've planned for each quilt to have a different pattern and different color combinations. My sewing machine is very busy these days! *(Grandma, USA)*

Shopping with grandchildren is an adventure in itself—not for the child, but for the grandmother! I've learned three things: (1) Never promise anything ahead of time. What they are looking for may not be there and *nothing* else will take its place. (2) Give them an either/or choice, because decision making is right up there with eating broccoli. (3) Be sure that they have something to look forward to once they leave the store so that you do get out again. *(Grandma, USA)*

Several years ago, when our grandchildren were four, three, and eleven months, my birthday was approaching, and I decided I really didn't need any more *things*. I wrote out a questionnaire and mailed it to my daughter, asking her to fill it out and return it for my birthday.

That was all the birthday gift I wanted. It asked, besides name and age, for the child's favorite activity, favorite book, favorite toy, favorite chore, least favorite chore, what they want to be when they grow up, what they like best about their mommy, their daddy, and each of their siblings. Then I gave them space to tell me anything else they want me to know. It is now seven years later, and I have three more grandchildren. Every birthday, those questionnaires are all the birthday presents I want. It is great fun every year to go back to what each child has written in the past and see what has changed and what is pretty much the same. **(Grandma, USA)**

In an age when people seem more likely to live at or well above their means, I see humility in the fact that my grandparents lived well below their means, choosing instead to save and invest so that others could enjoy the opportunities and peace of mind that come along with financial security. This

When I was four years old, I went to my grandma's house for Christmas. She gave me so many presents. She gave me a remote control, Lego, and more. I liked that day because we sang together. The best part about the day was sleeping at Grandma's house.

After that day, I went to the beach and sat in the boat. We ate fish and rice. Then, I went back to Grandma's house and said thank you very much. That was my best day ever. (Grandchild, Indonesia, age 10)

is not to say that they aren't willing to spend money; they are plenty willing to spend a good deal of money on something, but only if it is of real value and doesn't detract from generosity. The other thing I admire is that they truly seem to enjoy what they do have. I love that my grandmother wears her jewelry. Whereas others might feel the need to keep them locked away, my grandmother chooses to enjoy them for their beauty. In a time when people seem to prefer quantity over quality in their possessions, I admire that my grandparents own relatively few items, but each item is valuable and has a purpose, be it practical or aesthetic in nature. Moreover, they take good care of what they have. Their sacrifice in living below their means has meant that all of us grandchildren have had many opportunities that we otherwise wouldn't have. Not only has their sacrifice blessed their family, but they have also used their "talents" to support ministry. *(Adult Grandchild, USA)*

As a college graduation gift, my mom took each of our daughters shopping for small appliances (microwave, coffee maker, toaster oven, etc.) and kitchen supplies (pots and pans, measuring cups, utensils, etc.) for the first apartments they would be occupying as each went on for a Master's degree. Our younger daughter does not drink coffee, so she asked Grandma if she could have an ice cream maker instead of a coffee maker. She has not used it quite as frequently as one would use a coffee maker—but it has certainly made many batches of frozen goodness! *(Mom, USA)*

One grandma I know has a rule regarding opening presents: if the items are clothing, the grandchildren are required to say, "Oooh, aaah." It is humorous to watch the children open their gifts. When the boys open clothing, they glance at it, quickly say "Oooh, aaah" and move right on to the next gift. *(Grandma, USA)*

● Look for an attractive, colorful Christmas manger scene, a sturdy one the children can safely set up and play with. This makes a great pre-Christmas surprise along with a book that accurately tells the beloved account of Jesus' birth. *(Grandma, USA)*

● Giving gifts to our grandchildren is one of the delights of being a grandparent. The joy and pleasure it brings them brings joy and pleasure to us. How can we resist? It's easy to go overboard in this area, though, so we're wise to use restraint and caution. Often I check with my daughters so I do not duplicate things the grandchildren already have. I also ask my children what they want their children to have. It's wise to heed what our children say about this so we do not cause hard feelings. *(Grandma, USA)*

● For every birthday for at least five years, my grandma has given me fifty Canadian dollars. I've been able to buy many things with that money, and I'm very grateful to her. *(Grandchild, Sweden, age 14)*

● I'm careful not to favor one grandchild over another. I make it my goal to be fair and to give equal gifts on each occasion. I enjoy giving small, inexpensive gifts for no reason. This tells them I'm thinking about them and love them. *(Grandma, USA)*

● Go shopping and plan for them to buy something— younger children love the dollar stores. Most items give a few hours of pleasure. *(Grandma, USA)*

● I find it fun to buy presents for all my grandchildren. I mostly go for clothes and books. We get lovely baby and children's clothes in Southeast Asia, so it makes a lot of sense. I'm not so much for toys. I have seen that almost all little ones enjoy being read to, so I like to get books for them. My husband ordered the entire Narnia series for Alisha, but someone else had already presented her the same thing, so we have kept it for Manarah. We also have a good many Reader's Digest children's books in store for them to be presented when the occasion demands. *(Grandma, Singapore)*

Years ago, we started educational trusts for each of our grandchildren. With growth in the ensuing years, it has been enough to pay their college expenses. We feel we can't give a better gift than their education. The side benefit is that the grandchildren watch this investment grow, can graduate debt-free, and perhaps have some left over for adult years. (The funds have to be handled by an executor until the child is twenty-five or so.) *(Grandma, USA)*

My husband's grandmother was a collector. She collected thimbles and purple glass, and she involved her grandchildren in collecting, too. She had hundreds of thimbles; many had been given to her by her grandchildren, who collected them for her as they traveled, for they knew how much she loved them and treasured her collection. (Even in her nursing home room, she proudly displayed a small portion of her collection.) When the grandchildren became old enough, she began a collection for each of them. My understanding is that she allowed the grandchildren to help her choose the target of their collection. For birthdays, Christmases, and other special occasions, she would give him or her an addition to the collection. My husband's collection was a series of leath-

> *My grandma had a great sense of humor. My grandma always brought me toys. It is hard and painful to lose the people you love. (Grandchild, USA, age 7)*

er-bound literary classics; one granddaughter collected music boxes. *(Adult Grandchild, USA)*

My mom is always looking for ways to help me with the children. Because my children are preschool age, it is very difficult to run errands with them. Mom often takes it upon herself to do the errands for me. With rapidly growing children, it seems they need a new wardrobe every season. Mom will shop all the stores in town, looking for the best deal, and bring me a variety of options to choose from. She'll even buy them the more expensive outfits and give them as a gift. Sometimes she'll even ride along on errands with me and sit in the car with the kids and let me run into a store. Having this help has been invaluable. *(Mom, USA)*

As a grandmother living alone, I am thrilled to have grandsons and sometimes granddaughters and their parents help with things like lawn care, snow removal, and gardening. This help they are giving me now is preparing them to be responsible adults. I often pay them, so it is a good way for them to earn money for their future needs. *(Grandma, USA)*

When my oldest son was born, he was the first grandchild on both sides of our family. My husband's parents were ten years older than my parents and were definitely excited about finally being grandparents. My son was born on March 4 and warmly welcomed home. In my mother-in-law's excitement, she brought him a gift on the fourth of the month for the entire first year! It was her way of celebrating for the whole year. *(Mom, USA)*

Some years ago, when working full-time, I was able to take my granddaughter (then twelve) on a shopping expedition. I told her she could have a certain amount of money to spend on clothes she needed at the beginning of the winter season. I prayed in advance that she would not choose anything that was outlandish or inappropriate that I would have to say no to. I prayed that she would choose wisely. I was so thankful that she did and that God blessed our day. We found great bargains and the amount allocated went further than she expected, which was a lesson—as well as a happy experience—for both of us. *(Grandma, Australia)*

One of the greatest gifts a grandma can give a grandchild is the gift of time. The beauty of this gift is that it benefits all involved. Grandmas can have a wonderful impact on their precious grandchildren, but it involves taking time to be with them, play with them, and get to know their likes and dislikes—who they are as individuals. As a mom, it warms my heart when my mother/mother-in-law takes time to be with my children. This can look like a one-on-one play date, making cookies together, going shopping, or just hanging out at Grandma's house. When the children are little, it means getting down on the floor and playing Polly Pockets or Legos, and as they get older it means going out for a special lunch or establishing traditions such as before-school shopping trips. From a distance it can mean intentional phone calls to talk with each child one at a time, letters or postcards sent just because, or even something as simple as calling on their birthday to sing "Happy Birthday" and communicate that you are remembering them on their special day. All these things communicate I love you and you are special to me, and all of them require time and effort to make them happen. *(Mom, USA)*

Since I travel out of the country, I frequently bring my granddaughters dolls from places such as Britain, Holland, Russia, Peru, Turkey, Norway, China, and Mongolia. For grandsons, I purchase airplanes or cars. *(Grandma, USA)*

Grandma Poem

Grandmas are so cool.
Grandmas play with you.
Grandmas go with you.
They give you the coolest birthday presents.
But the coolest thing about them is they love you.

(Grandchild, Ethiopia, age 10)

Grandma sponsored a grandson to attend URBANA 2007 and has generously supported the various missions trips taken by the grandkids. *(Mom, USA)*

When it comes to gifts like birthday presents and Christmas presents for my grandchildren, I have usually tried to make something for them. It has not been financially possible for me to buy all my grandchildren what they would have wanted, so instead I have made them different things. One Christmas I made white pillow cases with lace for all the girls and embroidered their names on them in colors that matched their bedrooms or were their favorite. I have also crocheted many hats and scarves over the years. Another Christmas I made them twelve blankets that matched each of their own bedrooms and another year fourteen aprons with their initials on their chest. Five of my grandchildren are confirmed, and as a gift on this special day I have given them cross necklaces. *(Grandma, Finland)*

A couple of ways that we are trying to help with the college education of these grandchildren is through Bright Start and uPromise. We have also helped with tuition at our grandchildren's schools when things were especially tight for our daughter and son-in-law. *(Grandma, USA)*

My mom is crafty and quite the quilter. She has made each of my children a crib-sized quilt before he/she was born and another twin-sized quilt when he/she has moved into a "big kid" bed. *(Mom, USA)*

Starting at birth and putting small amounts into an education fund can amount to quite a bit by college time! *(Grandma, USA)*

My mother-in-law pays particular attention to being fair and always spends the same amount on presents for the children, right down to the nearest dollar, using socks or chocolates to make up the difference. *(Mom, Australia)*

We make it a practice to buy something practical or toys for the young grandchildren, but the major part of our gift is a check for their bank account. They need a little something to open, but most kids today have way too much stuff. *(Grandma, USA)*

Grandma Soderstrom always bought me my new dress for Easter. When I was young, she picked it out. As I got older, she sent the money and let me do the choosing. My Mom then bought me the accessories—lace socks, shoes, gloves, and hat. I know this description dates me, but I've got the cutest black and white photos of me all dressed up for Easter. My Mom did the same for my daughters. It was a wonderful and greatly appreciated tradition. (It certainly helped out on the budget.) *(Mom, USA)*

For Christmas, we get each grandchild three gifts: something to wear, a book, and a toy or fun gift. We have eleven grandchildren, so that keeps the gift giving achievable. I find that my daughters-in-law are happier if I shop off of a list. I have often needed to return items if they were not on the list. Some years I do much of my shopping online. *(Grandma, USA)*

We always try to visit for our grandchildren's birthdays, and are greeted with shouts of "Grandma! Grandpa!" as they run into our arms with big hugs. The next thing they do is eye our bags very carefully, with one of them usually saying, "Sometimes you bring us a present when you come." *(Grandma, USA)*

One of the things I know I will appreciate down the road is the college savings plan that my mother started for her grandchildren. Even though the amounts deposited may not be huge, they are growing and will be a help to my children once they enter college. I appreciate her long-range perspective to grandparenting. *(Mom, USA)*

For birthdays, I give each grandchild one gift that I have chosen for them and some money so they can choose one thing for themselves. If they are too young, their parents can choose something they know the child needs. *(Grandma, USA)*

For my parents and in-laws, birthdays and Christmas are times for equitably lavishing gifts upon their grandchildren. Big events, like births, baptisms, and graduations, are cause for donating money to the children's college savings accounts. *(Mom, USA)*

We send valentine cards to our grandchildren with ten dollars and Easter remembrances when they aren't close by. Sometimes, we take them book shopping and let them choose their own books. *(Grandma, USA)*

Grandma outfitted our children's nursery with some of the big-ticket items such as the crib, changing table, and glider-rocker. My husband was in school at the time, and we never could have afforded these things on our own. *(Mom, USA)*

When the first grandchild arrived in each family, we exuberantly purchased all we thought necessary to pacify and delight all the senses of our little cherubs. Now, with *many* grandchildren, we have become wiser and saner. Something to wear, something to read, and something to do is our goal for each one. (Sometimes, we only hit on one of those three; something to wear does not usually win extra points!) Now, we often ask the parents for ideas, and they readily comply. *(Grandma, USA)*

My husband and I saved money to make a trust fund for each grandchild for college expenses and even graduate school, seminary, or medical school. We believed if they received a good education, they would be prepared for life. We visited them in college at least once and wrote regularly. *(Grandma, USA)*

Grandma always has time for her grandchildren. She never busies herself with chores or dishes when the kids are around. Whenever I would come to pick up the kids at her home, I'd find dishes still in the sink and craft supplies everywhere! *(Mom, USA)*

My husband and I like to help in a financial way, when possible, toward a camp or Christian school experience. *(Grandma, USA)*

In this materialistic culture, kids have more things than ever. What grandchildren need is not more stuff, but more of grandparents' *time*. As parents, my husband and I try to limit the amount of toys our children receive for Christmas and birthdays. Cards and home-baked goods sent in the mail are fun for grandchildren to receive, too. *(Mom, USA)*

● Each year, we try to buy one gift for each family that they know is just from us. We gave them a computerized globe this past year, and it has been a huge hit. The kids are now studying countries and languages. *(Grandma, USA)*

● At birth, we gave each grandchild a zero coupon bond, and each year we add a small amount to their educational fund. When our grandson started ninth grade, we asked him if he would like us to give him a hundred dollars on each birthday and Christmas for his car fund rather than a gift. (We still got him an inexpensive gift.) He agreed and was happy upon graduation for the down payment he had. I don't know if the other grandchildren will make this same choice; we will leave it up to them. *(Grandma, USA)*

● Because of the sheer number of grandchildren (twenty-eight), we tend to do things en masse, though we (now I) give generous financial gifts for high school and college graduations, and for weddings. Fifteen grandchildren are married. We've also contributed to their short-term mission trips, and there have been quite a few. *(Grandma, USA)*

● My mom asks us (the parents) what she should get the grandkids for birthdays and Christmas. It could be anything from a basketball hoop to a contribution to the college fund to a pair of Tinker Bell socks. *(Mom, USA)*

● To keep Christmas gift-giving manageable (we have ten children and twenty-eight grandchildren), individual families have their own celebrations before coming to our house. In recent years we have contributed undesignated gifts (valued at twenty dollars or so) and drawn numbers. Others can take an opened gift if they wish rather than open a new gift. Lots of laughter and bargaining! *(Grandma, USA)*

For this Christmas, I made a throw pillow for each grandchild with a front insert of their favorite Christian song in print and done over a shadow of their favorite sport. I used fabric and trim to match their bedrooms. Some of their choices were "Oh God, You Are My God," "Trust and Obey," "It Is Well with My Soul," "O, For a Thousand Tongues," and "I Am a C." They see the words of their choice songs daily as the pillows rest on their beds. That idea originally came from our oldest grandchild when he was only four. He took me into his bedroom and looked around and asked me if there was anything in it that I had made especially for him—that was this grandma's incentive! *(Grandma, USA)*

For birthdays and Christmas, my husband and I give our grandchildren a substantial gift. Throughout the year on other special occasions, we give simple, inexpensive gifts. We begin with things that are needed: clothing, shoes, furniture for bedrooms, educational toys, riding toys, board games, sports equipment, bikes. The most prized gifts are toys the grandchildren want (within reason). We give them books—lots of books! We also give them appropriate videos, DVDs, and CDs that teach morals and manners. *(Grandma, USA)*

Long-Distance Grandparenting

During the months I was compiling this book, I often rose around 4:30 a.m. "Early morning hath gold in its mouth," said Benjamin Franklin. When the house was quiet, I could go about my business without neglecting anyone or being interrupted. My favorite part of those early morning work times—after coffee with vanilla creamer and time reading my Bible—was sitting down at my computer and opening new e-mail. I was privileged to be the first one to read each message as it arrived. The morning I opened the e-mail from Janice (Canada), I needed a tissue. Several mornings later, I picked up an e-mail from Janice's daughter Melody (Russia). I needed another tissue. This section begins with the touching thoughts Melody and Janice sent me. Did I mention that you might want to grab a tissue?

- My mom has successfully maintained a relationship with a toddler from ten thousand miles, and that's no small feat. The first Grandma and Grandpa movie that my parents made arrived in time for my Abigail's birth-day. It was a definite hit right from the start. Abigail

177

loved the one-on-one attention and that Grandma used her name and talked to her. She also loved the repetition, always knowing what Grandma would say and do. I think it makes her feel secure. The Grandma and Grandpa movie holds Abigail's attention better than any other kid's movie, not because it's action-packed but because it is directed lovingly to her. Some might remember watching *Romper Room* on television. At the end the lady looked through the mirror and said, "I see Ben and Allison, I see Kathy and Jonathan." I remember waiting and waiting for her to say my name, too (which she never did; Melody is not that common!). But Abigail has whole movies that are just for her! I've even put a photo of Grandma and Grandpa on the DVD box.

I don't feel quite as guilty using the television as a temporary babysitter when it's Grandma and Grandpa she's watching. And this way, Mom helps me get my housework and homework done even from a distance. I think the videos will make it easier for Abigail the next time she does see Grandma and Grandpa. They won't be strangers; they will be movie stars! She will know who they are and that they love her and are interested in her. From a missionary perspective, I also appreciate these videos of everyday life back home. I work at helping Abigail to feel connected with her home country, and these videos definitely help. The activities and crafts my mom does on the video are great. Now, when we make something, Abigail wants to film it and show Grandma.

Sometimes I wish I had more immediate answers to parenting dilemmas, such as when Abigail isn't eating well and I don't know how to help her. But I know Mom makes a big effort. It would probably be easier for her to push her grandmothering instincts to the back of her heart, thinking that they are not needed right now. But she's courageously put the effort into communicating over the distance. Great love includes opening our hearts to the risk of great pain. That's sacrificial love, the greatest gift anyone can give another. Abigail's Grandma loves her, and Abigail knows it. *(Mom, Russia)*

● I have always valued the role of being a grandma and planned to be available to my grandchildren. Having my daughter, Melody, and her husband called to long-term missions half a world away makes this look different than I had always expected, but it does not absolve me of the privilege or responsibility to be Abigail's grandma. It just means God called me to be a long-distance grandma.

When that ten-month-old baby boarded the plane, I pondered during the first few rather sleepless nights how I could stay real to a baby and how I could help her mom in a tangible way. When we talked on the phone via the Internet, I could hear Abigail cry upon hearing my voice and not being able to find me. I realized that babies needed voices, faces, and one-on-one interaction. Thankfully, little ones are more than willing to see or listen to the same thing over and over, so I made a movie of me and mailed it to her. I took movie clips on my digital camera of me talking to her as I put her toys away, reading a book to her, playing peekaboo, and looking for Grandpa, and I burned them all on the same CD. Each was about one to two minutes long, so strung together the movie ran about seventeen minutes. It was hard to do things we usually do with a baby in front of a camera, especially when my husband was behind the camera laughing! But I kept imagining Abigail, and that helped. I had to stop only once or twice to cry when the image became too real and too impossible to hug or get a response from. It was easier when I asked my husband to try the other side of the camera. Then it was something we were doing together.

I think the hardest thing about doing this is that the more we invest in the relationship, the more we miss the response. I hurt more by missing her more. But that will change as she grows, and it's my job to do the work now. Loving always takes the risk of hurting.

What I didn't consider was how this was going to be a big help to my daughter. Abigail often watches me read a story on a movie clip while Mel gets supper on the table. Abigail doesn't seem to mind that I read the same stories over and over. In fact, Abigail watched the first movie two or three times before she realized it wasn't live.

The ideas for the movie clips just come to me. Some have worked better than others. Reading stories is the best all-round choice, but it is the hardest to film. To focus on the book without glare is harder than it looks in a non-studio environment. It takes concentration to read to an absent child while including all the stops to comment on things that go along with the book.

Grammy takes me to plays at Florissant Civic Center. Grammy lets me ride in her golf cart when I'm in Florida. Grammy is going to take me on a cruise. Cuddle me. Love on me! Play with me. Grammy lets me sleep in her room. (Grandchild, USA, age 6)

I filmed myself doing a number of basic Sunday school crafts with Abigail. That was easier to do. I sent along the things they might need for the crafts with the CD. Mel got the stuff out for Abigail to do as soon as the movie was finished. I cried the day I saw Mel's blog entry where she was making the craft I had done on the CD. As I explained to my sister that there should be a picture of both of our hands on the same craft, she reminded me that as far as Abigail was concerned, she did do it with me. I am the one that knows what is missing. Abigail only knows what she has.

My husband, Martin, filmed us picking apples from our apple tree, complete with a step-by-step walk up the ladder with the camera held at toddler height. We also filmed ourselves raking leaves and looking for mushrooms. We shared the things we would do if she were with us for a day.

I filmed myself building a tent in the family room. Then I took the camera into the tent and peeked out the door to the mural of deer on our wall. That one was fun but took more editing. With practice, I am getting better at editing. My son-in-law, Paul, said the parts Abigail likes the best are when I say her name. That makes sense to me. She wants me to be talking to her, not to anyone that may be listening or watching. She is relating to a grandma who loves her.

Recently, we visited Mel and Paul and Abigail for seventeen days. It took a couple of hours for Abigail to figure out what was going on. While we were traveling to a resort, she said to her mom, "Grandma, Grandpa show"—her words for the video clips. From then on, she knew who we were, and it was easy to build on that foundation. We had a wonderful seventeen days together doing all those things I have always wanted to do: walking and talking, exploring the world of flowers, swimming pools, sand, and elevators, stirring coffee, reading stories, and just sitting and looking into each other's eyes. The last day I told her a few times that we were going back to our house and described how it was in the videos. She was quite upset when she realized we were leaving, but she didn't ask for us after we left. I think she is beginning to understand the idea of away but still alive! She tried to talk on the phone last time we talked. It is worth saying goodbye to be able to say hello.

I am quite amazed at how much you can love such a little girl. *(Grandma, Canada)*

I enjoy going to see my grandma for many reasons. First, I get to go on an airplane. I love going on airplanes over the ocean because I like looking at the water. Second, I love looking at all the dolls and pictures my grandma has. I also love to see Sophie, her cat. Next, I love Sweden. I love all the cool sights and all the friendly people. I love seeing Grandma! Those are the reasons I love to go to Grandma's house. *(Grandchild, USA, age 8)*

My mother-in-law is Japanese-Hawaiian and has American grandchildren (my sons) and Australian grandchildren (my nephew and niece). She is always intentional about teaching her grandchildren about her cultural heritage so they can have a better understanding of her and a better appreciation for their own cultural heritage. She also hopes that when they come to visit Hawaii they will fit in better. My mother-in-law frequently gives our boys children's books with stories that take place in

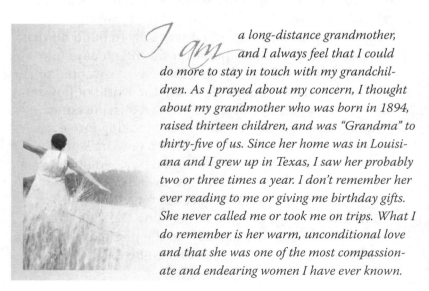

I am a long-distance grandmother, and I always feel that I could do more to stay in touch with my grandchildren. As I prayed about my concern, I thought about my grandmother who was born in 1894, raised thirteen children, and was "Grandma" to thirty-five of us. Since her home was in Louisiana and I grew up in Texas, I saw her probably two or three times a year. I don't remember her ever reading to me or giving me birthday gifts. She never called me or took me on trips. What I do remember is her warm, unconditional love and that she was one of the most compassionate and endearing women I have ever known.

Hawaii as well as vocabulary word books. When she visits and when she talks on the phone she frequently uses Hawaiian words, and my sons have enjoyed learning the language. She tells them stories about their relatives in Hawaii and how they live, hoping to teach my boys cultural skills that will help them when they visit. She also sends them CDs with Hawaiian music and prepares (or sends) local food. *(Mom, USA)*

To stay in touch when the children were little, I would read stories on a cassette tape and send them through the mail. My daughters would play them at nap and bedtimes, and even now the kids remember the stories. My daughters would set up the tape recorder and have the grandkids talk and sing to us so that we could hear their little voices. This was before electronic mail and Internet phone service. Now with the right equipment, it's far easier to stay in touch than it used to be. *(Grandma, Peru)*

Since our grandchildren live in St. Louis or Pennsylvania, I am a long-distance grandmother. I often send

Grandma was comfortable with who she was—no makeup, no fancy clothes, no need to prove herself. She was unhurried, gracious, and available to sit and talk. I felt comfortable in her home because we could touch and play with anything in the house. She always made me feel special; in fact she made everyone feel special. She has had a lasting and profound influence in my life because of who she was.

It is comforting to remember that authentic love shortens any distance and is ultimately the most precious gift I can give to my grandchildren. —Cynthia Heald

surprises in the mail for them, especially at times like Valentine's Day. Gum is something they like as well as books and window stick-ons. I try to purchase matching dresses for the girls and matching outfits for the boys at least once a year—usually at Easter. Trying to get them all to pose for a picture is quite a challenge since all nine are seven and under, but we seem to get at least one good one each year. Patience, patience, patience! *(Grandma, USA)*

My son and his family live and work in North Africa. We spent a wonderful five months together when they were home for the birth of grandchild number two. Upon their return to Africa, I worried that our two-year-old grandson, Ezra, would forget me. We had a web camera and looked forward to our weekly "visits" with them. However, due to difficulties with their Internet connection, we could have only visual and no voice. So, I would make all kinds of faces and make stuffed animals dance in front of the camera to capture Ezra's attention. His parents kept him in his high chair so that we could have good, long interactions with him. We'd blow kisses and delight at his every smile. However, you can only keep a two-year-old in a highchair so long. Once, when our daughter took him out of his chair for a nap, he toddled over to the web camera, and suddenly all we saw was his eye. The next typed message we received was, "Ezra just kissed the camera." I then knew we didn't need to worry about him forgetting us. *(Grandma, USA)*

I remember coming downstairs many weekday mornings as a child to see my mom on the phone chatting with her mom. It was cheaper to call early in the morning and better to call in the morning because of the time difference. My mom and my grammy spoke several times a week while I was growing up. Now my mom and I talk several times a week as well. I was blessed as

a child to see the close, positive, and loving relationship between my mom and my grammy. Although my
grammy was halfway across the country, I still felt close
to her; she never made the geographical miles seem
that lengthy because of our frequent communications.
I am trying to instill that same closeness between my
mom and my children. Although my parents live almost
halfway across the country from their grandchildren,
my children, too, feel close to their grandparents. From
infancy I've put my children on the phone so that they
recognize my parents' voices. I am thankful that our
local phone company offers an affordable unlimited
long-distance package because it allows my kids to talk
to their grandparents whenever they want for as long as
they want. My parents, especially my mom, will listen to
them jabber on for an hour about everything that's on
their minds. *(Mom, USA)*

● Long-distance grandparenting is challenging. We miss
our grandchildren's activities and seeing them for a few
minutes here and there. The grandchildren that live in
another state spend one week with us during the summer. We try to make that time special for them. This
summer, we are looking forward to taking them fishing
and camping. *(Grandma, USA)*

● When we lived a day's journey from our grandchildren,
we could make planned trips unique. When the grandchildren came to visit us in Minnesota, we always went
to Camp Snoopy, a clean, fun amusement park in the
center of the Mall of America, just eight miles from our
home. The children were hesitant about our move to
Illinois to be near them, because they could no longer
go to Camp Snoopy! We also had a whirlpool tub that
I would fill with warm water, pour in a very few drops
of dish soap, add some tubby toys, and push the button. Voila! Anyone two and older was allowed in, and

A long time ago when my mom was still a young kid, my grandparents decided to go to Vienna to start working there so that all their kids could eventually move here with them. They wanted their kids to have a good life. They started working at some hospital, while my mom and her siblings stayed with their grandparents until my grandparents sent enough money for them to all fly over to Vienna. Eventually, all of them came over to Vienna safe and sound. (Grandchild, Philippines/Austria, age 13)

they would disappear in mountains of soapsuds with only little cherub faces showing. We had only to sit and watch until the water turned cold, pull our pink toddlers out, wrap them in fluffy pink and blue towels, and let them escape for their evening romp through the house. **(Grandma, USA)**

As my sons were growing up, I often dreamed of becoming a grandma. I dreamed of going out for walks with the children along the river in our hometown, singing for them, playing with them, and going on boat trips with them. But instead, I found myself as a "grandmother across the ocean." I experienced long-distance grandparenting for thirteen years, and during this time I was blessed with twelve wonderful grandchildren (in three different families). I had to accept that my grandchildren would grow up on the other side of the world. My oldest grandchild, Mia, came to Finland to see Fammo (father's mom) and Faffa (father's father) when she was only three months old. My next grandchild, Andreas, was nine months old when I saw him for the first time. The rest of my grandchildren were born and are all equally dear and special to me. Some of them I had the opportunity to see for the first time as newborns, others not until they were closer to a year old. As time went by, we started dreaming of living closer to our grandchildren. To spend two weeks with them around Christmas or four weeks during the summer was not enough to develop a close relationship with them. When I wasn't with my grandkids I was longing to see them. When I knew I was going to see them soon, I was scared they wouldn't remember me or they would be afraid of me.

After thirteen years of being a long-distance Fammo, my dream finally came true. I was able to move close to my grandkids and become a full-time grandma. I was now finally able to have them over to my house on a regular basis, and I could also visit them more often. When I was planning my relocation, I often prayed the well-

My grandparents, my second uncle, my parents, and I visited the United States's national parks (such as the Grand Canyon). My dad, second uncle, and mom took turns driving the car from Los Angeles to the national parks. It was fun, and I remembered Grandma always having big plastic tablecloths with her so they would protect the luggage that was tied to the top of the car. It was like we were in a desert, almost like pioneers with a car. Grandma always had the right supplies—medicines and ointments for when we got hurt. Even without the ointment, it wouldn't hurt anymore because Grandma was near me. (Grandchild, Taiwan, age 16)

known prayer: "God grant me the serenity to accept the things I cannot change; courage to change the things I can; and wisdom to know the difference." One Wednesday night during the first year I lived in America, one of my grandsons handed me a coffee mug with this same prayer written on it. I think it's a good prayer for all grandparents to remember. We live in a different time with different values and customs than when we were growing up. Our main job is to love our grandchildren and show them our love. *(Grandma, Finland)*

One thing my son absolutely loves is when a grandma draws for him. He especially likes it when she draws a picture with crayons or markers, labels the people or things in the picture, and sends it to him along with a story. Preschoolers and early grade schoolers enjoy pretending, especially when people they love are in the story. Then the next time they speak on the phone with their grandma, it sparks all sorts of conversations. *(Mom, USA)*

For our grandchildren in Indiana, I try to keep contact by mailing books, cards, or small gifts. I want them to know that I am thinking of them. I also take digital pictures of my husband and me using gifts they have given us and send them as e-mail attachments. For example, they gave us bowls for Christmas that said Souper Grandma and Souper Grandpa, so I sent pictures of us eating our soup. *(Grandma, USA)*

My mom is a wonderful, godly grandma. Her love for my children and her other grandchildren is profound. Because she lives a thousand miles from me, she played her role long-distance. My husband and I went away once a year when the boys were little, and she spent a week at our house with them. I highly recommend that for long-distance grandmothering. My mom knew and loved my boys well because she spent that time here. She had them help bake pies, homemade bread, and homemade paste. She spent hours talking, listening, telling them Bible stories, and playing the Memory game. *(Adult Grandchild, USA)*

It was sweltering hot. We were saying our goodbyes to our grandchild's other set of grandparents. Tears were streaming down Jamee's face as he hugged his grandma, and he cried like a forsaken child. He wouldn't let go of her. His sweat mingled with his tears, leaving a big wet spot on her shoulder as she held him close to comfort him.

To visit our son's family was a huge investment that took a great toll on our budget and physical strength. But it was the only means to connect with the growing toddlers and to help them understand that they have family living across the ocean that loved them and yearned to strengthen this bond with them.

I was amazed at the strength of the relationship and the outburst of emotion in the four-year-old boy. I had not thought this possible between a child and anybody other than his parents. Deep down, I felt left out from this circle of love, and wondered if ever a grandchild of mine would love me with such intensity.

Children know genuine love. They understand its gestures but cannot comprehend the many reasons why this love cannot be available to them always. I tried to acquaint myself with this bubbly little boy, understand his likes and dislikes, attend to his needs, read him books, and color a picture or two together. He was happy and affectionate, but the attachment was only as deep as the two weeks I stayed with him. Next year, if I were to come back, I would have to start building that bridge of love and attachment once again.

Being a grandma offshore, I have missed precious moments in Jamee's life. Accumulating pictures in my purse, bragging about him to my friends, shedding tears of joy every time I heard him say across the telephone line, "I love you, Teta," did not make him love me any more. I was a name, a face, and a memory. Even now, after I have moved across the ocean to be near these adorable grandkids and their parents, I still have these feelings.

One day Jamee expressed his feelings out loud and bluntly. A visitor asked Jamee, "Who do you like more? Grandma or Teta?" I was stunned by the direct question and even more so when Jamee said, "I like them both. I like my Grandma in Florida two lapses (gesturing a turn twice around his body) and Teta one lapse. This is because I knew my grandma for a long time and this Teta only for a short time." Baffled at the forthright answer, the lady asked him if he preferred the cooking of one to the other. Jamee said, "I like my grandma's chocolate chip cookies and Teta's cinnamon rolls." Then he added, "This teta is awesome! She can do all kinds of nice art and crafts." I was very happy. Children express their feelings truthfully and forthrightly.

I had been living around Jamee for less than three months when the visitor drilled him with these questions. He was becoming more familiar with me and more willing to respond to my love and attention. I realize that it's important for me not to compete with his other grandma, but to seek to complement the circle of love being offered to this child from all who surround him. I thank God that it is never too late to give love. *(Grandma, Jordan)*

Even though our granddaughters lived more than eight hundred miles away, we took some vacation time to drive to be with them when they were baptized. We also took along a great-grandmother. We made a plaque with a special Bible verse for each one.

We are planning to take vacation time again to travel to be with a grandson on grandparent's day at his school. *(Grandma, USA)*

It didn't matter that I lived in Illinois and Grammy lived in New Hampshire, for her love spanned the miles. From my birth she let me know that grandparents are love. To her it wasn't about going above and beyond the call of duty, but just about being a grandma. She once told my mom that it amazed her her grandchildren seemed to love her as much as she loved us, but I don't know how that could have been any other way. *(Adult Grandchild, USA)*

When our grandchildren came to visit, I sometimes made up travel bags for their trip home—a few snacks, some surprise toys (Target's party favor aisle was great for this), and a roll of Scotch tape. *(Grandma, USA)*

My son lives in San Diego and has a little daughter almost three years old. To try and get her to know me better, I ordered a picture book that had about twenty-four different sleeves in it. On each sleeve was the op-

If I have a problem, my grandma, granny, and Granny Mac will do everything they can to help me sort it out. My grandmas are good Christian influences to me and give me someone to look up to. One grandma lives overseas, and she sends regular e-mails to see what's new in my life and how things are going for me. My grandmas take an active interest in what I do. (Grandchild, Australia, age 13)

portunity to leave a two-minute message, which can be changed as the pictures change. She heard me say, "This is Grandma and this is Grandpa Abbott. This is your Aunt Christie, etc." I told her a little about each of us. *(Grandma, USA)*

When my husband and I hugged our families in New York goodbye and took our three young daughters to Peru in 1968, I had little idea what my mother was suffering in parting with three of her grandchildren. I also had no idea that twenty years later, my own daughter would take my four-month-old granddaughter to Peru to serve Christ with her husband for three years. In that short time, they had another daughter and son. We were fortunate that we were serving in the Andes Mountains and were an eight-hour drive away, so we were able to be with them at times, but we still missed our stateside grandchildren. In 1991, our missionary kids were reassigned to Papua New Guinea. During their fifteen years there, they have added three more girls to their family. Again we were blessed to spend six years serving in Papua New Guinea and enjoyed our seven grandchildren there when we were in the same area. The Lord is good. *(Grandma, Peru)*

Sometimes I would call my daughter, Janna, and her daughter, Hannah, and have to leave a message on their phone. Janna would later play back my message. At an early age, Hannah would indicate that she wanted Janna to play the answering machine as soon as they entered the house to listen to me. She also loved to talk on the phone with me most every day; she continues to talk to me at least four or five days each week even now! *(Grandma, USA)*

Over the years we have had many wonderful visits from grandparents. And since both sets live a long distance away, we have had the privilege during these visits of living together for as much as a week at a time while our children were growing up. We have always looked forward to these visits and let our parents know that. We welcomed them with open arms, letting them know how glad we were that they had come to visit. We made sure that their guest room was well cleaned, neat, and inviting. The children were involved in this preparation. It wasn't a problem to help; it was exciting because Gramma and Grampa or Nana and Papa were coming.

Our two children benefited greatly from these visits as did my husband and I, because it meant that there would be sharing of childcare, time for Mom, a special date for the two of us, fun times while preparing and cleaning up from meals together, many wonderful times of laughter and sharing around mealtimes, lots of stories for our children on grandparents' laps, playing catch or skating with Papa, and hearing life lessons and important sayings from four wise grandparents. So even though distance separated us from getting together regularly, the times we were together were special and made wonderful memories. Likewise, our two trips a year to visit grandparents (and aunts, uncles, and cousins, etc.) have been wonderful times for our children and for us. *(Mom, USA)*

After living nearby and visiting us frequently, our granddaughters, two and four, moved out of state. Soon after, my husband and I made a video for them. We started it by opening the front door and greeting them as if they were coming to visit. We walked through the house, talking to them about eating in the kitchen, napping, playing, etc. Then we sat on the couch and read one of their favorite books showing them the pictures. At the end we said goodbye at the door and waved to them as they left. They watched this video over and over. Apparently it even eclipsed *Cinderella* and *The Little Mermaid*. Eat your heart out, Disney! ***(Grandma, USA)***

My husband and I made a Build-A-Bear for our granddaughter. Since there are four paws on the stuffed animal, when Anna presses the paws, she hears either Grandma or Grandpa's voices saying things such as, "Grandma loves you, Anna, and so does Jesus." Our daughter-in-law plays all four paws every night before Anna goes to bed, so our granddaughter is learning the voices of her long-distance grandma and grandpa. ***(Grandma, USA)***

When we were overseas and away from our grandchildren, we made good use of video cameras, which are wonderful for recording family events and sharing around. Packages were also a wonderful way to reach out to our distant grandkids. Even in countries where postal security makes packages a risk, a few stickers tucked in a card with a stick of gum will always bring a smile. ***(Grandma, Peru)***

I lived in Japan for twenty-two years and in Switzerland for two, and never lived near my grandchildren. I wrote them letters about where I was and what I was doing. I sent dolls, jewelry, and toys from different lands where I traveled and sent them slides and pictures of the countries I visited. ***(Grandma, USA)***

For my children, my parents are long-distance grandparents. We see my parents about three or four times a year for three days to two weeks at a time. We live together when we're together, either at our house or at theirs. We speak with them very frequently on the phone between our times together. When we're at my parents' house, they make special beds on the floor of their bedroom for my children. When my parents are at our house, they invite the children to have a sleepover with them in our basement guest room. *(Mom, USA)*

We read stories on tape and send the cassette and book so that our granddaughter could read along with Grandma and Grandpa. *(Grandma, USA)*

We live two hundred miles from our grandchildren, so we can't just run over to see them without working out schedules. However, my husband and I started a tradition when we had just one grandson, which we've carried out for nearly twelve years.

When our first grandson was three-and-a-half, our daughter drove from Michigan with him, and we had a few days to visit. Then, she left him and his teddy bear with us for a week. During that time, we catered to his interests and the foods he liked, and we took him to age-appropriate places. Our daughter who lives nearby has no children, so she took him swimming or to the playground, which gave Grandpa and me a rest.

We did the same with our granddaughter when she was three-and-a-half—juggling schedules so we could work both children in during the summer. Their aunt continued to take them swimming, to McDonald's, etc. Our granddaughter liked to bake, so one time we made muffins together. Her mom was surprised that she filled twelve muffin tins with batter, because she'd never done that before. She did a fine job.

Our third grandson was left with us on his fourth birthday. It was harder for him, and he didn't last a whole week. The thing that helped him most that first year was that he discovered his mom had left her sweatshirt by accident, so he slept in it every night.

The older the kids become, the more challenging it is to get all of our schedules together. *(Grandma, USA)*

I have been blessed by an amazing grammy, as well as watching my mom interact with my three children. My mom is a fabulous long-distance grammy, but that's partly because she had an amazing example to follow in her own mother. My mom will tell you that she's nothing special and that she doesn't do anything original, but I know that's not true. She might be right that nothing she does is original, but she's found just the right combination, and she does everything with love, which makes it extra special. My children love her supremely, as she loves them; sometimes it's like watching myself with my grammy. *(Adult Grandchild, USA)*

Thirteen

Manners and Discipline

Often it's the grandparents who pay attention to the grandchildren's manners. In one family, though, it was the grandchildren who paid close attention to the grandparents' manners. "When my four children were preschool- and elementary-school age," one mom explained, "we were working on table manners. I placed a toy pig in the middle of the table at mealtimes. If anyone was spotted chewing with his mouth open or forgetting to say please when asked for something, the pig was moved to his spot at the table. No words were necessary. He had the pig until someone else earned it. This continued throughout the meal, and whoever had the pig at the end of the meal helped Mom do the dishes. One night Grandma and Grandpa were eating with us. I had forgotten to bring the pig out, but when Grandma broke a good manners rule, the kids were quick to see that she got the pig. The children were careful not to earn the pig themselves, and took great delight when Grandma was the one who still had the pig at the end of the meal. She laughed with the kids and cheerfully helped with the dishes while the kids watched with glee. Her cheerfulness helped the kids see that everyone can be a good sport about manners and help with the dishes!"

● I always expected my grandchildren to obey, and they seldom disappointed me. Sometimes it was harder when I stayed with them in their own homes, because they tried to convince me that they were allowed to do something that we didn't want them to do. (Most of the time they were just trying to get something past Grandma and Grandpa.) *(Grandma, USA)*

● In my child-raising era, we used to separate our young children when they fought with each other, making them go to their rooms. We also had clearly defined rules for some important matters; open defiance of those rules met with a count to three to stop, or we would administer our paddle to the softest part of their bottoms. In this day and age, there is less spanking and more effort to "re-direct" or take "time-outs." It seems to me that there can be a healthy balance. Parents can be extreme: some spank just because they are in a bad mood, venting their own frustration. Some are so afraid of damaging a child's self-esteem that they let the children run the household, and then wonder why others don't invite their family.

I like that Grandma takes me to Starbucks and lets me share her mocha. (Grandchild, USA, age 4)

Balance, to me, is the goal worth working toward—never spank in anger and use it sparingly for open and clear defiance of a known and established rule of the home. Time-outs are effective for lots of things, especially children fighting with one another, but as old-fashioned as it seems, I still believe that too much leniency will end up harming the children, making it difficult for them to follow rules at school, obey traffic rules, and submit to authority wherever they go.

This is an important area that needs much prayer. That's where grandparents can be resourceful mentors—but only if they are asked! My husband and I always follow the guidelines that our adult children have established in their home with their children when we babysit, and we don't believe that anything more than a time-out is ever appropriate for a grandparent to administer. For parents, it's finding the balance between "spare the rod and spoil the child" and "fathers, do not exasperate your children." With lots of love, prayer, and time spent with the children, the balance of discipline as it becomes needed, will all work out well. *(Grandma, USA)*

I had guests over, and we were talking when Manarah interrupted us:

> Nani: "Manarah, you mustn't interrupt when two grownups are talking."
>
> Manarah: "I know I mustn't. My daddy says I have good manners." *(Grandma, Singapore)*

At the grandchildren's birthday parties, no one may take a bite of the cake until the birthday child has had the first bite. At a nine-year-old grandson's birthday, he announced "I am not taking a first bite—just go ahead and eat." We all waited him out until he finally gave in and took a first bite. Then he muttered, "It's my birthday. I can't believe that I am going along with a rule that I don't even like!" *(Grandma, USA)*

I try to help my grandchildren with good manners and courtesy. It helps them to show consideration and kindness for others. One daughter asked my husband and me to hold "E & E" classes for our grandchildren. After my husband taught them about electricity, I trained them in etiquette. We had boys and girls present at the same time, which allowed me to walk them through their varied roles. Now, it is a joy to see them practicing their good manners at our family celebrations. *(Grandma, USA)*

If I get in trouble with one of my parents, Grandma always makes me feel better by telling me that I won't do it again or by saying that everything will be all right. *(Grandchild, USA, age 13)*

I usually try to make discipline an explanation of the reasons for things. I try to re-direct unpleasant behavior into something acceptable, rather than being too demanding. Sometimes this is a challenge with a child who is especially strong-willed. *(Grandma, USA)*

Having grandparents next door is a privilege, and I want to make sure that my children don't take advantage of them. I ask my children to respect their grandparent's time and home. I remind them to knock, remember their manners, and return the things they borrow. *(Mom, Australia)*

When the cousins come for a week, I create a job schedule. This includes the ordinary tasks of living together, such as preparing meals, cleaning up after a meal, sweeping/vacuuming the floor, etc. I post the schedule in the kitchen, and they love to work together. I usually put two of them together for a meal/day/task. However, each one makes her own bed and picks up her clothes. When they were younger, Grandpa had the idea of giving a quarter to each person each day if they passed a morning check on their beds and suitcases. He would also throw in extra jobs, like washing a car, as ways to earn a little extra. *(Grandma, USA)*

When a parent is disciplining one of the grandchildren, my husband and I stay out of it. We found that if we got involved, we not only confused the grandchild, but undermined the parent's authority. This practice has been a lifesaver in more ways than one. If we disagree with what or how something is being done, we talk with the adult later. The only time we step in is if it is clear that the parents didn't see what happened or weren't aware of other circumstances. Then we talk with them on the side, and they can decide what to do. *(Grandma, USA)*

The thing that is nice about my grandma is that she is kind and has a lot of patience with me. (Grandchild, Philippines, age 10)

My children's great-grandma was of great comfort and wisdom to me. I recall one day being heartbroken about my toddler's willful and wild behavior. Great-grandma gently, but firmly, took my hand, looked me in the eyes, and said, "She *will* be all right." In that moment, I sensed that this wise and experienced loved one was offering me the perspective I was not able to have. It was a phase that my daughter would pass through along with many others. I took a deep breath, and Great-grandma was right; that willful toddler is a magnificent young woman today. Great-grandma saw what I could not see many years ago. *(Grandma, USA)*

Once, when my granddaughter was visiting, I was in the kitchen while my husband was watching tennis. Manarah kept talking and disturbing him. He asked her to be quiet. She came to me and said, "You know, Nani, I'm really, really upset with Thatha [Grandpa] because he talked to me, he *talked* to me [he scolded me]!" She then went to the living room and said the same thing to him! *(Grandma, Singapore)*

When the grandchildren's parents are around, I try not to give the children any words of admonition. When I am with them by myself, I use a time-out chair for the small children. I talk with the older children and ask them not to continue in their unpleasant behavior. Usually there are very few problems. The biggest issue is the sibling teasing and arguing. I try to follow their parents' model of asking the kids to ask for forgiveness and restore. *(Grandma, USA)*

The first couple of times my grandchildren came over, I cleaned up after them. But then I realized that we needed a new rule: No clean up, no play. They learned in a hurry! *(Grandma, USA)*

My mom didn't correct the boys very much (she just loved on them), but my dad did! He only had to tell them once—they took him seriously. The things my dad taught the boys were important, and any grandma could teach them as well:

- Don't be hoggish.
- Be generous.
- Love the Lord with all your heart, be devoted to Him.
- Flee from evil; flee very fast.
- Look at the person who is speaking to you.
- Be quick to shake hands when you meet someone.
- Be nice to your little brother. *(Grandma, USA)*

I am conscious that our grandson is watching us and learning habits, so I am careful to teach him good things, even social habits such as saying, "Thank you." I also teach him to appreciate people. He sometimes says, "My grandma is a good cook." He appreciates when I tell him stories or show him a video, and he says, "My grandma always entertains me." He also says, "Thank you, Grandma, for taking care of me." Sometimes he says through the telephone, "Take care, Grandma." God is helping me to create an atmosphere where our grandson feels welcome and comfortable in our home. *(Grandma, India)*

Setting the table or sweeping a floor takes some patient instruction. Carrying food to and from the table does, too. I don't assume that children know how to do these simple tasks. *(Grandma, USA)*

One day when shopping with a grandson, I refused to buy something that he wanted. He made me chuckle as he tried hard to convince me. When he finally gave up, he said, "My other grandma is nice." I simply replied, "Yes, I know your Grandma Powers. She is nice." *(Grandma, USA)*

Bad behavior cannot be tolerated, but I've often found that if you expect better of them and say so, you will see them do better. *(Grandma, USA)*

My granddaughter has a habit of disappearing in public places like parks and malls. We've tried to correct that by warning her of the obvious dangers. When told that she could get lost if someone took her away or she wandered off, her reply was, "But Jesus would find me like he found the lost sheep." Now, how do we refute that? *(Grandma, Singapore)*

● Grandma Rules:

- The only place in the house grandchildren can eat is at the kitchen table.
- No carrying around Sippy cups or bottles.
- No jumping on beds or furniture.
- No closed doors.
- Please honor us by changing diapers in the diaper-changing room (equipped with a full supply of diapers of all sizes, baby wipes, and anything else that's needed).
- Please pick up toys before going home. ***(Grandma, USA)***

> *"Grandmother-grandchild relationships are simple. Grandmas are short on criticism and long on love"* *(author unknown).* *(Grandma, USA)*

● One time we took two grandsons to a hotel with a pool. The pool happened to be right outside our door, so when the boys were finished swimming, we let them go in before us with instructions to take off their dripping suits at the door. The ten-year-old was very modest, wrapped a towel around him before we came in the room, and quickly got dressed. The eight-year-old ran around free with no clothes on and enjoyed jumping on the beds. He made us laugh, though, because when it was time to get dressed, he went into the bathroom and locked the door, because: "My mom said I should get dressed in privacy." He sort of got the right idea. We loved his innocence. ***(Grandma, USA)***

● A book I have found very helpful is *Manners Matter* by Hermine Hartley. Manners today seem to be a lost art with the younger generation. ***(Grandma, USA)***

● I taught my grandson to say, "Thank you, Jesus" before every meal. After the meal or drink he used to say, "Thank you, Grandma." *(Grandma, India)*

● Manners are a delicate subject for grandparents, but a simple reward speaks volumes. One time when the kids were visiting, I said that if they could eat without spilling on the floor or their chair each meal, they would get a quarter, and at the end of their visit we would go shopping. We saved a lot of clean-up time that week. Now we work on other table manners: not speaking with our mouths full, putting the hand we are not using in our laps, cutting and eating a few bites at a time, asking to pass the food, etc. *(Grandma, USA)*

● My kids are very aware that grandmummy doesn't tolerate disrespect or rudeness in any form. *(Mom, Nigeria)*

● I loved having tea parties with my granddaughters. I had some china cups and plates (a child's set), and I'd put a tablecloth on the table, cut the crusts off the bread for small sandwiches, and serve cookies with milk. It was a good opportunity to talk about using our best manners—hoping they'd remember to use them as they grew older. *(Grandma, USA)*

● When you have two kids who want to play with the same toy, get out the broom and pluck out two pieces of straw. Whoever gets the longest straw gets to play with the toy he or she wants. *(Grandma, USA)*

My grandma is a great influence on me, except when she licks her plate! (Grandchild, USA, age 10)

Fourteen

Overnights

I have the impression that many grandmas think over-nights with grandchildren are best either with one child or in small groups. If you've ever entertained the thought of having all your grandkids over at once, you might want to read Marge Gieser's story:

> Because all our grandchildren live in town, it's easy to have two or three cousins spend the night at my house every once in a while. It's often three little girls together or two to four little boys. Once, I gave in to the request to have an all-cousins' sleepover. The two teenagers declined, and one grandchild was too young, but nine little live wires came for supper, a video, reading time, and a sleepover. I reluctantly let the six boys (ages six to twelve) sleep in the basement, while the three girls (ages eight to eleven) slept upstairs near our bedroom. I put the two twelve-year-olds in charge—they promised there would be no scary stories and no getting out of bed (sleeping bags on the floor). I checked on them as

we were going to bed, and all seemed reasonably quiet and under control.

Ten minutes after we were in bed, the six-year-old came flying into the room; the stories were way too scary. He ended up in our bed for the rest of the night. We were sound asleep when we were awakened by the burglar alarm and a twelve-year-old leaping up the stairs breathlessly saying, "I'm sorry! I'm sorry! I was just kidding! I didn't know the alarm was on! Are the police going to come?" (To bluff his cousins, he had said he was going home because they wouldn't stop talking and had started out the basement door.) When the alarm went off, it scared them all half to death, and they thought they were all in trouble. My husband and I had a big laugh, and tucked six very subdued little boys back in bed. We also decided that maybe we should stick to sleepovers of two or three.

When I was little, my grandparents invited me over to spend the night once a month. This usually involved my favorite dinner, playing with the dog, and playing with Grandma's special toys. But the best part was falling asleep to Grandma's stories and then waking up to see her next to me. After I'd get ready for bed, Grandma would get me snuggled in my sleeping bag, and she would turn on the lights of the miniature town she had set up in front of the windows. This little town was made up of tiny ceramic houses and a church, a school, a grocery store, a library, etc. But my favorite parts were all of the little things that made the town come alive: the miniature lamp posts, the little

My grandma tucks me in bed every night when she visits me or I visit her. (Grandchild, USA, age 13)

When I was three years old, my mother had tuberculosis. Her mother, Grandma Wulff, moved in with our family and took care of my brother (five) and me (three) while Dad worked and Mom convalesced. Grandma made a very difficult time much easier on all of us. She made a casserole we all dubbed "more"—because no one could have just one serving. My grandmother did not know how to be idle. Once, when the electricity went out, my dad wondered what the clicking sound was.

people on the glass pond ice-skating in the winter, the cotton Grandma would put down for snow, and what-not. She would tell me the most detailed story about one of the little homes in this town or the church and the life of the pastor in it. I remember only some of the stories, but I will never forget the way that town looked all lit up in the dark room and my Grandma telling me story after story until I fell asleep. *(Adult Grandchild, USA)*

My mom has been a terrific Grandma. She gave me a Valentine's Day gift one year—to have one of my young children overnight once a month at her house. I don't know who loved it more—the one who went to Grandma's house or the one who got special time alone at home with us! This gift continued until the kids were in high school. There is nothing like special attention from Grandma. *(Mom, USA)*

One time when my parents were going to have a late night out, I went over to Grandma's house to sleep over. I had already eaten dinner, but she cooked up an amazing batch of cookies and said they were all for me! There was no way I would have been able to eat all of those cookies. We played lots of games, and it was a lot of fun, especially because I was not home alone. The next morning

*Grandma had continued to knit in the dark with-
out dropping a single stitch! When Mom was well,
Grandma returned to her almond orchard and
vineyard. We all missed her. She came with us
on many family vacations, and each summer, my
brother and I would spend several weeks with her
at her home. She took us to church and on Sunday
drives to Lake Merced. The rest of the week, she
turned us loose to romp and swim in the irrigation
ditches. Many of my fondest childhood memories
include Grandma Wulff.* —Francine Rivers

when I woke up, Grandma had made about ten things for
breakfast, all for me. Grandma is an amazing cook, so I
ate well for breakfast that day. *(Grandchild, USA)*

I have vivid memories of overnights at my grandparents' houses. One set of grandparents lived locally, and
I could be with them more often. But when we went
to Detroit to see Oma and Opa, it was for an extended
period, and that was special. They always made me feel
specially loved. They would be sure to look at me in
the eye and really care about what I said. My grandmas
both let me look in their fun drawers; I especially loved
their jewelry boxes (they would let me try on anything
I wanted) and my Oma's sewing box (she was a seamstress and had a huge drawer full of beautiful buttons).
They would always prepare my favorite foods. They lavished their time and attention on me and made me feel
like I was their favorite (I have found out that my siblings felt the same way). *(Grandma, USA)*

Sleepovers offer the best times for listening. It seems
that in the dark, when little legs have stopped running
and minds are a bit relaxed, deep thoughts often arise.
Luke (age four) asked me one night, "Who do you think
was the first person to go to heaven?" *(Grandma, USA)*

My grandma tells the best stories. She makes up stories about Jiminy Cricket and his adventures. Going to bed at Grandma's house is a lot of fun on the nights when she tells us a story. *(Grandchild, USA)*

We love overnights! Papa gets sent to the guest room while the girls and I take over our room and the queen-size bed. There's always a bedtime story before prayers. In the morning, we play I Spy before getting up. *(Grandma, USA)*

It's fun to do a really late night when the grandchildren are here. We might rent a movie, have popcorn, and stay up late. Once we took them to a college observatory to look at the night sky through a telescope. Of course, we had to wait until after 9 p.m. It was almost scary to walk up several flights of stairs to the top of the building, where we met a professor who could explain the stars and planets to us. We had an awesome time, marveling at God's night secrets. *(Grandma, USA)*

We have many overnights with the kids and usually take them

Grandma always had candy for us when we came over. And she didn't cry—even when my brother told her one time that her meatloaf tasted like dog food (how would he know anyway?). Whenever we'd go to stay with her while our parents were away, she'd take us to the toy store and tell us each to choose a toy that we liked. Also, she made a point to have us over for sleepovers, either with our cousins or our friends. (Adult Grandchild, USA)

out to dinner. Depending on the time of year, we might go to a park or come home to all the toys, books, and videos that I have collected from garage sales. I buy only the best, don't have to spend much, and have a basement and cupboards full of things for them to do. My husband always fixes pancakes for the children the next morning, and that is a huge tradition with them. Often we will offer to keep the kids for twenty-four hours just to give the parents a break. *(Grandma, USA)*

> *Grandma takes me places. Grandma lets me come to her summer classes. Grandma lets me come to her house for sleepovers. (Grandchild, USA, age 6)*

In past years, my son's children stayed with me a lot because of the parents' schedules. I created a space in two bedrooms for them to call their own. Both of the grandkids seemed to love having a place just for them to study and to read. *(Grandma, USA)*

When Kenedy stays over night, she often wakes up early with me. I make her a cup of coffee (a lot of warm milk and sugar with a few drops of coffee). She has her own journal, pen, and Bible, and she sits down with me during my quiet time in my special quiet time place. *(Grandma, USA)*

Once my cousin, my sister, and I went to my grandma's house to sleep over, and we all brought our American Girl dolls. We put them in the living room, and my grandma put hers there, too. Then we all pretended to go to Chicago and get them. My grandma also pretended to pay for each of them. *(Grandchild, USA, age 7)*

211

- Overnights are *big*, and we try for at least one for each grandchild a year—with enough time for us to recover between visits. We usually go to some special place (bowling, out to eat, shopping, a park, etc.), then bake a favorite dessert, make a snack, or have a special treat that they get only at Grandma's house. Sometimes we sew or make a craft and have story time (reading or telling). The grandchildren love to hear stories about when we were kids or what their parents did as children. Grandpa usually takes them to breakfast (their choice); last year I delivered breakfast in bed to our grandson on a tray with a picture of him on it and a note saying how much we loved him. Sometimes they stay two nights or until their smile begins to slip. *(Grandma, USA)*

- When the children spend the night at our home, we usually have a popcorn and movie night. I put a couple of sheets down on the family room furniture and floor to protect against buttery popcorn fingers. We watch a movie together while we enjoy eating in the family room. At bedtime, we always read a book, ask about their favorite part of the day, and pray with them. *(Grandma, USA)*

- When our oldest grandson was two and had a new baby brother, I wanted to help him adjust to being one of two children and no longer just one. He came over one night a week, for the afternoon, dinner, and overnight. When the others came along, we had them one at a time, one a week. We didn't necessarily do anything special, but they had our full attention. I made goodies they liked and could help make. We read and told stories (with them as the characters) around my little Dickens' Village house. We prayed together each night. We did these overnights until each grandchild was fourteen or fifteen. I had a box up on the shelf, full of little things—a ball, crayons and paper, hot wheels cars, tiny dolls, fancy pencils, etc.—and they could pick one thing out to take home. *(Grandma, USA)*

When our grandkids come to our house, they sometimes ask to use our computer, which is great. We'd feel awful, though, if they ever stumbled onto something they shouldn't have seen. In this day when all kinds of awful influences are available on the Internet, it's wise to make sure our grandchildren will be protected on our computers when they come to visit. We can do this by installing an Internet filter, making sure we're around when they use the computer, announcing that the computer is off-limits overnight, and keeping the computer in a visible place—not in a secluded area with a closed door. It's good for our grandchildren to know we want to protect their minds and hearts. *(Grandma, USA)*

Grandma always made life special growing up. I have so many fond memories of going to her house and sleeping over. She always made those times fun, and she always made me feel loved and safe. *(Adult Grandchild, USA)*

Bedtime is special when we are visiting at our grandchildren's homes. I like being part of nighttime devotions and prayers, because great conversations often take place then. One question was, "How can I be happy in heaven if someone I love isn't there?" I have tried to find a blessing to give my granddaughters each time we are together, such as, "Fill

My granny is kind and giving. She has us after school when mum is at work. She fixes my soft toys and writes letters back as Dr. Granny. She taught us how to knit. My granny knows me really well. (Grandchild, Australia, age 11)

your heart with beautiful things, and you are and will continue to be lovely." With the little girls, I gently draw a heart on their chests with my finger. *(Grandma, USA)*

Grandma sometimes invites her granddaughters for an overnight. During their time together they have learned to bake pies and trifle, sew simple outfits for their American Girl dolls, and construct a dollhouse out of boxes and household items. One time each girl came home with a small photo album documenting the weekend together. *(Mom, USA)*

Fifteen

Photos

A close friend of mine, Ruthie Howard, is so good with a camera and pictures that her extended family members affectionately call her Aunt Flash. I enjoy walking into her home and spotting the pictures she's hung in her living room and hallway of six generations of her family. I don't take as many pictures as Ruthie, but I take a lot. One of my brothers-in-law teases that I've documented every meal the family's ever eaten together. I haven't worked so much, though, at acquiring photos from several generations past. The ideas I've received for this book have prompted me to think more about that.

- My first family picture was taken when I had just come to America. It was when I was one-and-a-half years old. I sat on my grandma's lap. She was thrilled when she saw me. *(Grandchild, Taiwan, age 16)*

- I have photo albums for all seven grandchildren. Parents are often too busy to keep them, so I carry a camera almost all the time and manage to get some wonderful shots. I also have a storage box for each of them, and whenever they make a picture or send a note or card, I put it into the appropriate box. One day they will go back to the grandchildren. I did this for a single mom I knew, and when she received it, she said she had to sit down and have a good cry. She hadn't kept a lot of things, and this became a price-less gift. *(Grandma, USA)*

My mother-in-law is a "scrap-booker," and she is making a scrapbook for my son (and other grandchildren). We give her access to our snapfish.com pictures, and then she orders the ones she wants for her scrapbook. I think she does a few pages for each year of his life. It is fun for her because she is so far away from us, and then she can show it to her friends and other family members. *(Mom, USA)*

One of the neatest things my mom has done for each grandchild is to compile a scrapbook. In this are excerpts from all the letters I have ever written to her about that child. Starting from before they were born, she has clipped and pasted it all. In each book she has inserted the pictures I have sent, so the clippings and the picture often go hand in

I've never seen my grandma. She died even before my mom got married. But my mom told me a lot of things about my grandma, so I can draw a picture of her: generous, kind, and friendly with a bunch of wrinkles on her face. According to my mom, Grandma was one of the richest people in her village. She owned three facto-ries (an umbrella factory, and I can't remember the other factories). But my grandma was kind and loved to help people. (Grandchild, South Korea, age 13)

hand. Upon their graduation from college they get their book. It chronicles their life through their mother's eyes. Of course most of my correspondence was through snail-mail letters, but modern grandmas can do this with e-mails, or they can write down snatches of conversation with the grandchild's parents. *(Mom, USA)*

I love pictures, and I have a million of them. I put them in photo books that the grandkids can look at. They love to see themselves in pictures and hear the stories about each one. And I put pictures in frames all over the house. The children are so happy to see themselves, and they notice when I put a new picture in a frame. I take a lot of my own pictures and am good about sharing copies with my daughter-in-law. *(Grandma, USA)*

One year for Christmas, my daughter made picture frames with our grandchildren's names at the bottom. It has been such a nice gift that I update their pictures each year. *(Grandma, USA)*

Before my husband's grandma died, she'd been collecting a box of mementos and photos that pertained to each of her six grandchildren. When she and Greg's grandpa were preparing to move to a retirement center, she put these items and photos into separate photo albums for each of her grandchildren. What a gift I received when my mother-in-law gave me Greg's books from his grandmother! Some of the treasures included in his books were his birth announcement, the thank-you notes I had written to her for the bridal shower and baby gifts that she'd given to us, Greg's high school and college graduation announcements, invitations to all of the events surrounding our wedding (showers, engagement party, etc.), newspaper and newsletter clippings about Greg and our family from over the years, a postcard from Greg thanking her for the cookies she'd sent him at college, a typed transcript of the message Greg's grandpa left at the church office for Greg's grandma telling her of the birth of Hannah (their first great-grandchild), a Polaroid of Greg's grandpa holding newborn Hannah at the hospital for the first time, and a program and napkin emblazoned with Greg's name from a high school honors dinner given in his honor. My sister-in-law (who received her husband's books) and I have been blessed with the opportunity to delve into the years of our husbands' lives before we met them. Those years have been preserved by the grandmother who loved them so much. *(Adult Grandchild, USA)*

● Keeping close to our families over long distances does not happen without effort. When we are blessed to be in the same area with our grandchildren, we try to make happy memories rather than just being there expecting good times to come to us. It's important to enjoy the times that we do have with family and record them on film or make scrapbooks. *(Grandma, Peru)*

> *When my grandma was only eight years old, she drove her dad's milk truck. (Grandchild, USA, age 7)*

● I take many candid shots of the grandchildren almost each time we are together. I make doubles of them to give to their families, since they are usually too busy to take pictures. Many of my daughters' framed shots on the walls of their homes are photos I had given them. *(Grandma, USA)*

● Just recently my husband and I went through years of photos and pulled out about two hundred pictures that provide a review of my granddaughter growing up. The work to do this will be greatly rewarded by her enjoyment of the album! *(Grandma, USA)*

Debbie's two boys were born at a hospital in our area, so I was there within the hour. I took pictures of the family going home from the hospital and entering their home for the first time. Before the birth I had videotaped getting the nursery ready and the very pregnant mom. Anne lives in Indiana, so we were there within a day or two and did the same thing. We recently watched our granddaughter's video on her third birthday; it was fun to see how she had grown. Neither Debbie nor Anne has a video camera, so this was something I could do for the sake of history. I also got footage of Grandpa Cal and Great-grandmother expressing their hopes for the child to come to know, love, and serve God. In the early years I taped birthdays, trick-or-treating, and Christmas. I have made copies, but want to put all this on DVD so several people have it in case of fire, flood, etc. Anne's husband has no baby pictures, because his house was destroyed in a fire. *(Grandma, USA)*

> *The things my grandma and I like to do together are go to Fannie May, the mall, and the park. We love to walk together also. I love my grandma. (Grandchild, USA, age 10)*

Sometimes I send my grandchildren thank-you notes (made out of plain stationery from a craft store) with a picture of each child and me on the card. *(Grandma, USA)*

The first summer we invited grandchildren for a week of Cousins' Camp, I took pictures throughout their time here. After they went home, I found simple albums and created a mini memory book for each one. They were nothing fancy—just pictures, labeled with names, places, and dates in a small booklet. It soon became a tradition. As the number of grandchildren increased, it took me several weeks to complete the project, and I nearly gave up. Then my twenty-three-year-old granddaughter (who has now graduated from camp) came to visit and proudly brought her picture books to relive those earlier memories. I realized what a treasure they had become.

I used this idea even when babysitting for a younger grandchild for ten days. (She had never been to camp.) As we took special outings, I would take a few pictures. After she had gone home, I created a little memory book of our time together and mailed it to her.

During our week of Cousins' Camp, Grandpa would take each girl out to a restaurant for a special meal just for the two of them. He spent the time talking, sharing, and listening to each one, as well as enjoying food together. The girls looked forward to their date with Grandpa and would voluntarily dress in their best clothes. Since Grandpa's death, the girls have treasured those special times they had with him. At his memorial service, each grandchild contributed a drawing/poem/letter for a collage of memories; several mentioned those special one-on-one occasions when they shared laughter

> *One of my memories of my grandma is that once when I had bronchitis she was in Vienna, and every day I had to go for a walk for thirty minutes. Many times she would go with me and we would talk and have fun. She was always so caring to me, and she is just so awesome. (Grandchild, Sweden, age 14)*

and dreams with him. (I later took those drawings/poems/letters, interspersed them with pictures of that child with Grandpa, and created a *Remembering Grandpa* book for each family.) *(Grandma, USA)*

We have rehabbed several baby squirrels, and they are a riot as they become active. We have made a couple of videos of Grandpa trying to put them back in their pen. The videos are simple, but the grandkids roll with laughter as Grandpa gets one in but another pops out before he can close the door. Grandpa hams it up a good bit of course. Not everyone would be willing to try this one. *(Grandma, USA)*

Last summer, my husband celebrated one of the big birthdays. I solicited his cousin, Mona, an artist, to do a painting of our seven grandchildren as a surprise for him. She painted a magnificent watercolor that was the marvel of even the subjects themselves. It hangs over our piano as a focal point in our living room, reminding us daily of God's gift to us of our precious grandchildren and declaring to them the richness of their value in our lives. *(Grandma, USA)*

I have a special album with pictures of all my quilts in it as well as each of the quilts with the grandchild for whom it was made. *(Grandma, USA)*

One simple way to journal a grandchild's growing-up years is to write a few lines each birthday regarding highlights of the year. It might include the circumstances of his first steps, his climbing escapades, his awareness of God, and something you love about him. Include one picture of him, and so begins a little book you can give him one day. *(Grandma, USA)*

I keep photo albums of each grandchild, and after they marry, I send them the album. *(Grandma, USA)*

I regularly take pictures of my grandchildren at various ages and stages playing with their toys. I want to help the kids remember what toys they played with. I also capture pictures of their bedrooms and pets. *(Grandma, USA)*

The little book, *Whose Feet Are These?* was one of my first projects years ago using a Print Shop computer program. It included all the grandchildren's pictures. On the front cover was a picture of Grandpa's big feet with a pair of little feet (a grandchild's) between them. The two had just splashed down into a swimming pool on a float, but all you can see on the picture is the two sets of feet. The question, Whose feet are these? is eventually answered at the end of the book, but each grandchild and a puppy and a whale are featured as the mystery unfolds. There are a few special pictures included to remind the grandchildren of fun times together (Sea World, a hike in Korea, etc.). The poetry is simple. *(Grandma, USA)*

I have made a picture album for each grandchild. The child is featured in the album, but other pictures of family are in it also if he or she is in the picture. Those who have seen their book enjoy going through it and recalling the activity or event when the picture was taken. *(Grandma, USA)*

After taking my grandchildren to the zoo one day, I took lots of pictures and later gave them each their own photo album of all the animals we had seen. It was a great way for them to review the animals. *(Grandma, USA)*

I have a photo of my great-grandma, Grandma Soderstrom, Mom, and me (when I was about two years old). I like that picture so much that I was inspired to replicate the same scene some years ago with my grandma, my mom, me, and my two daughters. Two of those precious ladies are now in heaven with Jesus, and I smile every time I dust that picture in my living room. *(Mom, USA)*

Sixteen

Prayer

few times each month (once a week when I'm on top of things) I send out an e-mail to my husband, three sons, and daughter-in-law titled Request for Requests. It's a request for their current prayer concerns, and they each send back two or three. When they send them back, I put together another e-mail affectionately titled Mom's Musings. At the top, I type a short paragraph about what everybody's doing. Then I include a few encouraging verses from the Bible and list each family member's prayer requests, from the oldest to the youngest. I send the e-mail to each family member and print out two hard copies for myself. I put one in my prayer notebook and the other in a three-ring binder where I have now collected several years of family history through prayer concerns. This plan to pray for one another has worked well, and I intend to keep it going when we have grandchildren old enough to be included in the e-mail rounds.

● The first thing that comes to my mind when I think of Grandma is prayer warrior. While she may be less than five feet tall, Grandma has put on the whole armor of

223

Her name was Gertrude. My paternal grandfather bought her off an Indian reservation for two mules and a sack of flour. Of mixed race, he chose her because she looked strong and healthy.

My grandmother gave birth to eight children. Her husband often left for several months at a time to find work in different towns. The Depression made life hard, and the family lived in poverty. To survive she made and embroidered pillowcases and dishtowels, which she sold. She sewed clothes from flour sacks for her children to wear.

Years later, I remember going with her to other people's homes where

God. Every time I need prayer, the first thing I think is *I'd better get Grandma praying. (**Adult Grandchild, USA**)*

- When Micah was little, I used to place a hand on him and pray that he would grow physically, mentally, socially, and spiritually. Grandmothers play a significant role in praying for grandchildren and teaching them to pray. (*Grandma, India*)

- I know that my grandma prayed for me every day, because she told me so. She often told me the exact things she was praying for me. She said that she was praying for my husband, and that she had prayed for him from the day I was born. My mom has done the same thing for each of my children, and I am doing that for my grandchildren. God has blessed and answered those prayers. (*Grandma, USA*)

- I pray for each of my grandchildren every day, specifically. I pray for their salvation and relationship with God. I pray for their future spouses. I pray for specific things that are

she scrubbed floors and washed laundry. She lived as a widow for forty years until her death at age ninety-three. She never complained or felt sorry for herself. My grandmother didn't have much, but she worked hard and helped others. She loved having her large family visit, and at Thanksgiving she made delicious pies and cornbread dressing. My fondest memory is of her sitting in her rocking chair and singing old hymns. She lived out her faith in God and His sovereignty. Her prayers and love for the Bible have had a lasting effect on four generations. —Rebecca Lutzer

happening in their lives (swim meets, piano recitals). I pray for areas of their lives that need work (self-control, getting along with a brother). I pray for their health. I pray that God would use their individual character traits (generosity, enthusiasm). I pray for their education and their futures. I pray Scripture for them (such as Eph. 1:16–19 and 3:14–19). This all means that I need to, and am privileged to, know them well. *(Grandma, USA)*

● My grandma prays. A lot. This is what I cherish most about her because it encompasses who she is—a woman of faith, a woman who seeks after God, a woman who looks for God's grace in the darkest of situations, and a woman who loves not only her family and close friends but strangers also. I believe this is what keeps my grandma and me connected over the miles that separate us. We pray for each other every day; she knows everything that is happening in my life, and she prays for all of the things that I am going through, whether good or bad. And I do the same for her. The beautiful thing is that she has taught and modeled to my mom to pray, too, and they have both taught and modeled to me to pray faithfully, wholeheartedly, and often. I praise God for the work he is doing in my family generation by generation. I hope and pray that I can one day pass this heritage of faith and prayer on to my own children and grandchildren. *(Adult Grandchild, USA)*

Someone wrote a prayer list of topics to pray for kids, a different topic for each day of the month. My mother printed this list out with relevant Bible verses and laminated it. Each family has a copy to keep near the dinner table. Each day we pray for the topic according to the date of the month. For example, one day we might focus on praying that we might have greater compassion for those around us. Another day might be that we have a heart for missions or integrity in our lives and in the lives of those we love. *(Mom, USA)*

My grandma brings back many memories. One is her awesome cooking. I think all grandmas know how to cook. She is also very caring and interesting to talk with. She always tells jokes and has some funny stories. She also dresses really funny. She always wears Hawaiian type clothes. She's understanding, patient, loving, and peaceful. The last time I visited her, I felt at home and welcomed. It's fun playing Boggle with her. She always wins, though. It's because she was a schoolteacher before. (Grandchild, Philippines, age 13)

● Once when Mormor was at our house, she was praying. When she was done, instead of saying amen, she said bye-bye. We all laughed really hard. *(Grandchild, USA, age 8)*

● As a long-distance grandmother, I feel my greatest gift to my grandchildren is prayer. For the older grandchildren, we have asked them, "What can we pray about for you?" I pray that my grandchildren will revere God and live in harmony with his will, because as Mary says in her song, "His mercy extends to those who fear him, from generation to generation" (Luke 1:50, NIV). I pray that the Lord will guide them in their choices and keep them from harm and evil. I also pray Numbers 6:24–26 for them: "May the Lord bless and protect you; May the Lord's face radiate with joy because of you; May he be gracious to you, show you his favor and give you peace" (TLB). *(Grandma, USA)*

● I have many memories of my grandma Knoedler praying, but that alone wouldn't count for much if I also didn't see her as one of the righteous people whose prayer is powerful and effective before God. I know we don't really have saints in the Protestant tradition as our Catholic brothers and sisters do, but I do believe my grandmother is a special saint among the communion of saints. I believe that through a life of diligent and persistent seeking after God, she has developed a special sensitivity to the movement of the Holy Spirit. My grandmother's life, although graced in many ways, has also had its share of hardship, burden, and suffering—both spiritually and physically. I cannot imagine what it must be like to pray to God after having a son be diagnosed with M.S. and watching him slowly deteriorate physically, until finally he is taken to heaven before her. I know my grandma worried much over my uncle and closely felt the sufferings he experienced. It is her faithfulness during these times—her submission to the ultimate will of God—that means the most to me. It is because of this that I find the most comfort when I hear that Grandma Knoedler is praying for me; this is my mystical belief that God gives special attention to her prayers as He did to Moses, Abraham, and other such individuals toward whom God "bent" His will because of their faithfulness. This is her spiritual legacy to me: when God feels far off, and God's ways seem unclear, I can look to my grandma as an example for guidance. *(Adult Grandchild, USA)*

Our granddaughters are blessings sent from God. It is our joy to pray for them. I keep a card file of prayer requests for my granddaughters' events, special occasions, and challenges. As I read God's Word, I look for verses to pray for each one. I also record answered prayer. *(Grandma, USA)*

Philippians 4:6 has been my guide for praying for and with my grandchildren: "Do not be anxious about anything, but in everything, by prayer and petition, with thanksgiving, present your requests to God" (NIV). I have so much to be thankful for; I have sixteen precious grandchildren, of whom one has already gone to be with Jesus; I am so thankful that I now live close to my grandchildren. I can get to know them personally and finally be a part of their everyday lives. I have suffered from insomnia for many years, so I have had all the time in the world to pray for my grandkids. It is a blessing for me to be able to talk to my Lord about them and to pray for their struggles and needs. As a grandmother, I tend to wonder about their future. This is why I frequently pray for needs they may not even be aware of yet. I pray, for instance, that God would lead them to occupations in which they will be a blessing to others and that God would bless them with loving Christian spouses. But the most important prayer for them is that they would remain in their faith. When I have prayed together with my grandchildren, I have tried to lead their thoughts and prayers so that they would not only include their own needs, but that they would include the needs of others. I have taught them to pray for the needs within their family, the extended family, their church community, their friends, and the world. *(Grandma, Finland)*

I find myself praying a lot for my granddaughter—for her salvation, for purity, for protection, and for wisdom for my son and daughter-in-law in raising her. Because I don't experience her daily life with her, I have more time to pray. I feel that one of the great callings of my life right now is to do that. I remember when my grandfather died, I felt a profound sense of loss because he prayed for me so much. That is a legacy I would like to leave to my granddaughter. *(Grandma, USA)*

It is an ongoing privilege to pray for our grandchildren and their parents daily. As I was driving one of my grandchildren to grade school one morning, my six-year-old granddaughter expressed concern for the day. I sensed her worry. What to say in the few moments before I dropped her off? I suggested that we talk to God about it. I prayed for the day, and then said I would be praying for her after I left. Our hearts were calmed, and she was soon talking with a schoolmate. *(Grandma, USA)*

I keep a collage of photos at my computer station. That way, I'm reminded to pray for each child while booting up my computer *(Grandma, USA)*

I have felt privileged to pray for these precious little ones practically since their conception. *(Grandma, USA)*

Grammy wanted to know anything I would share with her about my life halfway across the country. When I started high school, I sent her a letter about all of my new friends from church and school. I even included photos from our youth group photo directory, so she could see my friends. She hung that letter and its accompanying pictures inside her pantry door so she could refer to it whenever we spoke. She remembered the names and details of those who were important to me. She prayed for me and for my friends tirelessly. *(Adult Grandchild, USA)*

Praying is a given for every Christian grandmother. While I often include all eighteen of mine in daily prayer, I sometimes concentrate on just one for a particular day. I can lift up him or her to the Lord throughout the day. *(Grandma, USA)*

My children know that their grandparents pray for them every day. Grandmas often tell us of a particular Scripture they came across in their daily Bible reading that prompted them to pray for us. Because they are up-to-date in our lives, they can pray specifically and then ask us how things are going. What a treasured gift this is to us—a precious ministry in our lives. Recently my mom said, "Wait a minute and let me read this verse to you. I am so excited! I just came across this in my Bible reading and know that this is for David." It was Acts 13:22: "He [God] raised up David to be their king, concerning whom He also testified and said, 'I have found David the son of Jesse, a man after my heart, who will do all My will'" (NASB). She also shared it tenderly with ten-year-old David, my son and her grandson, giving him a vision for his life. *(Mom, USA)*

I had a grandmother who loved me and prayed for me even though we lived miles apart. We visited her every summer while I grew up. She was a wonderful Christian lady whom I looked up to. I could only hope that I could fill her shoes one day. Now, I'm a grandmother and want to share my life with my grandchildren. The best way I know how is to pray for them. They are in my prayers morning and night. I entrust them to God's care and pray that they will grow into caring Christian people. *(Grandma, USA)*

Grandmummy was a lovely, warm, kindhearted, and prayerful woman. Grandmummy taught us all the essence of prayer and the love of Christ. *(Mom, Nigeria)*

My husband and I attend a church where each Sunday we pray something called The Prayers of the People. One prayer is: "Praise God for those in every generation in whom Christ has been honored. Pray that we may have grace to glorify Christ in our own day." I am grateful and blessed to be able to say that many names come to my mind when we pray this. But I must say that Grandma Knoedler especially and almost immediately comes to mind because I know that Christ has been honored by her life, and I pray that I, too, will honor Christ with mine. *(Adult Grandchild, USA)*

My husband's parents are ninety and know each of their great-grandchildren well by name, because each day they pray for them and have done so every day of their lives. We all count on Grandpa's prayer each day, and he has taught us much about a consistent, specific prayer life. At the memo-

Although I have many places to go, I love my grandma's house the most for three reasons. First, we usually play Apples to Apples. Second, she always lets me ride my bike in the street. Third, in the summer she lets us play in the sprinkler. (Grandchild, USA, age 8)

My Grandmother is hip, fun loving, and always understands me. She is an amazing cook, and I always get tingly inside when I hear that we are eating dinner at her house. My favorite memories are at the Rib House (her restaurant). I would work for her and get paid, but I felt good around her. I feel like I can always be myself around her, which I can't even do around some friends sometimes. I call my Grandma Granny. I could never call her Grandmother, because that does not sound right to me.

I admire my Granny so much and she has done a lot of things for people; especially my PaPa. She has taken care of my grandfather ever since he started being sick. Sometimes she gets frustrated, but she is always a good Granny.

(Grandchild, USA, age 10)

rial service for my father, the pastor said, "I could always ask Arnold to pray for anything, knowing that he would." Now, who will take his place to pray for the needs of our people and this church? My father prayed for his family as if he were looking directly into the face of God, with a faith to believe that God would answer. *(Grandma, USA)*

From the time my grandchildren are born (even before), I pray that the Lord will provide the mate that He feels would be best for them. I prayed this for my children, and the Lord answered abundantly. I also pray regularly that all my grandchildren come to know the Lord. This has been precious to see! *(Grandma, USA)*

● I've always prayed for the grandchildren. Now that most of them are parents, my husband and I pray even more for them. Much of the time prayer is the only input we have in their lives aside from some e-mail, an occasional phone call, and birthday greetings. The wonder is that God does the work, and we watch what happens in their lives as a result. I saw great changes in my sister's children as the result of continued love and prayers of their parents and their grandmother and me. The ones who strayed the farthest were prayed for the most and today are faithfully serving the Lord. *(Grandma, USA)*

● My grandma is tender and ever so loving. She prays for me non-stop when I'm in need of prayer. *(Grandchild, USA, age 10)*

● In our extended family, we draw names for the coming year's prayer partners. Each person gives his requests on an index card to the one who is to pray for him. Many of the younger family members pray for their partners daily. This provides for special generational bonding during the year, since our family members are scattered across the country. *(Grandma, USA)*

● We will never forget the day that our phone rang, and our three-and-a-half-year-old granddaughter was on the other line. "Grandma," she said, "I asked Jesus into my heart today. I'm going to heaven. Grandma, are you going to go to heaven too?" She then insisted I get Grandpa, so she could tell him the same news. Our daughter-in-law later told us that she and our son had been praying for their daughter's

I'm thankful that grandma gardens with me. (Grandchild, USA, age 7)

salvation. The stories taught in Sunday school, the books they read to their daughter, and the Christian music they played in their home all set the foundation for questions. Then as our daughter-in-law was driving home from an errand with the children in the car, this three-and-a-half-year-old asked her mommy if she could ask Jesus into her heart. Our daughter-in-law was happy and surprised, and said that they would talk more about that when Daddy got home that night. "No!" she insisted. "I want to ask Jesus in my heart right now. Please, Mommy, let's pray and ask Him right now." My daughter-in-law, remembering the verse about "suffer the little children to come onto me, and forbid them not," decided that the Lord was moving in her daughter's heart. She pulled to the side of the road, and there she prayed with her little girl, who in the complete authenticity of a three-and-a-half-year old, asked Jesus to come in her heart and forgive her for any bad things she had done, because Jesus loved her and gave himself for her. There will be many choices along her life to reaffirm that important decision and to grow as a Christian, but there is no question that God was working in this little life, and we are so blessed to have the knowledge of this little one's tender heart toward God and dependence on Jesus! *(Grandma, USA)*

Prayer is the most important thing I can do. I have my grandchildren's individual pictures before me in my prayer journal. To help me concentrate on them and their specific needs, I put my fingers on their faces and gently cover them even as I ask the Holy Spirit to cover them, protect them from evil, guide, design, and direct their day, activities, and relationships. I pray that God will orchestrate their lives in every dimension. I have shown them what I do—and they are pleased. It makes them feel special to me and to God. It's important for us to let them know that we pray for them often. *(Grandma, USA)*

It is important to tell our children and grandchildren that we are praying for them. My ninety-eight-year-old mother-in-law is a wonderful example of this. For many years she has prayed daily for her extended family, including spouses: five children, fifteen grandchildren, and thirty-six great-grandchildren! What a blessing and heritage to pass on to the next generation. *(Grandma, USA)*

When Micah was three years old, and he and his parents were leaving for Kodaikanal, he told us that he wanted to pray. As we all bowed our heads, Micah said, "Lord, we are leaving for Kodaikanal. Help us not to die on the way." His prayer was short and directed to the Lord. The next day, when Micah and his parents arrived at their destination, our son called us and said, "God answered Micah's prayer. We did not die!" *(Grandma, India)*

My daily prayer now is that God would mold me into the grandma He wants me to be. Among many other things, I hope to give my grandchildren perspective and time. *(Grandma, USA)*

God has blessed my husband and me with wonderful children who love Him. He has also given us many grandchildren, whom we pray will also learn to love God and want to serve Him as they grow up. I need to do my part by praying faithfully for each one and setting a godly example before them. May God help me meet this challenge! *(Grandma, USA)*

At high school graduation this year, our extended family gathered around our first graduate, and each person shared memories and gave him a blessing. His mom gave all the guests a slip of paper with Colossians 1:9–12, and asked us to pray this prayer for her son often in the future. *(Grandma, USA)*

How I need wisdom and understanding to point my grandchildren to Christ as He would have me. And so I pray:

- That I will trust in the Lord with all my heart and lean not on my own understanding, regardless of how much I think I know and how much of life I've already walked through (Prov. 3:5)!
- That I will use my words with restraint (Prov. 17:27).
- That I will weigh my words (Prov. 15:28).
- That I will hold my tongue and guard my lips, for a woman of understanding does this to guard her life as a mother and grandmother (Prov. 11:12; 13:3).
- She who guards her mouth and guards her tongue keeps herself from calamity (Prov. 21:23).
- That I will run to the Lord after those sleepless nights tossing and turning for the lives of my children and grandchildren—for counsel and sound judgment come from God (Prov. 8:14).
- That I will remember that a kindhearted woman gains respect (Prov. 11:16).
- That I will never forget that my heavenly Father loves them and cares for them even more than I do. God can work all things together for good for those who love Him—even their mistakes, as He has mine. *(Grandma, USA)*

Prayers for our step-grandchildren are very important, as they have to deal with many extra feelings and issues in their lives. *(Grandma, USA)*

My grandma taught me how to pray in Spanish when I was around four years old. *(Grandchild, USA, age 13)*

● The most important thing I have done for my children and grandchildren is to pray for them every day—from before birth to the present time. *(Grandma, USA)*

● It is a privilege and responsibility to pray for our grandchildren. Since we have already been through the child rearing years, we have the advantage of knowing how tough the growing-up years can be for little ones. Sibling rivalry. Illness. Learning disabilities. Shyness. Discipline. Family dysfunction. Peer pressure. Abuse. Divorce. How do we pray for these precious children so dear to our hearts? We can begin by praying for their parents to have wisdom, patience, emotional and physical strength, and the ability to discipline in love. As we beseech God for these children of our children, we pray for their salvation, protection from illness and accident, that they learn obedience, for a hedge of protection from sexual abuse, that they be able to stand against the temptations of bad peer pressure, for their education, and against

My grandma was a stout woman, but very strong physically and spiritually. She felt sad when she lost her youngest child in a fire, but God told her to keep on loving her family. She was a great woman of God and followed God's path for her. When I turned two, Grandma made me a big patch blanket. She made it by hand.
I didn't really understand because I was a little child, but it was precious to me. I loved it when I got older. It is a prized possession that I will never throw away because that's all I have of my grandma. I know she loved me, and now I love her more than ever. (Grandchild, USA, age 10)

the negative and evil influence of the media through TV, movies, videos, and DVDs. *(Grandma, USA)*

I have used the Praying for Our Children calendar to pray for my grandchildren. This calendar has widely circulated and includes praying for character qualities based on Scripture. I also pray for their salvation and for their circle of friends, victory over temptations or peer pressure, and future mates. *(Grandma, USA)*

My grandma could probably win the world record for the longest prayer ever prayed by a grandma. The only thing that bothers my family is that the food gets cold. Once, I tried to take food while she was praying, and she banged my hand with the chopsticks. *(Grandchild, Taiwan, age 16)*

My maternal grandmother was a wonderful spiritual force in my life—she prayed for me and my siblings and cousins daily. I lived with her and my grandfather for four months when I was in first grade and again for the summer between my seventh and eighth grades. I was their first grandchild and had lived with my mother at their home until I was eighteen months old because my father was away fighting in World War II—we were always very close! Grammy Scales wrote a book on answered prayer, which I cherish. *(Grandma, USA)*

While parents often say a quick exhausted prayer as they collapse into bed, we grandparents often spend much time in prayer, even during the night, for our grandchildren. While our children's prayers may be for the moment or for a particular situation, our perspective as grandparents allows us a bigger picture view of each grandchild. We see inherited traits, good and bad, of our own or those of our children, or we observe potential in our grandchildren that we can bring before our heavenly Father in faithful prayer over time. I view it as both a duty and a privilege to bring each of these precious gifts of grandchildren daily before the Lord in prayer. *(Grandma, USA)*

Once we found out our son and daughter-in-law were expecting, we began praying for that unborn child and his or her salvation. Since the child was born, we have prayed for her salvation and even her future mate as we did with our own children. *(Grandma, USA)*

My mom and mother-in-law have both been prayer warriors for their grandchildren. I can always call them to pray for a specific request for the kids and know that they will drop what they are doing to pray for the children. This is the most important thing that they can and will do for my children. *(Mom, USA)*

When eight months old, my grandson had never passed a hearing test and had two sets of tubes in his ears. Prayers. Now he has a third permanent set. More prayers! He finally passed a hearing test and is talking up a storm. He has some emotional problems and trouble sleeping, so those have been the subject of many more prayers. I don't know what grandmas who don't pray do! *(Grandma, USA)*

I pray often for my little flock, not only for their immediate needs, but also for virtues and fruit of the Spirit to be developed in them. *(Grandma, USA)*

We frequently tell our grandchildren that they are in our prayers many times a day. What a comfort it is to know that the Lord hears and acts on all of our prayers. *(Grandma, USA)*

Many times after struggling during the night with the desires in my heart for my children and grandchildren, I wake up and open God's Word to find peace and guidance. I have learned that even after our children are not directly under our roof or in our care, the heart God gave me as a mother to point them to Christ and to guide them is still the same. Yet the circumstances are very different. I must honor their adulthood and my new position. And so I begin by praying in the quiet of the early morning: "Father, remove any obstacles that hinder the open expression of your love through me. May I move toward my children and grandchildren out of knowledge and understanding. May my words and my hands bring healing, for the tongue of the wise brings healing rather than piercing like a sword (Prov. 12:18). If left to myself, I'm fearful that my words might pierce." *(Grandma, USA)*

Grandparenting is such a blessing. Getting to know the children as individuals is so important, especially so that we can be specific as we pray for them. *(Grandma, USA)*

Sometimes I am frazzled with the many different roles I have throughout the week: being a good wife, a caring mother to a grown daughter, son-in-law, and teenage daughter; being a good daughter in assisting my parents in their needy stage of life; being a fun and loving grandma; and being successful at my career (I still have one more child to get through college). I often feel guilty for not spending more time with my two young grandchildren. I see other grammas who seem like perfect models. Daily I get on my knees and ask God for guidance, wisdom, and grace. *(Grandma, USA)*

Despite the fact that my family all lives a distance apart, I believe that there is no distance in prayer. I am duly bound to pray for my family each day and consider it a great privilege. Many great men and women of yesterday and today are the product of words from their parents and grandparents' prayers. *(Grandma, Nigeria)*

Seventeen

Pregnancy, Adoption, and Childbirth

The evening that my husband Jim and I first met our daughter-in-law, Brit, we were fascinated with her sparkling personality. She also captivated us with the story of how her parents adopted her and her sister from Colombia, South America. Here's the warm account, written by Brit's Mom, Linda Jensen:

Adoption. The word alone has so much meaning to me, first because our girls are adopted and second, because as God's beloved, He chose to adopt me into His family through Jesus Christ. Foreign adoption had always been tickling our minds, even back in college. I am still amazed that we were able to adopt our beautiful girls. I can't tell you how many times we have heard people say, "Oh what lucky girls!" No! We are the blessed ones. I talk to many people who have adopted, and they echo the same story. The hoops we jumped through were endless; certifying, authenticating, and documenting, not to mention fingerprinting, drawing up a will, and a whole lot more. The only thing they didn't ask me for is my banana bread recipe. Then the wait began, and it seemed like we would be drawing social security before we would be parents. But in God's perfect time, we got the word to go to Bogota.

I remember sitting in my kitchen with my friend, Carol, lamenting that travel to Colombia was banned because of some political problem. It was down to the wire. Our suitcases were packed with diapers, and we were scheduled to leave the following day. Carol said, "Linda, what would you need God to do to risk traveling to Bogota?" I said, "I'd need the ban lifted on travel." She bowed her head at my kitchen table and boldly asked the Lord for exactly that. Through a series of telephone calls, which included being put on hold with the United States embassy, we were told that we could travel at our own risk. I had struggled with fear as long as I could remember, but I was so bonded to a little girl in Colombia that I would have swum with the sharks to bring her home. I will never forget my sweet mother-in-law asking my husband why he would go to a place that was so dangerous and take such a risk. His answer was quick. "Mom, if I were there, would you come and get me?" Needless to say, we left with such a strong desire to meet the child we always knew—we just did not know what she looked like. Now we know, and it has been a

My grandma is called Pat, short for Patience. She is very neat, clean, loving, funny, and pretty. My grandma is sixty-four years old and still has spunk. She doesn't have a job, so she works around the house and does a great job. (Grandchild, USA, age 10)

kiss from God to have our two daughters from Colombia in our family. They have truly blessed our lives.

Before our grandson was born, I started praying for him right from the beginning and was thrilled about his growth during the pregnancy. I counted days and waited for our grandchild's arrival. When he was born, I became a grandma! I was promoted from mother and mother-in-law to grandmother. I praise God for our grandson, who gave me this promotion. *(Grandma, India)*

Grandma came to help after each of our kids was born. She was willing to do whatever was necessary, whether it was cooking meals or keeping my sick two-year-old out of the house while I took care of the newborn. *(Mom, USA)*

All three of my grandchildren were born at Elmhurst Hospital, in the labor and delivery unit where I work! *(Grandma, USA)*

Being the mother of sons, there are certain experiences I never expected to have, like buying a wedding dress or being present for the birth of my grandchildren. However, God sometimes surprises us. Our son, Jeremy, and his wife, Stephanie, were home from North Africa for the birth of their second child. We knew the baby was going to be a girl, and we were thrilled because girls were a rare commodity in this genetic pool. A month before her due date, Stephanie was sitting in the living room with me. Stephanie hadn't been feeling very well, and as she got up from the couch, she started hemorrhaging. Our two-year-old grandson started crying. Miraculously, my son and husband were both in the house. We got Stephanie to lie down on the couch and called 911. She was in a lot of pain and crying because she hadn't felt the baby move in the last hour.

I sat by her side and prayed with her that God would spare this little one's life. The paramedics arrived quickly and checked for the baby's heartbeat and couldn't find one. They reassured my daughter-in-law by saying there was too much noise (Ezra was crying up a storm). Then they moved to transfer her to the stretcher. This is a scene that I will never forget. My son waved off the paramedics and reached down and gently lifted his wife up into his arms and placed her on the stretcher and accompanied her to the hospital. We later followed. Upon our arrival, we learned that Stephanie had a ruptured placenta, and they were considering a C-section. However, the baby seemed to be doing well, and they decided to allow her to have a natural delivery. Since I am on pastoral staff at my church, I was able to go into the delivery room where I again prayed and asked God to preserve them both.

I'm thankful that grandma and I both like to cook. (Grandchild, USA, age 8)

After a couple of hours, our little granddaughter was born, and I watched as my son cut the umbilical cord. God did indeed preserve her life and her mother's life. My son decided to name her Joy Abigail, which means Joy, a father's joy. He named her in the ambulance because he said, "If this turns out well, there is going to be a lot of joy." She is not only her father's joy, she is my joy as well. *(Grandma, USA)*

We have friends that have two sons, one through adoption and the other biological. It was a weekly tradition of the grandparents to take the grandsons out to breakfast every Saturday morning. At one of these breakfasts, some long-time friends stopped by the table to chat. The lady visitor questioned the grandmother as to which boy was adopted. The very wise grandmother responded

"Now which one is it? I can't remember. Is it you Scott or is it Todd? Hmm. I just can't remember." The boys went home to tell their parents. "Guess what! Grandma forgot which one of us is adopted." *(Mom, USA)*

I was living in Nebraska at the time when my granddaughter was born. My husband brought me to my daughter's home (in the Chicago area) several weeks before the due date because she had been having early labor. Our granddaughter, Marisa, arrived a bit early. Grandpa got to see her, but was called back to work. I ended up living with my daughter and son-in-law for six weeks. Later, I heard that my son-in-law told friends he wouldn't have imagined his mother-in-law living in the same house for six weeks! There are a couple of things I did to make it work. First, the house was cleaned up and supper ready when he arrived home. Often I ate early and made plans to be gone for a few hours in the evening so they could have family time. My son and his wife were moving to a new house, and I also helped them pack and move. *(Grandma, USA)*

I made a special wall quilt for our granddaughter's nursery before she was born. I shared the material with my daughter's mother-in-law, and she made the window treatments and the crib dust ruffle to coordinate the decor. It was a labor of love for both grandmothers, and we formed a close bond with our new arrival before she was born. *(Grandma, USA)*

I like to go for walks with Grandma. (Grandchild, USA, age 8)

I helped Janna and Greg for two weeks after Hananah's birth and then was able to see her about every six weeks for the first fifteen months of her life before we retired to Florida. During that initial two-week period, Janna would bring Hannah to me to watch for a couple of hours after she nursed her in the early morning so that she could go back to bed for a little more rest. Hannah and I would rest together, or I would take her for a long walk while I prayed for her and talked with her. *(Grandma, USA)*

I have to admit, when I realized that my son and my daughter-in-law were seriously considering adoption, I wondered how it would feel to have an adopted grandchild. They had planned to adopt a child from Guatemala, but God had greater plans for them, and a while later they received twins from Guatemala. It is like being pregnant; you don't know how many babies you will be blessed with. I got the opportunity to travel to Guatemala to help them take care of Arianna and Brayden during the adoption process. The moment I saw the babies for the first time is a moment I will never forget. I took them in my arms and felt the same love that I had felt when I saw my other grandchildren for the first time. Arianna and Brayden are mine! I had the opportunity to be a part of their lives at an early stage and to begin to build our relationship then. They were only five months old when I met them for the first time. The love and closeness I feel for them is no different than what I feel for the rest of my grandchildren. *(Grandma, Finland)*

When my granddaughters were born, I spent a week at my daughter's helping out in any way I could. What fun to help care for a baby again! I spent one day a week with them and sometimes more—other times they came to our house. They are now five and seven and in school, so we don't visit quite as often. But we do have our special times. *(Grandma, USA)*

As a mom, I am blessed watching my children interact with two very different grandmas. My mom is Grammy, just as her mother was to me; my mother-in-law is Grandma, just as her mother was to my husband. When we were pregnant with our first child, who was the first grandchild for both sets of grandparents, we asked all four grandparents what they would want the baby to call them. No one had any ideas that were set in stone, but my mom did mention that she'd like to be Grammy if that was okay with us. I thought that was wonderful, for "Grammy" to me connotes an amazing, loving woman with whom I had a very close relationship despite geographic distance. *(Mom, USA)*

Being a labor and delivery nurse for the last twenty-seven years has helped a lot when it comes to answering questions from my daughter and daughters-in-law during their pregnancies and even during labor. When my daughter was in labor with her first child, so were quite a few other women that day, and the nurses were very busy. I felt very useful as I helped with comfortable positions, breathing techniques, and encouragement while her labor was progressing. Seeing that first grandchild come into the world was amazing, bringing tears to my eyes. Children and grandchildren sure are a blessing from God! *(Grandma, USA)*

When Debbie and Dave and their five children lived in Korea, it was important for the extended families to stay connected and especially to keep the cousins familiar with each other. Debbie and Dave's youngest son, Nate (American) was born in South Korea only a couple of weeks before Tori (Korean) was born in the same town in South Korea. When Debbie's sister and brother-in-law adopted Tori and arrived in the United States five months later, I made a card with pictures of her arrival at the airport. The other side of the card included pictures of Nate. The fact that the two cousins are American citizens, but Korean-born cousins seems to enhance their kindred spirits. They are so close and love each other very much to this day. Even when they were very young, they would walk down the street together holding hands and laughing at any single word the other would say. The fellowship of kindred minds is like to that above. **(Grandma, USA)**

It is customary among Indian families for the daughter to go to her parents' home for her confinement or for the mother to go to her. This is of tremendous practical help to the new mother and helps her to recover easily after childbirth. In my case, I went to be with my daughter, Preeti. It was awesome and exciting since this was my first grandchild. I stayed with Preeti and David until Alisha was two months old, helping out with housekeeping and baby-care when needed. Those two months with Alisha were very special. I would hold her in my arms and pray over her. It seemed as if she were taking it all in. David's parents also drove up once in a while to see her. Now, when I tell Alisha that I

My grandma would always cook for me whenever I was hungry. She would cook my favorite meal. Whenever my parents had to work and there was no one to take care of me, my grandma would come to our house and watch me. I was a very sick baby. So every time I was sick, my grandma would take care of me— give me medicines and cough drops and make warm tea for me. (Grandchild, Philippines, age 14)

took care of her for two months after she was born, she feels special. She is growing up to be a beautiful person. She calls me Nani, as do the other grandkids. Nani is Grandma in Hindi. Manarah is our second grandchild and the firstborn of our son Pranay and his wife Vani. She is four and was born in Cairo, Egypt, where her parents were based at the time of her birth. Vani's parents from India were there to help her at the time of her confinement. My husband and I made a trip there to see Manarah and attend her dedication service when she was two months old. I stayed on for a month to help out after Vani's mother left. Ameiyah's birth (another grandchild) almost seems like a miracle because her mother had had three miscarriages in a row before she was born. This little one was covered with prayer before her birth, and we thank God for her. Vani's mom was there again to help, and we made a trip to see her when she was just three days old. Ashray is our only grandson. He was born in a rural mission hospital in Bangladesh, and again I took two months off to help. He was born exactly a day after the tsunami, so we call him Tsunami, for that is what he is like. He is a little man of action, very lively and busy! *(Grandma, Singapore)*

I had the privilege of driving to St. Louis and painting the nursery, with some help from Greg's mother, for Janna and Greg while they vacationed a few months before Hannah's birth. *(Grandma, USA)*

> *I like that Grandma makes French toast for me. (Grandchild, USA, age 6)*

My mom has generously offered to help us out after the birth of each of our three children. With Hannah, my mom stayed for almost two weeks after delivery to help me. With Carter's delivery,

I had some complications, and she stayed about five weeks, until I was able to drive and carry the baby on my own. Elizabeth was a sick preemie, so my mom again stayed about five or six weeks to help out. *(Mom, USA)*

Our daughter and her husband have adopted three children that they have raised since birth, and that has been very special. One thing I did for their quilts was to use fabric from clothing that I had made for myself, my husband, and our children to help blend their lives with our family. *(Grandma, USA)*

After raising four sons, my husband and I were elated to have our first grandchild be a little girl. We could barely get enough of her, with her little bow in her baby fine hair, lace booties, and pink ruffled dresses. On the night she was born, our daughter-in-law and son invited us into the labor and delivery room to see her, and we were amazed at how her little eyes tracked us as we moved! We knew she must have an incredibly high IQ to watch our movement like that, and we also knew the gracious miracle of the birth of a grandchild. *(Grandma, USA)*

One granddaughter was born in our house right after Christmas twenty years ago, when Mary Lee went into labor and couldn't get back to Wisconsin for home birth there. *(Grandma, USA)*

Eighteen

This and That

My husband, Jim, and I recently made a weekend trip to Atlanta to help our son Nate and his wife, Brit, move into their first home. Brit's wonderful parents, Larry and Linda, were there, too. They had been helping with painting and decorating. While a bunch of people were standing in Nate and Brit's kitchen talking about this grandma book, somebody asked what I planned to do with good stories and ideas that were unique to the categories I originally outlined. Linda and Larry offered a suggestion: "How about a category called *This and That*?" So that, my friends, is what you're about to read in this chapter.

● Not having had grandparents around as a child due to being overseas, a grandparent's role was a mystery to me. Now, my children have the luxury of having their grandparents not only in the same city but also next door.

This provides a never-ending supply of love and support to my children. When I am too tired or busy or cranky to offer the encouragement they need, there is always a granny next door to provide sticky tape, an

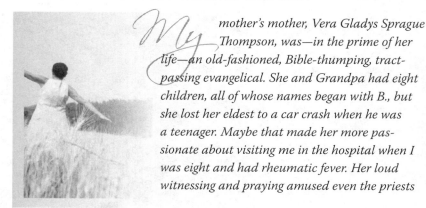

My mother's mother, Vera Gladys Sprague Thompson, was—in the prime of her life—an old-fashioned, Bible-thumping, tract-passing evangelical. She and Grandpa had eight children, all of whose names began with B., but she lost her eldest to a car crash when he was a teenager. Maybe that made her more passionate about visiting me in the hospital when I was eight and had rheumatic fever. Her loud witnessing and praying amused even the priests

egg, milk, pegs for the washing, hems and buttons, and especially a cuddle. When grandchildren are sick, there are constant inquiries (are they warm enough, have they had a lemon drink) and always Granny's yucky medicine! *(Mom, Australia)*

When I married at the age of nineteen, my grandmother gave me all of her china—a beautiful blue and white pattern I still have displayed in my china cabinet today. When I asked her why she gave it to *me* (she had seven grandchildren), she said that whenever I was at her house as a child for family dinners, I always asked to be seated facing her china cabinet so I could look at her dishes. I hadn't remembered, but she did. She knew me as an individual. *(Grandma, USA)*

As I embark on this new journey of being a grandma, I want to:

- Listen more than I speak.
- Encourage my daughter-in-law in her efforts.
- Be available to watch my grandchild whenever I am needed.
- Pray for them a lot; when I hold my granddaughter I pray out loud so she hears my voice.

and nuns in the wonderful Catholic hospital where I had landed, as she—of course—tried to get them all saved. My favorite memory is of her high, warbling, vibrato as she threw her head back and sang, "We'll talk it over, in the bye and bye. We'll talk it over, my Lord and I. I'll ask the reasons, He'll tell me why, when we talk it over, in the bye and bye." I believe they're already talking it over, and one day it'll be my joy to join them. —Jerry Jenkins

- Be intentional about quoting Scripture.
- Read stories.
- Have my children and grandchild for dinner at least once every week or ten days. That gives them a break, and we get to see our grandchild.
- Pray for wisdom and discernment for myself in what I say and do in front of my grandchildren.
- I think that grandparenting, like parenting, is not a formula thing. Grandchildren will sense that we love and care for them in our faces and in our tone of voice.
- I sing to her. I do this in private because I am voice-challenged, but I love to sing simple childhood songs.
- When she is older I will tell her stories about Daddy when he was a little boy. I loved to hear my grandparents' version of their childhoods and my parents' childhoods. ***(Grandma, USA)***

Often, missionaries who are apart from their blood relatives for years at a time bond with those around them. On our small center of Yarinacocha in the jungles of Peru, we were referred to as Aunt Linda and Uncle Glenn by the missionary children. Later we were adopted as grandparents by other families in Papua New

Guinea. It's good to remember that we are the body of Christ, and if we can reach out to others who are far away from their families and give the hugs that far-away grandmas cannot give, we are being the arms of Christ. *(Grandma, Peru)*

One night, I was tucking our granddaughter into bed. We had already read several storybooks and said prayers together, when all of a sudden my granddaughter said, "Grandma." I said, "Yes, honey?" Looking up at me with such sweetness, she said, "I just really, really love you." My heart about soared right above the ceiling! I told her I really, really loved her too. This is what I think grand-parenting is all about. It makes that second half of life so worthwhile. *(Grandma, USA)*

My parents were great storytellers. They told my boys stories of the Swedes and Norwegians coming to America and settling in the farming community where we were raised. My mom and dad also had tons of stories about farming, the Depression, and selling cars. The boys sat spellbound, never getting their fill of those stories, even as teenagers and young men. *(Grandma, USA)*

While watching Micah, I allowed him to help me with things like cooking and washing. He was happy to bring clips to hang out clothes and later to bring me the dried clothing. He was always happy to hear me say, "We did it together." He would say proudly, "I help Grandma." Yes, grandchildren want to help us. *(Grandma, India)*

I love it that my parents try to find common interests with my daughters and that they also like to spend time with the girls alone. The dynamic is completely different than when mom and dad are around. *(Mom, USA)*

I want my grandchildren to know that God is most im-portant in my life and that living according to His Word is the way I want to direct my life. I also want them to know that their grandfather and I love them uncondi-tionally, pray for them, and always cheer them on. As always, it is the heart relationships that matter most, not things. *(Grandma, USA)*

I enjoyed just being with my grandparents, out of doors, away from city noises, smells, and business; to be able to just *be* is one thing that I enjoy, especially when outside and in nature with people that I love and who also love me. *(Grandchild, Austria, age 17)*

I remember my grandmother singing the following song to me (this song helped shape my attitude toward life and all of God's creation):

> Little drops of water; little grains of sand;
> Make a mighty ocean and a pleasant land.
> Little deeds of kindness; little words of love;
> Help to make earth happy just like heaven above.

She also sang the following, which helped me to see who my grandmother was:

> Pass me not, Oh gentle Savior,
> Hear my humble cry.
> While on others Thou are calling,
> Do not pass me by.

And also:

> Will there be any stars, any stars in my crown,
> When at evening the sun goeth down?
> When I wake with the blest in that mansion of rest;
> Will there be any stars in my crown?
> > *(Grandma, USA)*

We have been blessed with four grandchildren—two boys and two girls. Never could I have imagined what joy they would bring to us, even with trials and tribulations. Each one is precious. What a joy it is to watch our grandchildren grow and become independent little individuals! *(Grandma, USA)*

My grandma was realistic. She taught me wrong from right, and didn't overlook when I was doing something bad. She trained me in a way that I would become a man. At first, I felt that she was being too hard on me, but later I figured out that she was showing me the path of life. *(Grandson, Nigeria, age 17)*

I think Hannah was around five when she started having nightmares and was afraid at bedtime, so when I visited during that time I would go in and sing, very softly and almost monotonously, the song "In the Garden" and then talk very quietly about how we can meet with our Savior and talk to Him about how we're feeling. After I returned home, she called me a couple of evenings and asked me to sing it to her over the phone. I was thankful that God used me and that song to help her through a difficult time. *(Grandma, USA)*

A recent musical highlight for my mother was to have her seven grandchildren play their various instruments during her oldest granddaughter's wedding reception. Because of her encouragement in their lives, the children felt free and honored to share their music at the reception—they had plenty of performing practice! *(Mom, USA)*

Blessings:

- The joy of seeing my first grandchild.
- Taking grandchildren to and meeting them from school.
- Having a grandchild in my Scripture class.

- Sharing the first awareness of God's creation when out on walks with a toddler in stroller, appreciating anew myself as I point things out to him/her.
- Having the opportunities to attend:
  School autumn fairs.
  Swimming carnivals.
  A Girl Guide jamboree.
  Easter hat parade.
  School and sports award presentations.
  Ballet concerts.
  Band concerts, music Eistedford/competitions.
  Netball, baseball, soccer matches.
  School concerts.
  Pre-school nativity plays. ***(Grandma, Australia)***

My own grandmother lived with us until she died, and what I remember and treasure is that she spent time with us, the grandchildren. She didn't do any housework, but she read to us, played games with us, and told us stories—real ones from life and stories she had been told by her parents. She taught me to sew, to embroider, and even tried to teach me how to knit. She gave us her time and attention. ***(Grandma, USA)***

My grandma is one of my favorite relatives. I am really interested in medieval weapons, so the last time I visited my grandma, she asked a smith to make me some stuff. She also made the tastiest Indian food for me. (Grandchild, India, age 14)

I set aside spending money for the grandchildren to use when they come. I save my extra earnings from substitute teaching and give each grandchild a certain amount to use on the activities we participate in so Grandma is not putting out each time we go somewhere. They learn to manage their own money and also decide whether they want to spend it on a particular activity. This works well for the young child with no earning power. I also give them jobs to do; they earn a little spending money, and I get the job done. *(Grandma, USA)*

My children's granny never forgets her promises. Words that are said are always carried through. *(Mom, Australia)*

My grandma has shown me how to love my children un-conditionally—in the best and worst of circumstances. I will never forget her courageous faith during the winter months of 2006 when her son (my uncle) was dying. My grandma was inspirational in those times. *(Adult Grandchild, USA)*

With each of my three grandchildren, I rock them for a minute or two at bedtime and sing "Jesus Loves Me." When Hannah was younger than three, I said to her af-ter singing that song one evening, "You know that Jesus really does love you, don't you?" She looked at me very seriously and said, "No, Grammy, He loves you—that's what you've been singing." I was flabbergasted that she took that song very literally at that young age. So now, with the younger two, I quite often follow up that song with an explanation that the "me" means them as well as me. *(Grandma, USA)*

God gave us two children—Shini, our daughter, and William (Billy), our son. As parents we had the joy of seeing both of them give their hearts to Jesus Christ at an early age. They chose partners who loved the Lord and got married with our blessings. Fibroid surgery revealed that Shini and Rob could not have children of

> *My nana, who is a grandma, is a lovely one. She likes to build puzzles, read, play games, and pick me up from school. She even helps with homework. Sometimes my nana gets tired at night, and when she means one thing she says another. Here is an example. Time for bed. Time for dead. I think she's funny. That's my funny grandma!*
> *(Grandchild, USA, age 7)*

their own. In the meantime, Billy and Beth had a son, Micah. When friends ask us, we say that God has given us the grace to accept both situations, and He's prepared us to be better counselors. When those who do not have children come to us for counseling, we can boldly say, "We know your situation because our daughter has no children." When those who have children come to us, we can say, "We do understand your situation because our son has a son." Thus God has helped us to be a blessing to all. Having grandchildren is a blessing, but if some of our children do not have children we must understand that in the providence of God it is not a waste. Both ways can be a great blessing to many. *(Grandma, India)*

I enjoy taking care of my grandchildren individually on occasion. When Ben is at summer camp, I take Jeremy (who feels a little left out) to do something special, like visit the bumper boats or go to Chucky Cheese. *(Grandma, USA)*

Mom keeps little toys in her purse (small flashlights, novelty items, etc.) to entertain the kids when they are bored in a restaurant or other public setting. It works every time! *(Mom, USA)*

● As a granny I have more time to:

- Listen to a prepared school speech.
- Hear a school reader being read.
- Sew up a hem or stitch on a button.
- Make pikelets (similar to pancakes) and hot chocolate after school. *(Grandma, Australia)*

● At family gatherings, when grandchildren love to run and play with their cousins, I try to find a moment here and there to connect with each grandchild—to give them a hug, make an observation, or ask a question about their world. *(Grandma, USA)*

● I don't consider myself a good seamstress, but my grandmother was. She lived with us for many years before passing away, and she sewed many dresses for my dolls over the years. Those are special memories I have of her as well as the many times she allowed me to observe and help her cook. She always used to say her recipe was in her head: "a pinch of this and a dash of that." She knew whether the yeast dough was right by the feel and look of it. *(Grandma, USA)*

● My mother-in-law is interested in each of the grandchildren's achievements and can never see any fault in them. They never misbehave and are never made to clear their plate! *(Mom, Australia)*

● I look forward to visiting my Grandma H. because she always has some sort of surprise for me. *(Grandchild, USA)*

● My mom will do whatever it takes to see our daughters whenever they are back in town, no matter for how brief a time. She adores them—and they know it and absolutely love her in return. My mom will soon be a greatgrandma for the first time, and I know she will be just as great a grandma to our newest family member as she has been to her two granddaughters. *(Mom, USA)*

My maternal grandmother lived in Minnesota, and we lived in Michigan. She would come to visit each summer in her green (her favorite color) travel coat. She would always bring a small iron piggy bank filled with shiny new copper pennies that we fished out with a table knife. When it came time to distribute her belongings a few years ago, we adult grandchildren almost fought over that pig. *(Grandchild, USA)*

Grandmas get to become like children. As our grandson, Micah, was growing, he caused us to run after him, sing for him, and play with him. Our grandson made us to behave like children again! When our children were growing, they had their grandmothers to take care of them. Now I was able to give full attention to my grandchildren. My grandchildren have helped to keep me active. *(Grandma, India)*

When our first grandchild arrived, I found a company that made grandmother necklaces. On a black silk cord I threaded silver faces, one for each grandchild. I could choose whether the silver face would be that of a girl or boy, and whether that child would have blond, brunette, black, or red hair. I could even choose between curly or straight hair. There was enough space on the back of the silver pieces to write each child's name and birthday. With twenty-four grandchildren, it was quite a necklace. It became a decoration in my bedroom. It is fun to see some of the younger ones still wanting to look at it with their cousins and siblings. *(Grandma, USA)*

All the grandchildren love to hear stories of when their moms and dads were little, and so we love to relive and retell those stories. *(Grandma, USA)*

● I think it's nice that my grandchildren call me Mimi. It was the name selected by a granddaughter when she was very young. My daughter-in-law said I seemed too young to be called Grandma! *(Grandma, USA)*

● I have found my grandma's perspective on money very helpful to me as my wife, Tiffany, and I plan our financial future. We often say that we want to leave a similar material legacy for our children and grandchildren: one that appreciates all that is beautiful and finds joy in what is valuable while simultaneously understanding that as with Abraham, blessings are given primarily so that we can in turn bless others. *(Adult Grandchild, USA)*

Four-year-old Luke was conversing with his great-grandfather recently. From his perch on the table, he looked carefully at Grandpa and asked, "Grandpa, how old are you?" Grandpa replied, "I'm ninety-one," to which Luke quickly responded, "So you'll go to heaven soon, right?" (Grandma, USA)

● Helping with homework or music practice can be daunting. I'm OK in the early stages, but as the grandchildren progress to higher grades, I don't improve alongside, unfortunately. My piano accompaniments were far too slow for the talented clarinet player, so we gave that away. Also, I did make a mistake in a math question one day. That particular grandchild wasn't keen on getting help after that. *(Grandma, Australia)*

● My pastor, Andy Stanley, challenged us with the truth that we all have been given power in our life, whether it is as a big brother or sister with power over a little brother or sister, power in our jobs with authority over others, power as a teacher or a coach, or power as a parent over children. All of us have power to some extent; that power has been given to us for a time, and it's a stewardship. We are accountable for it! In John 13, Jesus, "having loved his own who were in the world, now showed them the full extent of his love" (v. 1, NIV). During the evening meal just before the Passover Feast, Jesus "got up from the meal, took off his outer clothing, and wrapped a towel around his waist. After that, he poured water into a basin and began to wash his disciples' feet, drying them with the towel that was around his waist" (v. 4–5, NIV). The most powerful person in the room got up from the meal, shed his robe—the clothing that in that time and culture was the symbol of his position and authority—and took the place of a servant by washing his disciples' feet. My mind went to the many times I have had the privilege to get up from our family meal, give our daughter the rare moment to enjoy her meal without interruption, and pick up the crying baby or take the toddler "potty" at the restaurant. I was given an opportunity to show the full extent of my love. We are given opportunities to show the full extent of our love when we selflessly serve our children in those kinds of ways. In the world and arena of our life as grandparents it might look like this:

- Offering to stay with them the first or second week home from the hospital to wake up in the night with the baby so the parents can have a little more sleep.
- Offering to change the diaper when we are with them.
- Offering to give baths when we visit, as even baths can become a chore when parents are tired at the end of the day.

There are many other practical ways that we can serve our children and grandchildren at the same time, taking the example of Jesus to use our power as parents to serve them, all the while developing a special bond with them. *(Grandma, USA)*

One of the greatest thrills my husband and I experience is when we first arrive at our grandchildren's home, and the little ones come running to the door with open arms, wrapping themselves around our necks with kisses! This is one of life's greatest joys! *(Grandma, USA)*

Mom has made herself the biggest fan of my children. Even when they act naughty around her, she always believes the best about them. They know that they receive unconditional love from her at all times. *(Mom, USA)*

If a child is upset, or is tired and doesn't want to sleep, or if we both need some snuggle time, I make up rhyming songs about how Jesus loves them and how much I love them. I sing them over and over until it lulls him to sleep. *(Grandma, USA)*

Each grandchild is unique and much loved. When they drop in, if possible I stop what I am doing, give them a hug, and give them my full attention. *(Grandma, USA)*

My sincere prayer is that my children and my grandson will be proud of me and remember the impact of my life and care in their lives always. *(Grandma, India)*

On the windowsill over my kitchen sink, I keep art projects made by my grandchildren (and their parents). I don't know if a decorator would like the look, but when I see the clay sun with the happy face, or the scratch art picture of hearts, it always brings a smile to my face as I think about the little people who made them just for me. *(Grandma, USA)*

[One college-aged young man wrote the following as a remembrance to his grammy, and it was read at her memorial service.] "I will miss you! You raised a wonderful daughter—thank you for my mother. I hope you know how much I appreciated everything. I wish that I had written more and called more. You are the greatest, Grammy! I love you. I will never forget you. I can only hope that who I am and what I become makes you proud. I know that God will greet you with a smile. I wish, I really truly wish, I could be with you now. I wanted to see you, or at least talk to you, one more time. 'I can't believe I'm/you're really here!' (That is a reference to a running joke that I had with my grammy. We used to race to see who could see the other person first and say it when we got to their house. Throughout the years we came up with creative ways to beat each other—like one time when my grammy hung a sign out of the second story window of her house that overlooked her driveway with those famous words emblazoned on it: 'I can't believe you're really here!') Visiting you meant so much to me. I never understood how my friends couldn't love their grandparents. You weren't perfect, but you always meant the best. Your intentions were supremely loving. You have taught me important lessons about family, love, kindness, generosity, fun, friendship, humility, imagination, brilliance, marriage, maturity. I know you will be happy forever with God. I love you; I will miss you! Thank you, thank you! Goodbye, Grammy." *(Adult Grandchild, USA)*

I am a school librarian, so I enjoy showing my grandchildren fun things on the computer or sharing new children's literature with them when they come over. *(Grandma, USA)*

My grandchildren have given me three different names. You would think they would all be the same, but. . . . My oldest granddaughter couldn't pronounce Grandma so I became Nama. The second prefers Gramma. My grandson lived in Germany about the time he was learning to talk, and he and his brother call me Oma! It's kind of nice; I can immediately tell which child/family is calling me. *(Grandma, USA)*

Once in the car on the way home from Grandma's house, my four-year-old gave me a moment of great insight: "Mommy, Grandma has *time*." Mom is all about the business of raising the child, and time is very scheduled by necessity. Grandma has the incredible luxury of endless time to listen, read, cuddle, play, and love. Time is a priceless gift. *(Mom, USA)*

This Granny has the best:

- Homemade choc chip cookies (recommendation of step-grandson, age nine).
- Brand of perfume or hair products to sample.
- Patience to read the same story countless times.
- Choice of toppings for ice cream.

This Granny has the worst:

- Toleration for the shrieking of little girls.
- Music and DVD collection.
- Allergy to sticky fingers.
- Reaction to grandchildren's creepy crawly collections. *(Grandma, Australia)*

Pure enjoyment of the simple things in life makes Grandma a pleasure to be around. *(Mom, USA)*

One day when Grif was in kindergarten, he came to eat lunch at my house. Here is a brief conversation that we had over our meal:

Grif: "Grandma, did you know that you are not my dad's mom?"

Grandma: "That's right; your dad's mom is in heaven with Jesus. However, I am your dad's stepmom."

Grif, looking shocked: "Well you're not evil or anything!"

Grandma: "Thanks. You know, not all stepmoms are evil. Cinderella's stepmom was evil, but not all stepmoms are evil."

Grif, after thinking just a bit: "No, not all of them are evil. Actually you're nice!" *(Grandma, USA)*

For my grandma, kindness, gentleness, and love were part of her everyday way of life. The other day when I was asked what I remembered about Grammy, I was hard pressed to remember an incident or story because all I remembered was a feeling—unconditional love. Sure, I can remember lots of things she said or did, but the first thing that always comes to mind is how loved and special and comfortable I always felt around her. *(Adult Grandchild, USA)*

Hannah has always been my "special punkin." Carter is my "sweetie pie," my "snuggle bug," and my "cuddle bunny." Elizabeth is my "sweet big girl." Carter asked me once a few months ago why I called him "sweetie pie" on the phone, and I explained that we often have special names for those people that we really love, so he told me that he would have a special name for me when I arrived for Elizabeth's birthday. When I got there, he had made up some silly word for me, but then he promptly forgot what it was, and so did I! *(Grandma, USA)*

I've always tried to attend events that are meaningful: ice skating programs, grandparent day, etc. These mean a lot to the children. In return, they show up for my events. Last winter they surprised me by being in the audience when I played in a bell choir concert! Two of the girls went to a "personal safety for me" class, and at the end parents were invited to participate and run the course. No one went forward, so I did. Not only did I learn something, but the girls were more enthusiastic about doing the same thing. *(Grandma, USA)*

Both grandmas to my daughters are Christians, and it is wonderful to have such great role models of godly women for them to aspire to. *(Mom, Australia)*

When my two grandchildren, Stacy and Eric, were small, they were always drawing pictures for Grams. I kept them in a neat stack on a shelf in the closet. As they grew in numbers, I decided I would use thumb tacks and put them on the dry wall going into the basement along the stairs. Stacy named it the wall of art. She is now twenty-four and Eric is twenty, and the pictures are still there covering the sides and some of the ceiling. I haven't the heart or the desire to remove any of them. *(Grandma, USA)*

My mother was the typical chubby Grandma who always wore an apron because she was always baking great things in her kitchen. She was the most gentle, loving, caring Grandma. My mom used to babysit for Matt, our firstborn. The whole time she spent talking to him, reading to him, and playing whatever games he liked. She never told Matt, "No, Grandma doesn't know how to play that game." She just joined him. She once told me that she was sure that she had played Star Wars for a total of one hundred hours, or at least it seemed that long to her. She said, "I still don't know the names of most of those characters or what they're supposed to do, but I do know Luke Skywalker, Darth Vader, and Chewbacca." *(Grandma, USA)*

When grandma used to live with us, she made chicken and rice (my favorite meal) almost every day. So when I came back from school, I always had something to look forward to. When I was a kid, she used to ask me to help her bake cakes. Once, for my eighth birthday, we made a special cake together. It was really big, and had "Happy Birthday" written on it with sugar. It was really cool! Sometimes, my grandma suddenly starts crying when she's talking to people. She doesn't do that all the time, but there are special occasions when she's talking to a stranger about her life and she suddenly starts crying. She also has a habit of kissing everyone on their shoulders; whenever she meets a new person, she kisses them on the shoulder. But she's a really nice and cool grandmother on the whole. (Grandchild, Iran, age 16)

Our grandchildren loved to hear us tell the story of how Grandma and Grandpa met as well as hearing about our dates. They also loved hearing stories about their great-grandparents. They also enjoyed getting out the old photo albums. *(Grandma, USA)*

One of the best experiences I had was when Marisa, then about three, wanted to water my flowers. She started looking at me through the corner of her eye, and I could see the wheels turning. Of course she turned the hose on me, I got soaked, she was laughing so hard she got soaked, and we both had to change clothes. *(Grandma, USA)*

- Both Grandmas have time! They listen, they laugh, and they love unconditionally. *(Mom, Australia)*

- When my grandma came for visits, she arrived on the train. Even when she was in her seventies, she still had a sparkle in her eyes. She was the kind of grandma who got into trouble with us grandchildren at the dinner table for giggling! *(Grandma, USA)*

- While working in my garden a few days ago, I was reflecting on a sweet moment with our two-year-old grandson, Kade. He was crying and feeling very tired at the end of a long day and said, "I want my Mimi." As I scooped him up in my arms, and he curled his little two-year-old body up in the same fetal-like position I used to hold him in as a baby, resting his head on my shoulder, tucking his arms underneath his body—words cannot describe the gratefulness I felt first for that place in his life and then for the love that swelled in my heart for this precious little boy. It was those feelings and emotions I was revisiting in my garden, whispering to God my deep gratefulness and my wonder of it all. Wonder at how did I ever earn that important, cherished place in my grandchildren's hearts and lives?

  It was in that state of worship and conversation with my Father in Heaven, that He in His most gracious and merciful way reminded me about my grandparents. My grandparents were the most important influences in my life on loving. I believe today that I am loved and cherished by my Creator because they spoke that truth to me over and over in words and in deeds. I became a grandmother with the deep desire to love my grandchildren in the same way and to instill in them the truth of who they are and whose they are. *(Grandma, USA)*

Nineteen

Traditions

Traditions that are passed from grandparents to parents to grandchildren come in many shapes and sizes. Some are reflective and thoughtful, like one tradition from Ken and Margaret Taylor's family:

This past Christmas, our extended family included forty-nine for dinner and gift exchange at our house, following brunch for thirty-eight. (One is always counting when dealing with numbers like this. Do we have enough chairs, places set, etc.?) Of the forty-nine, seventeen were grandchildren, ten with spouses, and eleven great-grandchildren. Thirty-eight adults sat at one long table through the dining room, living room, and front hall. Between dinner and opening gifts, it is traditional to recite the Christmas story from Luke 2. Grandchildren are now having their children learn it. This year we were led by six-year-old Bethany. Talk about heartwarming!

Other traditions are sentimental, like the idea sent to me from Becky Schulz:

When my daughter was born, my mother sent me a yellow chiffon dress that I had worn when I was a toddler. The dress was well-preserved and still looked nice, so I washed it and had my daughter wear it one Sunday when she was around two years old. To make it special for my mom, I took a picture of my daughter wearing my dress and mailed it to my mother. I thought it would be a nice tradition to start, so I saved a few special items from all of my children. Once my first grandchild was due, I got out the box with the memories from my children and rewashed two special items (one was a blanket that my mother-in-law had knit for my son), folded them, and put them in Ziplock gallon bags. I gave them to my daughter-in-law, letting her know why I saved them but also letting her know she was under no obligation to reuse them. My daughter-in-law is so sweet. She used the blanket for the baby, and we took pictures noting that the blanket had been knit by a great-grandmother. I then washed and prepared bags with the other clothing articles for my other children to send to them when they start having children.

Some traditions are downright silly and might not be understood to anyone outside a particular extended family. Don't underestimate the place that silliness holds in a family's traditions!

Happy families . . . own a surface similarity of good cheer. For one thing, they like each other, which is quite a different thing from loving. For another, they have, almost always, one entirely personal treasure—a sort of purseful of domestic humor which they have accumulated against rainy days. This humor is not necessarily witty. The jokes may be incomprehensible to outsiders, and the laughter springs from the most trivial of sources. But the jokes and the laughter belong entirely to the family.[1]

In this section, you'll find traditions that range from reflective to sentimental to silly—and others in between. Try some of the new, but keep the old as well.

● Around Thanksgiving, all of the grandchildren come over, and we decorate gingerbread houses. It takes some time getting ready for this event. For the past two years, some of the older grandchildren have helped me make all of the little houses. Then on another assigned day, we put all of the candy out and give each person a little house and a frosting tube. Last year we had one great-grandma, two grandmas, three moms, and eight grandchildren decorate houses. It is a great multi generational event. *(Grandma, USA)*

● One tradition I share with my grandkids is "Santa Claus Breakfast." In Finland, it is a tradition to eat rice pudding on Christmas Eve morning. So every Christmas Eve morning all my kids and grandkids come over to my house, and we celebrate this wonderful holiday by eating rice pudding together. We also enjoy other traditional Christmas treats from Finland, such as *glögg* (a spicy hot drink), gingerbread cookies, and other bakery goods. Sometimes my grandchildren come over to help prepare these treats and help me serve. These are good times! The tradition has now expanded to include friends and church family. *(Grandma, Finland)*

● For birthdays my mother takes a picture of her and my father doing something or in a place that is meaningful to my boys. Sometimes it's a picture of them with my son. She prints out the pictures (one in the front

1. Phyllis McGinley, *The Province of the Heart* (New York: Dell, 1959), 72.

Everyone agrees that it is a family that makes a house a home. For us—to a degree—it has been a house that has made a family! Let me explain. Twenty-eight years ago, Ken and I bought a summer place in southwestern Michigan that gave us access to a stretch of private beach on Lake Michigan. I say "place" rather than house because the property had two houses with a total of eight bedrooms. Later, we bought another house on adjacent property and now have thirteen bedrooms. From the first year, we gathered for ten days in late summer. Some of the twenty-eight grandchildren have come every summer, so they know all of their aunts, uncles, and cousins on the Taylor side of the family, a fact I particularly appreciate because our children also have twenty-eight first cousins, many of whom they do not know. When they were young, most of them lived in the far West while we lived in the Midwest.

and one in the back), usually includes a verse and a short birthday greeting, and then laminates it. This is her child-friendly birthday card to my boys. When they were really young they would play with these pictures, point to them, chew on them, and become more familiar with the faces of their distant grandparents. Now that my boys are a bit older, they use them as little placemats or coasters. *(Mom, USA)*

A fun game our family plays at Christmas when all come home is Amigo Incognito. We draw names. For two days, one does secret acts of kindness for the secret person whose name he has drawn. These acts vary from leaving pieces of candy on a pillow, writing notes of ap-

Traditions grow along with the family. A nighttime bonfire on the beach with singing and s'mores, picking blueberries, skit night, and going to Cap'n Mikes to ride go-karts are some of the traditions. Some years ago, we purchased a ski boat and a wave runner, and we spend one day at a smaller lake with hours of water fun. This requires packing a huge picnic lunch!

Recently, a twenty-one-year-old granddaughter wrote, "I know it has been expressed many times by many different family members, but I feel I should tell you again just how much the Michigan house means to me. It's a time I look forward to all year. My fondest memories are with my cousins and others in the family—times I never would have experienced without this wonderful gift from you and Grandpa. I will never be able to thank you enough."—Margaret Taylor

preciation and love, and completing household tasks before being asked. Once Great Nana even made a favorite pie for her amigo. At the end, we gather at Great Nana's, age ninety-five, for one of her annual tea parties where each person guesses who had his name. It is difficult because some family members do good deeds to other amigos to throw off their identity. *(Grandma, USA)*

● My family likes to celebrate, and we do it as often as possible. Every grandchild gets a birthday party with the whole family at Grandma and Grandpa's house—in addition to his or her own family's celebration. Sometimes, we double up with another cousin or an adult. Each party involves some sort of theme, party favors, balloons, decorations, and food specified by the honoree. On Hailey's fifth birthday, when asked what she'd like for her birthday dinner, she replied, "White rice and corn." "And what would you like to go with the rice and corn?" "Nothing—just rice and corn." So, we all had rice and corn. (I quietly slipped in a little chicken and salad for the adults.) ***(Grandma, USA)***

The wake-up song I usually sang to our two young children when I entered their bedroom and opened their blinds each morning was one of the many children's songs that I learned from my mother-in-law. It went like this: "The first thing in the morning when I get out of bed, I sing and sing a happy song that comes into my head. I don't know where it comes from; it just begins you see. And so I sing and sing and sing, as happy as can be." ***(Mom, USA)***

Our Swedish family celebrates Christmas Eve with a smorgasbord for our extended family. Called Jul Fest, here are some of the foods included in the feast:

Rice Pudding	Limpa Bread
Lingonberries	Assorted Cheeses
Meatballs	Relish Tray
Herring	Fruit Tray
Salmon (poached, whole)	Homemade Swedish Cookies
Baked Ham	Coffee Cakes (almond and
Shrimp	cardemum)
Creamed Potatoes with	Princess Torte (torte cake
Anchovies and Onions	frosted with marzipan)

Every once in a while someone brings lutfisk, the fish that is associated with a bad smell. It brings out lots of laughs, and everyone holds their noses! It's actually a mild white fish, and after soaking and cooking, it has no objectionable smell. ***(Grandma, USA)***

● One of our grandsons used to actually hop up and down most of his birthday (his junior self now allows it only on the inside). So it is with great joy that we make this balloon-waving, cake-eating, candle-blowing, game-playing, and gift-giving day a special one. If the whole family joins in—so much the better! Sometimes I help to make it a special time by taking pictures and helping serve cake and ice cream. Our grandson, Jack, wanted just his family and grandparents at his party. We played musical chairs and a form of pin the tail on the donkey, and had a great time. He loved seeing the grandparents play kid games. Our grandson, Ryan, had a family party as well, and we did many fun and silly games that his mother invented. *(Grandma, USA)*

● At my son's suggestion I invite each granddaughter to join me for lunch around her birthday. I have enjoyed taking them to various tea rooms and engaging them in meaningful conversations about their interests and current activities. I find great joy in encouraging them. *(Grandma, USA)*

● Weep for the poor souls who never celebrate birthdays! Even as a grandma, I still have that hopeful heart before the big day arrives. Maybe it's just to get a card from a family member or friend. I cried this year when I got a card from my husband that said I was his very best friend and

When I go to my grandparent's house, my grandmother gets excited about my arrival and cooks a lot of things for me. I always like every kind of food that is made by my grandmother. To me, she is the best cook in the world, but everybody else likes it, too. (Grandchild, Korea, age 16)

that he was completely in love with me and *always* will be and from my sister who said I was the very best sister (I'm her *only* sister), and again when my brother called that day. So you can imagine the anticipation of our grandchildren who are half a century younger than me. *(Grandma, USA)*

One tradition I have is making counted cross-stitch Christmas stockings for each grandchild with his or her name on the top. *(Grandma, USA)*

At Christmas, we make Teddy cookies, which are gingerbread cut-outs, and then decorate them. This custom was started when my husband was a little boy. We did it with our children and their grandmothers and now with our grandchildren. We look forward to it every Christmas. It's fun to look back at pictures from previous years. *(Grandma, USA)*

We try to buy each of our granddaughters a new matching Easter dress each year and each of our grandsons new matching spring shirts. We will do that as long as they will allow it! Matching may be un-cool one of these years. But for now, it makes a great family picture with everyone color coordinated. *(Grandma, USA)*

This idea depends on the climate where you live, but in the Chicago area the first robin sighted after a long winter is a reason to celebrate. I found a pillow with a robin on it and began a family tradition. As soon as a grandchild sees the first robin of the spring, I write the name of that sharp-eyed spotter and the date and year on the back of the pillow. We have since graduated to a framed print of a robin and this has become quite a competitive event in our family. *(Grandma, USA)*

I think one of the nice things my mom has done is to send my children birthday, valentine, Christmas, and Easter cards that are age appropriate. She always writes a letter to the child. I have saved several of these for my children to have someday. *(Mom, USA)*

Last Easter, my husband and I had an Easter egg hunt with our grandchildren, which was one wild race as baskets were filled. We hid one very large golden egg with the promise (which we fulfilled) that whoever found *the* egg would be the next one to have a sleepover at our house. That will become a tradition, because there's already talk of being the winner next year. *(Grandma, USA)*

My grandmother always makes me breakfast when I am at her house. (Grandchild, United Kingdom, age 14)

Mom wants to ensure that when my children come to her house, they have only fond memories. When our family's first grandchildren were born, she made sure to have a supply of toys (new and used), including some of the toys we had as children. She regularly updates the toys with a new book or puzzle. She never tires of playing the same old games with them. She knows that this builds a sense of tradition and deepened relationship. She will even keep food on hand that they love (small ice cream sandwiches) or create memories with food (pretzels in a cup each time we leave, to eat in the car). The kids love these simple routines, giving them a sense of tradition and making time at Grammy's house extra special. *(Mom, USA)*

I had decided that I would give the children a creative/learning experience for their birthdays. A lot of this has been theater, but I also try to tap into a specific interest of theirs. For instance, my little grandson will turn eight next week, and while he and I were reviewing the musical *Brigadoon* for my summer theater, he turned and told me how much he would love to play the bagpipes. A little light bulb turned on in my mind, and I later contacted a college professor who played bagpipes in full color uniform. For Robbie's birthday, I surprised him by taking him to a bagpipe performance with this professor and his band. The professor also taught Robbie about the instrument. We had taken Robbie to dinner beforehand and invited him to spend the night to complete some quality time with him. Birthdays can be a liberal arts education, introducing children to all kinds of new interests. *(Grandma, USA)*

As an extended family, we love to enjoy a Christmas Eve dinner gathered around a couple of fondue pots with heated cooking oil and chunks of lean beef sirloin for spearing and cooking in the oil. We share together in cooking our own meat, and it makes us gather for a longer time than usual as we experiment on just how long it takes to make our sirloin cook so it's done just right for our taste buds. I prepare small bowls with dips for the meat, including horseradish, steak sauce, barbecue sauce, dressing, etc. We take the time to visit and share with one another, often in an even more meaningful time than usual as we gather as a family. Of course, the typical salads, potato dishes, and veggies complement the meal. *(Grandma, USA)*

> *"Grandparents are similar to a piece of string—handy to have around and easily wrapped around the fingers of their grandchildren"* (author unknown). *(Grandma, USA)*

I have gone to lunch with my daughter and granddaughters twice now at the American

Girl doll store. It is a bit pricey, but we dress up and take the train downtown and make it a very special outing. Sometimes both grandmas go, and we have shared the cost of buying the dolls. *(Grandma, USA)*

This idea is perhaps more for mothers than grandmas, but the idea came from my mom. In an effort to teach us about giving at Christmastime, my mom always baked special Swedish bread called Yule bread. She made several loaves, tied them with a big red bow, and my brother and I delivered them to our neighbors. I wanted to do something similar with our girls, but I wasn't a good baker. However, I did make a good batch of English toffee candy. So that has become our tradition. The neighbors on our street know it's Christmastime when they get their special treat from our family. *(Mom, USA)*

I wanted to celebrate Thanksgiving with some time of expressing our gratitude to the Lord. One time I suggested we all sing "Praise God from Whom All Blessings Flow." Silence. Giggles. It seemed that though two of the families were in church regularly, no one knew that simple praise song that Vern and I had grown up with. The next year I called them ahead of time and asked them all to come prepared to talk about something for which they were grateful. The children could draw a picture of something or someone if they wished. That went much better. In fact, Vern went from person to person with a microphone and tape recorder, and we recorded what people shared. I still have that recording. *(Grandma, USA)*

I saved bed sheets for my grandchildren that were monogrammed by my mother. *(Grandma, USA)*

It had been a tradition in my family that whenever it was someone's birthday we would wake them up with the birthday song and breakfast in bed. There were not always fancy presents, but it did not seem to bother our children. The feeling of being remembered in a special way meant so much. I have wanted to do this with my grandchildren as well, and I have come to realize that it is much appreciated. On my grandchildren's birthdays I try to go to their houses in the morning and bring them a little something, although early school mornings sometimes make it challenging! *(Grandma, Finland)*

We try to have specific things that are only and always done at Grandma's house—going to the park together, taking silly pictures on the digital camera, making French toast or scrambled eggs, playing foosball, repeating Robert Louis Stevenson's *The Swing* while swinging, giving rida, rida, runka knee rides to the babies, and playing follow the leader. *(Grandma, USA)*

At some time during each child's birthday month, I have a Grandma Day with the birthday child. The grandchild spends the night at our home, and the next day we do something special or go somewhere such as:

- The zoo.
- The children's museum.
- The arboretum.
- The Sears Tower.
- The beach.
- A climbing wall.
- A long bike ride.
- A train or cab ride.
- A petting farm.
- The pumpkin patch.
- The nail place—to get a manicure and pedicure.

Some of the children have chosen just to stay at our house and make crafts. A twelve-year-old grandson and I spent a whole day making a large gingerbread house from scratch. Grandma Days are a special tradition that both the children and I anticipate and enjoy. *(Grandma, USA)*

For Thanksgiving, we often place five kernels of corn above each plate. After the meal is served, each person shares five blessings. We remind the children that this is a custom carried over from the Pilgrims. *(Grandma, USA)*

We usually spend Easter with my parents, so my mother has developed traditions with my boys to help them appreciate the holiday. Several days before Easter my mom and my sons plant wheat grass seeds in a small flowerpot on the windowsill. The wheat grass is fast-growing, and in a few days they can already see green grass growing upward. When they plant the seeds they talk about how the Bible says that unless a grain of wheat falls to the ground and dies, it will only remain one seed. But if it dies, it produces many seeds (John 12:24). She uses this as an object lesson to show how we must first die to self before we can produce fruit in Christ and to talk about Christ's death for us and the new life that we have as a result. She also has a small cardboard cut-out person that represents Christ. On Good Friday she takes the body of Christ and with my sons wraps the body up with long strips of cloth and spices and puts the body in a box that is placed outside and buried under a large pile of rocks. As she does this she reads the account of Christ's death with the boys. First thing on Easter morning she takes the boys outside to the pile of rocks that looks exactly as they had left it. The boys uncover the rocks, find the box, and open it. They are still at an age when they are shocked to find that the body they had left there is gone. Together they sing "Up from the Grave He Arose." And that is how we begin our celebration of Easter each year. *(Mom, USA)*

For the past seven years, our family has acted out the Christmas story complete with costumes. Each year, I wonder if the children are getting too old to participate, but so far everyone is still very willing. After Christmas, I make a photo book of our play for each family. Everyone enjoys seeing his own pictures, and it helps us get excited about doing it again next Christmas. Here is a poem that I enclosed in a Christmas card about our play.

My grandma gives great hugs, and I look forward to getting one each time I return to her house. I have always loved my grandmother's hugs. (Adult Grandchild, USA)

Our Christmas Dramas

A play doesn't just happen—to the basement we bound.

The roles must be chosen; the costumes all found.

Mary's part is easy. Lilly can't be here.

With only two girls, we alternate each year.

There's another good part where a girl can excel,

Since none of the boys choose to be Gabriel.

"I'll be the donkey, I'm strong and I'm tall."

It would be a shame for somebody to fall.

Boys are great shepherds. A cane's a fun tool.

A laser would be better. A sword would be cool!

We need Joseph, an innkeeper, Caesar, a king.

A whole host of angels and they have to sing.

Shepherds can be magi and have several roles.

We'll need some parents to fill in the holes.

The narrator is ready. We all know our cue.

The parts are assigned and the costumes will do.

It starts out with Mary alone it would seem.

Then Gabriel's visit and Joseph's dream.
Jesus is born. Grif plays "Silent Night."
Angels tell the good news. The shepherds have fright.
Jesus is worshiped and gifted by kings.
And Mary again ponders these things.
And that is our drama, *God's Gift to the Earth*.
We are blessed beyond measure by our Savior's birth.
   (Grandma, USA)

I have lived most of my life in Finland where we have some traditions that are not well known here in the United States. Now that I live close to my grandkids, I want to pass on some of the traditions that have been important in our family. The Lucia tradition, for example, has meant a lot to me ever since I was a little girl. The Lucia Day is a tradition that has existed in parts of Europe since the beginning of the 1800s. In Finland, this tradition has been recognized for about one hundred years. The story about Lucia began in Sicily during the time of the Roman Empire. The Emperor initiated severe persecution of the Christians, and as a result Lucia was to be burned at the stakes. But God heard her prayer, and the fire did not touch her. Later she died as a martyr by the sword. Lucia was a blind girl who visited prisoners in an attempt to bring some light and hope into their lives. To be recognized, she carried candles as she walked around the prison caves. This is why on Lucia Day (December 13), girls all over Scandinavian countries dress in white and carry candles as they bring hope to prisons, schools, nursing homes, hospitals, and businesses. Every year around December 13, I gather all my grandkids in my home and dress them up as Lucia, Lucia maids, "star boys," and elves. When it is still dark outside, we drive around visiting friends and family, singing the Lucia song and other Christmas carols as we bring coffee and gingerbread cookies to them. *(Grandma, Finland)*

For Christmas Eve, we attend our church service followed by a traditional meal. After this, we read Scripture and turn down the lights with the exception of the lit candles in the center of our table. Then each person takes his votive candle, lights it, and names a blessing for which he wishes to thank the Lord. Sometimes we have answered the question, "What do you like best about Jesus?" (This is good for younger kids.) After all the candles are lit, we often sing, "This Little Light of Mine." *(Grandma, USA)*

Our family has always written letters at birthdays. My mother sends my sons a letter for their birthdays including fond memories from the recent past and hopes and prayers for the future. She writes what she appreciates about the person and how she is specifically praying for them. It is something that we keep far longer than most birthday cards! *(Mom, USA)*

Each year, I try to have a birthday party for one of the dogs in the family. It's a party that the cousins can invite their friends to, so we often have quite a crowd. Typically, the birthday includes games about dogs. Children compete with the dog to see who can lap up (with their tongues) a pie tin of applesauce the fastest. Or they have barking and yelping contests. Or they have relay races, carrying the newspaper in their mouths on their hands and knees. Sometimes they play pin the tail on the dog. There is always a cake made of raw hamburger. One year, our big Newfie ate the cake in two bites—lit candles and all. We have hot dogs, of course, and three shades of Jello cut up in cubes to resemble cubed dog food. Each child is served a dog dish with his or her name painted on it to take home. The children bring presents for the dog—recommended edible treats that can be consumed on the spot. *(Grandma, USA)*

Grandma always did Christmas stockings for all the grandchildren. Christmas morning was so much fun as we watched the kids open their stockings from Santa! (She did a great job finding little gifts that would be just right for boys and girls at various ages.) *(Mom, USA)*

During December, we pay for babysitters for the grandchildren one night. Then, at our home we host a Christmas party for our adult children and spouses without the grandkids. We find that because we have quite a few grandchildren (eleven), it is difficult to find a time to visit as adults, so this has become a tradition that we enjoy, and our children enjoy it as well. *(Grandma, USA)*

Several years ago we started a tradition of my grandchildren—all girls—coming to stay overnight the night before Easter. Sunday is church followed by dinner at Grandma's house. Now that they are older I thought we might stop, but the girls have been asking for months so we'll work something out. *(Grandma, USA)*

Since I moved closer to my grandchildren and anticipated that they would be visiting more, I started a journal. The first grandchild named it *Grandchildren at Grandma's*. When my grandchildren are here for a day or longer— especially on their own—we keep track of what we do. They love going back to see all the things they have done when they've visited at our house. *(Grandma, USA)*

Twenty

Vacations and Trips

Sometime in my late thirties, my parents invited all their children and grandchildren (sixteen of us back then) to go to Florida for a week—all expenses paid. My kids could hardly contain their excitement. Neither could I! I'd never been on a vacation to Florida. My parents' generosity meant as much to my husband and me as it did to our children. To think that the matriarch and patriarch of our family would plan a trip like that for the whole tribe left me with a warm feeling of belonging. As our family boarded the plane, all sixteen of us wore matching caps, each with our first name printed across the front. When a flight attendant greeted our then eight-year-old son with "Hi, Nate," Nate said, "How does she know my name?"

My parents also like to plan extended family getaway weekends every now and then at a local hotel—a great way for the adults to visit and the cousins to spend time together. Even Grandma and Grandpa play "hotel tag" with us on these trips. Before we begin the game, Grandpa reviews the rules: no running allowed, everybody splits up into groups of two or three, and the person in the group who's "it" has to wear a silly old hat. What wonderful times we have enjoyed visiting and playing games with parents, siblings, cousins, and nieces and nephews. Those trips have provided my children with fond memories and stories that continue to be told at extended family gatherings.

I recently took my four-year-old granddaughter for a drive in the car. We live in a very beautiful part of New Zealand where a large lake is surrounded by mountains. I travel this route often, and I don't always notice my surroundings because I see them all the time. My granddaughter likes driving in my car as she can see out of it better than most others, so I took her with me to give her mother a bit of a break. The journey took about thirty minutes each way. I was amazed at the things she saw and pointed out to me—things I probably would have missed otherwise. She sometimes goes to the lake to feed the ducks and swans, but I didn't realize that she had no concept of the size of the lake. The part she usually visits is sheltered. All of our car trip was near the lake, but sometimes the lake was out of sight, and she would get excited thinking we were seeing yet another lake. I heard, "Look, Gran, look" so many times that I began to realize I missed a lot when I traveled on my own. Some of the area we traveled through was forest, and the size of the trees amazed her. They were so thick around that my granddaughter said, "You could hide behind them, Gran." I ageed that even her Gran could hide behind them without any trouble. But the greatest shout of excitement came when she saw what she thought was a big rock floating in the lake. It was, of course, an optical illusion. There is a small island in the lake, and as we were driving along it looked to her as though it was floating. I stopped the car and explained what an island is and that we were the ones moving, not the island. I could see by her expression that she was not at all sure about that. I then started the car again and she said, "See, it is moving." I stopped the car again, and she suddenly understood the difference. I had forgotten how children ask such difficult questions! It would do us all good to have our eyes opened to God's wonderful creation and look at things through the eyes of a child. **(Grandma, New Zealand)**

During the summer of 2005, we asked my parents to stay with the girls for about twelve days so that we could travel to England for our anniversary. They were happy to spend some quality time with the girls alone—without any interference from us. Before they arrived, my parents planned a mini-trip with the girls. They asked each of the three girls to research a historic site that they would like to visit. Then when it was time to take the trip, they visited each of the sites that the girls had researched. Let me tell you, my girls *still* talk about that trip with Grandma and Grandpa. (I recently e-mailed my parents to tell them this; I think that meant a lot to them.) They remember so many fun times—the hotel they stayed in, the restaurants they ate in, even the places they stopped for ice cream. And each of the sites that they visited were even more meaningful because they knew something about each one. These were really special days with my parents, and I'm sure none of them will ever forget the trip. **(Mom, USA)**

We are blessed with a lake house in the family, and my folks are generous in letting us use it with our kids whenever we are able. We have a traditional week there with our son and daughter-in-law and two grandkids. It is a wonderful time. We have the little ones sleep with us—it is special for us and fun for the grandkids, and it gives Dad and Mom an uninterrupted night of sleep! We get up with them early in the morning (so Dad and Mom can sleep in) and go outside. This is time for quiet talks, throwing pebbles into the lake, and exploring before the rest of the world awakens. We take a lot of photos during the week, and the memories are precious. We are amazed at what a two-year-old can remember the next year! *(Grandma, USA)*

Right after Christmas this past year, my husband and I went with one of our daughters and her children back to my hometown of Carney, Michigan. We tramped through my father's favorite hardwoods, and I showed my grandchildren where we brought the cows to pasture. I told them about the day a bear startled all of us in the brush beside the road! They also saw where I walked home from school each day with friends and then through the woods and up a steep hill to our homestead, where we had a 360-degree view for miles around. We visited my brother and sister and some of the family. We saw my home church, met the pastor, went through the halls of my alma mater where my senior class picture was hanging, and had great fun just getting the feel of my old small town. Now we have a point of reference for many future family stories. *(Grandma, USA)*

> *I think my grandma has the widest and most tender heart. She is very loving. I wish I could do more for her—as much as she has done for me. A family reunion wouldn't be a family reunion without grandma.*
> *(Grandchild, Taiwan, age 16)*

My husband has always enjoyed riding roller coasters. I'm scared to death of them and will not ride one. So he told the family that when they thought the grandchildren were old enough, we would take them all to an amusement park. The time finally came when even the youngest could ride, so all seventeen of us made the trip to Cedar Point in Ohio to ride all the roller coasters. We went to a water park the first day and to the amusement park the second day. Everyone rode the roller coasters with the exception of three of us. They rode from opening until midnight. The youngest grandchild was eight and the oldest was sixteen. My husband was sixty-five. It was a wonderful three days being with our entire family and seeing them have fun together. *(Grandma, USA)*

Mom is so hospitable—even when she is the guest in our home! She always works hard to make sure that everyone is happy and comfortable. She and Dad try to make the kids feel as if they are very special, whether it is planning things to do with them or affirming them with encouraging words. *(Mom, USA)*

Because we had a lake house, the grandchildren loved to spend their vacations with us. It was their grandfather's idea to give each one a silver dollar as they learned how to water ski. It was a fun incentive, and out of the fourteen grandchildren, all but two of the younger ones are skiers. *(Grandma, USA)*

I took a grandson on the Amtrak train twice last summer to visit old friends. What a delightful time! *(Grandma, USA)*

When grandchildren are old enough to appreciate history, my husband and I take them one at a time to a city such as Philadelphia. With our grandsons, the history of the city is interspersed with a baseball game. After we return, I put together a scrapbook for them. *(Grandma, USA)*

● During summer vacations, my children visit their grandparents and stay for two or three weeks at a time. It is
a good time for them to meet other members of the
extended family who also have come to visit or are just
stopping by. Frequently, a visit of one of these relatives
becomes a chance for Grandma to talk more about our
relatives and tell their stories, emphasizing their importance or contribution to the extended family. Most
family members visit the grandparents during vacation,
so Grandma's place becomes a place of family reunions.
Knowing that, grandmas can take advantage of these
visits to bring family members closer to each other.
(Mom, Burkina Faso)

● After a family reunion four years ago, we decided to go
back every summer to a lovely lake. What wonderful
memories we have of the beach, swimming, boating,
fishing, hiking, picnicking, puzzles, and just being together. I did this with my grandparents a few times, too.
(Grandma, USA)

● Vacations with grandchildren—how could life get any
better? This is especially true if their parents are there so
no one is homesick. The parents also care for their daily
needs and take care of the discipline. We've discovered
that this is the perfect way to bring cousins together, as
well. We have gone separately with each family to Disneyworld or some other warm spot, and we have also
met as an entire family at the beach and also at a water
park. Each of these vacations created lifetime memories
(and we have many photos to fill in the memory blanks).
I enjoy photography, so taking pictures of my grandchildren is almost compulsive! I usually prepare a small
album of our time together to give to each family following the trip. *(Grandma, USA)*

We try to take a family vacation each year, which is getting to be more of a challenge since our family is growing so quickly. The last couple of years we have rented a house by Lake Michigan that has enough bedrooms and bathrooms for all of us, and it's just a ten minute walk to the water. We all enjoy making sand castles together, looking for seashells, and playing in the water. Our kids take turns planning and preparing a meal, and one night my husband and I babysit all the grandchildren, and our children go out to eat together. It gives us special time with the grandchildren and them some peace and quiet. On those evenings, you can find my husband going on a bear hunt with some of the grandchildren (hand motions included) while I am either changing diapers or trying to get others to sit down for a story. Another thing we like to do when we're together is to sing our grace at the table. We have taught quite a few short choruses to the grandchildren and the harmony with the adults is really wonderful. We most always hold hands while singing or praying together. *(Grandma, USA)*

Because twelve grandchildren vie for our attention and most of our contact with them is en masse, we made a decision many years ago that we would make an effort to do things with one or two of our grandchildren at a time. Because my husband and I do so much traveling— usually medical meetings or mission trips—we decided that was a great opportunity to include a grandchild or two when they were old enough to appreciate the experience. It is, of course, our dream to take each one of them on a mission trip, but since we probably won't live that long, we can only take the opportunities as they come. It's been our joy and privilege to take our oldest granddaughter to India and Bolivia. We watched her heart be softened and broken to the needs of the world, and she is willing to "go" if called by the Lord. Whether the trips we've taken have been near or far away, it's been great to get to know these complex little individuals while they're away from Mom and Dad and all that is familiar to them. They don't have to compete with other cousins for attention from us, and the insecurities of being away from home are in our favor so far as teachable moments are concerned. It takes a lot of energy to travel with grandchildren for more than a few days (sometimes two to three weeks!). But it's a major investment into their lives that has already proven to have good returns. We won't be around forever, and there is no guarantee of good health around the corner. So while we have it, we'll continue sharing our travel experiences as we can. *(Grandma, USA)*

A special tradition with Grandma and Grandpa has been the many times that they have taken us on family getaways with all the kids and grandkids. Sometimes it was to a local hotel and other times it was to Miami Beach. Dad and Mom have played Guesstures, hotel tag (which Dad pretty much devised), and many other games with the whole family. What special memories we have—and lots of laughter. Mom made it her responsibility to have enough food for an army, and then she encouraged us to eat it all. *(Mom, USA)*

During spring break, we try to do something special such as go to our grandchildren's towns and get hotel rooms and let the grandchildren come over to the hotel and swim. Sometimes we have more than one family, and the cousins love being together. They love the breakfasts and snacks. One experience we had this year caused us to have a good laugh. Two of the grandchildren put English muffins on their plates and warmed them in the microwave, pouring pancake syrup on top. We were unaware of this until one walked over to my daughter and exclaimed, "These are the worst pancakes

I have ever eaten!" They were introduced to a new food and enjoyed them the next day straight from the toaster—no syrup. *(Grandma, USA)*

We have had several ski vacations with our family. Those have been very special times. We are responsible for our own breakfast and lunch and then have a different family prepare the meal for each evening. We find that going away on a vacation together is easy on everyone because we all pitch in and help and no one is really the hostess. *(Grandma, USA)*

When our granddaughter, Megan, was five, we took a trip with her family to Disneyworld. Her eagerness to see Ariel surpassed everything, so finally the moment arrived. We took the photos of Ariel hugging a melting, euphoric Megan. As we walked from the ocean cave, I said, "Megan, she really looked like Ariel, didn't she?" With assured wisdom, she looked up at me with huge, round eyes and said, "Grandma, *that was* Ariel!" *(Grandma, USA)*

> *I used to* love *to ride in my grandma's van, (so did all of my cousins and my sister), so whenever we had to go somewhere, she would always let us ride in it. (Sometimes I wonder how all of us fit.) (Grandchild, USA, age 14)*

As our grandchildren reach nine years old, we take them on an Intergenerational Elderhostel program. The first was Marisa to Williams Bay, Wisconsin, where we did farm chores, explored our family, and learned to make a pop-up book of her life. Later I made one for her with pictures of the week we had together. This summer we take Renata and Mikala to an Amish village in Indiana;

we'll try to do things alone with each one at some time during the week. *(Grandma, USA)*

When our grandchildren come to visit us, I try to keep to the routine they are used to. They do get treats every once in a way when they are with us. There is plenty to do and see in Singapore, which they enjoy. It is a treat for both to snuggle into our bed and sleep with us, so that is permitted when they are on a holiday. I enjoy taking care of them when they are with me so their moms have a break. We have had a couple of planned holidays together in Egypt, Malaysia, Thailand, and Dhaka. Our next combined holiday is planned for Christmas in the United States. *(Grandma, Singapore)*

Once a year my parents take all their kids, spouses, and grandkids to an indoor water park for four days. It is long enough to foster relationships within the family, but short enough that we aren't all sick of each other by the end. Grandma "Mimi" does all the cooking, and we enjoy watching the kids play with their cousins and grandparents. The boys look forward to this event every year. *(Mom, USA)*

My husband and I rent a cabin at Honey Rock camp (in Wisconsin) and take two grandchildren at a time for five days, involving them every day in nature, people, creation, wonderful food, and many simple pleasures. We are able to show them that we do not need TV or other entertainment there, because it is a place apart. It reminds us of God and His creation and community. *(Grandma, USA)*

We have two grandchildren who live away from us. We always enjoyed having them stay with us because it allowed us to get to know them better. One summer we had them for a week. We decided we would show them what life is like in a farming community. While we are not farmers, we have friends who are. Brent had already ridden with the farmer in the tractor when they picked the corn and took it to the elevator on a previous visit. This time we went to the corn field with both Brent and Sarah, who were eleven and eight at the time. They got to pick and shuck the corn. Later that evening, we cooked and ate it. We also went to another friend's farm where they had donkeys, mules, horses, chickens, etc. The kids got to pet the animals, feed them, and enjoy them. We also went to a butterfly house where there were hundreds of butterflies. Of course there were several trips to McDonalds during the week. We took pictures of each event and made a book of their visit for them to take home and show their friends. *(Grandma, USA)*

One summer, I took my four older granddaughters to Branson, Missouri. We stayed in a motel for a couple of nights. We visited Silver Dollar City and Celebration City (two theme parks). We rode rides and ate hot dogs and watched fireworks. We also attended Dixie Stampede and had dinner there. It was a fun girl time. *(Grandma, USA)*

We are blessed to have wonderful relationships with both my parents and my in-laws, and the two sets of grandparents with each other, too. We have been fortunate to never have to deal with feuding grandparents over who gets which kids for which holidays. My parents come to St. Louis for Thanksgiving every year, and we have Thanksgiving dinner at my in-laws' house. We occasionally seek out the wisdom of their years of parenting to help us with major decisions of parenthood, while still remembering that the decisions are ultimately ours to make as we are now the parents. *(Mom, USA)*

My grandma, my mom's mom, is the only grandparent who is still alive. When my dad's work took him to Vienna for a few years, my grandma came to visit us from Korea. When she went back, my brother, Dong went with her, because he wanted to go to Korea to buy some clothes and other things we need as Koreans. When my brother came back, he told me a funny story that happened in the airplane. My grandma had enjoyed her time in Vienna so much that she said to my brother, "I don't want anything else now. I don't want anything else—even if I die." (Grandchild, South Korea, age 14)

Our children surprised us with a family weekend in Door County for our fortieth wedding anniversary. They enjoyed it so much, they wondered if we couldn't continue. And we have, with a four-day weekend at a Lake Geneva hotel/condo, with us picking up the cost of the housing. One night is set aside for a pizza party when we have all seven grandkids so the parents can go out for a relaxing dinner. *(Grandma, USA)*

We took our oldest three granddaughters with us on vacation to Florida for a week a few years back. Two years later, we took our next two grandsons for a week to Great America and related activities. (This was their choice. The beach in Florida sounded too tame for them.) The next two grandsons, who are four years old, will vacation with us in a year or two. And, God willing, the two almost-two-year-old girls will be next when they reach an appropriate age. *(Grandma, USA)*

● We had a favorite family vacation spot in the North-woods of Wisconsin—Stormy Lake. As we got married and had children, we continued to enjoy these vacations together with extended family. It's a wonderful way to spend time together in a relaxed atmosphere—grandchildren with Grandma and Grandpa, as well as cousins, nieces, and nephews. Getting away together provides lots of family bonding time. *(Mom, USA)*

● We plan one trip every other year where our children and grandchildren meet us for a short family vacation. We have visited my father and step-mother as well as others of my family in New England; we have visited family in Wheaton, Illinois; and we are going on a short Disney cruise in August to celebrate our fortieth wedding anniversary. *(Grandma, USA)*

● My parents have always had a passion for traveling, so when the oldest pair of cousins was in first grade, they took them to Disneyland and on a grand tour of the numerous relatives and great-grandparents that lived in California. Because our family was young, we had not ventured into air travel, so our children loved flying and seeing relatives they had not met. The bonding between cousins was wonderful as well, since they lived several states apart. When my children were in fourth grade, the trip was to Washington, D.C. and Williamsburg. The grand finale was when they were juniors in high school, and they went to Europe for two weeks. Since my dad had led student academic groups to Europe for more than twenty-five years, his knowledge of the area and the friends my children got to meet were priceless. One family friend is a former naval secretary and member of Parliament, so they even got VIP tours in London. Another friend manages a large hotel in Paris, so they spent New Year's Eve with a French family attempting not to eat escargot! *(Mom, USA)*

● When possible, I had each grandchild visit me for a week or longer by themselves. I paid the airfare and took them to Disneyworld or the beach. *(Grandma, USA)*

● My mother's parents did not have much in the material sense, but I felt rich for being loved by them. They lived halfway across the country in New Hampshire, and we usually saw them just once a year. My favorite weeks of the year were the ones we'd spend each summer at their rural hilltop home in the woods. When we were at her house, my grammy would make us our favorite meals, read us the same books tirelessly, and play any game (real or imaginary) as long as we wanted. One favorite memory is that each summer she would take us to the grocery store and let us pick out a box of sugary cereal to eat while we were at her house since we didn't get to eat those kinds of cereals at home. Another favorite memory was of the long rides from the airport to my grandparents' house. My grammy found such fun ways to pass the hours we'd spend in the car. She always had some of our favorite books from her house in the car to read while we were on the road. She also would sing funny songs, many from her childhood or her teaching days, and over the years we learned them, too. My son Carter's favorite song to sing is a silly one that my grammy taught me with hand motions that starts, "Oh, Chester [point to chest] have you heard [point to ear] about Harry [rub your hair]. . . ." *(Adult Grandchild, USA)*

● We have a lake home, so the children come for an extended time—sometimes with parents and sometimes without. It is important for the grandchildren to know the grandmother's rules and the lake association rules. Children are always hungry near water. I take snacks as well as toys and give the children the responsibility of collecting the toys and carrying them to the cars. *(Grandma, USA)*

Grandma Prayer

Father,

We are grateful that your Word stands firm in heaven and your faithfulness extends to every generation. Thank you for creating and establishing families. In your Word, you've asked us to pass your truth and your message of unfailing love from one generation to another. Please supply us with wisdom, energy, and strength to carry out this wonderful privilege. We're grateful that, through faith in Christ, you have promised to be our Shepherd for all of our days. As we follow and serve you, may we leave a good and godly legacy for generations that follow us. We ask this in the powerful name of Jesus. Amen.

Ellen Banks Elwell is a fifty-something mom who enjoys seeing families grow as they practice God's principles for living. A graduate of Moody Bible Institute and American Conservatory of Music, Ellen has written piano arrangements for kids as well as *One Year Devotions for Moms* and *The Christian Mom's Idea Book*. She makes her home in Wheaton, Illinois, with her husband, Jim, and they enjoy taking beach vacations with their adult children—Chad, Nate and Brit, and Jordan.